THE LION OF PARLIAMENT: SYAMA PRASAD MOOKERJEE (1901-53)

THE LION OF PARLIAMENT: SYAMA PRASAD MOOKERJEE

(1901-53)

Foreword by

K. S. Sudarshan

Edited by

DR. ANITA ARYA

GYAN PUBLISHING HOUSE

New Delhi-110002

THE LION OF PARLIAMENT: SYAMA PRASAD MOOKERJEE
(*Biography, Politics, History*)

ISBN: 81-212-0745-2

Published in 2001 in India by
Gyan Publishing House
5, Ansari Road
New Delhi 110 002
Phones: 3261060, 3282060, Fax: 3285914
E-mail: gyanbook@del2.vsnl.net.in
Visit Our Website at: http://www.gyanbooks.com

Laser Typeset at Alphabet, Delhi
Printed at Chawla Offset Printers, New Delhi

Contents

Foreword

A few days back Dr. Anita Arya, popular political leader, parliamentarian and authoress of a voluminous work on women's problems, requested me to write a foreword to her forthcoming book *The Lion of Parliament Dr. Syama Prasad Mookerjee.* She has devoted several years to bring out this book on Dr. Mookerjee — worthy son of a worthy father Sir Ashutosh Mookerjee, former Judge of the Calcutta High Court and Vice Chancellor of the Calcutta University. The later post was subsequently adored by his illustrious son. A multi-faceted personality like Syama Prasad Mookerjee — an eminent educationist, an astute parliamentarian, a profound statesman, intense humanist and a nationalist to the core—cannot be epitomised in a few paragraphs. Several volumes can be written about this noble son of Bharat who was imbued with so many sterling qualities.

Under the influence of Veer Savarkar he joined the Hindu Mahasabha. This was welcomed by Gandhiji who accepted that somebody was needed to lead the Hindus after Malviyaji. Syama Prasad was invited by Gandhiji to join the first national government. He accepted the invitation in the hope that he would be able to influence the policies of free Bharat. But on broad matters of policy, particularly regarding Pakistan, his differences with Nehru were very acute. His heart writhed so much over the plight of the refugees and he virtually became benumbed at the mindless massacre indulged in by the Pakistanis against the peace-loving Hindus of East Bengal. When he found that Nehru was unwilling to accept his advice he decided to quit the cabinet and organize opposition to protest against Nehru's policies from outside the government. Syama Prasad decided to give shape to a new national leadership. As a result of his efforts, the all India Bharatiya Jana Sangh was formally launched in October, 1950. It was to be open to all citizens who owed unflinching allegiance to India and her great culture and heritage.

In 1952 Syama Prasad was returned to the Lok Sabha, together with two other members of his party. But he was able to bring together many smaller groups in the Lok Sabha and form a nationalist opposition group with strength, enough to make him the first leader of the opposition. His speeches were a treat to listen and were heard with rapt attention by a packed house.

During his visit to Jammu in August 1952 he had said, "I will get you the Indian Constitution or lay down my life for it." His concern for the plight of the Hindus and his passion for keeping the state of J&K within the Indian Union was so irresistible that he rushed in May 1953 to enter that state without any permit, which was a requirement in those days. He was arrested and put behind bars under inhuman conditions, where, because of lack of proper medical care and utter neglect he succumbed to his illness and became a martyr in the cause of Bharatiya unity.

G. V. Mavalankar, the then Speaker of the Lok Sabha observed, "He was one of our great patriots and his services to the national cause have been equally great. The situation in which he passed away is tragic......"

Several authors and authoresses have written books on this great personality of the twentieth century but Dr. Anita Arya's work is different from her predecessors in many ways. Dr. Anita Arya's book will definitely attract the attention of scholars, general readers and admirers of Dr. Mookerjee. Dr. Arya's scholastic approach is the main feature of this book. I congratulate her for bringing out a good book on Dr. Mookerjee.

K. S. Sudarshan

Margashirsha (Shukla) Panchami
Kaliyuga 5102

01-12-2000 A.D.

Preface

Dr. Syama Prasad Mookerjee was born on 6th July, 1901 in Calcutta. He is still recognised as one of the founding fathers of sovereign India and a great patriot, educationist, parliamentarian, statesman, humanitarian and above all a campaigner of national unity and integrity, India has ever seen. He moulded his character and future by inheriting a rich tradition of erudite scholarship, fervent nationalism and fearlessness from his father Sir Ashutosh Mookerjee, who was the Vice-Chancellor of Calcutta University and a judge of Calcutta High Court. Dr. Mookerjee's latent qualities and brilliance could be shone forth with the help of hard training he received at his home and school coupled with the filial care of his father.

After having passed through the matriculation examination with a scholarship S.P. Mookerjee he joined the Presidency College, Calcutta and at the University level too he imprinted very impressive track records. To prove his patriotic spirit he took up Indian languages for MA instead of choosing English in which he was proved to be proficient. He received higher degrees in law from England and Benaras Hindu University. Death of his father caused to bring him into the educational field even while he was still a student. He was elected to the University Senate and Syndicate in 1924 and represented Calcutta University as a Congress candidate in the Bengal Legislative Council.

By becoming the youngest Vice-Chancellor of Calcutta University in 1934, Syama Prasad took advantage of the opportunity to put his aims and ideals regarding education of his people in practice. It was under his Vice-chancellorship that Rabindranath Tagore delivered his convocation address in Bengali. He turned against Congress when it was found indulging in placation and propitiation of some particular sections of the society. When Muslim League Ministry was found striking at the educational structure of the Bengal Province he managed to muster the support of non-Congress Hindu forces and toppled the Muslim

League Ministry. By forging coalition with Krishak Praja Party under the leadership of Fazal-ul-haq, Dr. Syama Prasad became the Finance Minister in the coalition ministry and thus he established his position as a practical and far-sighted politician.

Under the influence of Veer Savarkar, Dr. Syama Prasad joined the Hindu Mahasabha and in 1939 he became its acting president and declared complete independence of India as the political goal of Hindu Mahasabha. He proved himself to be a principled and fearless politician when he resigned from the Bengal Cabinet protesting against the interference of governor and bureaucracy in the ministerial discharge of the affairs of the police and general administration. The speedy and practical devices he adopted for the large-scale relief of the famine-stricken people of Bengal in 1943 shows how humanitarian and practical he was. It was Dr. Syama Prasad Mookerjee who laid the firm foundation of the industrial development of India by setting up the three most successful gigantic undertakings. He proved himself brave hearted and dashing in difference with Pandit Nehru regarding Pakistan. Dr. Syama Prasad left the Congress ministry and Hindu Mahasabha on the issue of broad national concerns. He put his efforts and energies on creating a political platform through which the ideology and policies he stood for could be projected. As a result of this Bharatiya Jana Sangh was formally launched in 1950. He visualised Jana Sangh as the spearhead of the nationalist forces in the country and wanted it to be so broad-based as to be able to comprehend them into an effective political organisation.

Introduction

This book serves as a comprehensive and extensive biography of Dr. Syama Prasad Mookerjee who was one of the founding fathers of independent India, a great patriot, educationist, parliamentarian, statesman, humanitarian and above all an active campaigner of national unity and integrity. I have accommodated the details about the different phases of life of Dr. Mookerjee under different chapters. The book comprises nineteen chapters. Chapter one provides the reader with an outline on the life of Dr. Syama Prasad Mookerjee.

Chapter two deals with how Dr. Syama Prasad Mookerjee was influenced and moulded by the rich tradition of erudite scholarship, fervent nationalism and fearlessness of his father, Sir Ashutosh Mookerjee, who as the Vice-Chancellor of Calcutta University and a Judge of Calcutta High Court having occupied a unique position in the life of Bengal. Being an upper-class Brahmin family with a high social status, Mookerjee house in Bhowanipur, Calcutta, was known as much for its *poojas* as for its being the abode of *Saraswati*. Thus, Syama Prasad grew in an atmosphere of religious rituals and ceremonies and he also took advantage of listening to the discussion between his father and scholars from several parts of the world. This immensely helped him to pay respect to age-old Indian culture and felt a strong attachment to the western thought of learning.

Chapter three narrates Syama Prasad's education and how the hard-training at home and school coupled with the filial care of his father enabled him to shine forth his inborn qualities and brilliance. After having passed through his matriculation examination from Mitter Institute with a scholarship he joined the Presidency College, Calcutta. He came top in all university examinations. As a token of nationalistic spirit he imbibed in himself and refused to take up English in MA. He, therefore, took Indian vernacular—Bengali and other Indian languages. He received a number of law degrees from England and India. He got married in 1922 and his wife Sudha Devi died in 1934 after giving birth to four children. In 1934 Dr. Mookerjee became the youngest Vice-Chancellor of Calcutta University.

Chapter four minutely gives details about his major contributions as a prominent educationist of the time. He served Calcutta University with single-minded devotion in various capacities such as President of Councils of Post-Graduate Studies in arts and science, Dean of the Faculty of Arts and Vice-Chancellor. This chapter also describes his views on medium of instruction, on free elementary education, development of Hindi as a language. The circumstances which led him to make a shift from education to politics and his meeting with V.D. Savarkar are also described in very lucid manner.

Chapter five is all about his sincere opposition against the Congress and Muslim League's plans to Muslimise Bengal. The mention of his guides and mentors in politics have been given due merit in the chapter.

Chapter six mainly deals with his staunch opposition and confrontation with British Government against its interference in the ministerial discharge of the affairs of the police and the general administration and characterising the much talked provincial autonomy as a mere farce. This chapter contains the strong-worded letter he sent to Lord Linlithgow (Governor-General). There are also the clear-cut description on Midnapore Disaster, Riots at Dacca, Famine in Bengal, the Amritsar Session Surrender, Stafford Cripps proposals and all that.

Chapter seven explains the famine relief work in which Dr. Mookerjee had directly involved. At his own initiatives he set up a number of Relief Committees. Bilaspur and Amritsar sessions of Hindu Mahasabha are lucidly and extensively explained. Syama Prasad's opposition to the C.R. formula and one of his historical and strong-worded letter to Gandhiji regarding this are included. The major historical events like the attempts towards the Indian National Army, elections to provincial legislatives and Muslim League victory are also very duly dealt with.

Chapter eight is dealing with the wrongful accession of Hindu majority areas to Pakistan and accession of Hyderabad and Kashmir to India. Pandit Nehru is being criticised for his policy of appeasement and mishandling of accessions of Kashmir and Hyderabad. Dr. Syama Prasad was severely critical of Pandit Nehru regarding the wrong accession of Hindu majority areas to Pakistan.

Chapter nine explains the riots masterminded by the Muslim League capitalizing on its electoral success. The Congress is also blamed for its nervousness and favourable change in British attitude. Dr. Mookerjee was in favour of partitioning Bengal to save the minority Hindu population from majority Muslim population. Congress took advantage of the situation and accused Syama Prasad of causing partition in Bengal. However, Mookerjee's apt reply compelled Congress to keep quite regarding this issue. There is enough mention Radcliffe Commission on partition and Syama Prasad's role in Constituent Assembly of India.

A clear-cut account on the first cabinet amidst aggression and genocide in India is given in chapter ten of this book. Dr. Mookerjee's role in the first cabinet of free India as the Minister of Industry and Supply is duly explained and there is due mention of the industrial projects he had taken up. The chapter also covers Syama Prasad's conflict with Nehru on some major issues, assassination of Gandhiji, massacre of Hindus in East Bengal, Mookerjee's revolt against agreements and declarations with Pakistan, resignation from Cabinet and revolt against Nehru-Liaquat agreement.

Chapter eleven presents a poignant picture of Hindu minorities of Pakistan after partition. Pakistan remained insincere regarding the minorities in that nation. The chapter also allows the reader to have a peep into the major issues of the time like secret circulars on treatment of Hindus, Nehru-Liaquat Pact, assassination of Liaquat Ali Khan, mass exodus of Hindus, Nehru's visit to Bengal, East Bengal minorities conversion and Syama Prasad Mookerjee's last speech in Parliament.

Chapter twelve explains the background against which the Jan Sangh had emerged as a major political party. It is clearly described in the book the lack of the national outlook of the political parties which were in existence during the time. Though the RSS was considered as a non-political organisation the need of its political affiliation cameforth later on.

Chapter thirteen comprises Syama Prasad taking over the presidentship of Jan Sangh. He commissioned Jan Sangh as the spearhead of all national forces. In his historical presidential address he broadly put in the aims and objects of Bharatiya Jan Sangh. He thought that it should be served as a spearheading force of nationalism.

Dr. Syama Prasad Mookerjee's great and genuine interest in Indian culture and his sincere effort to impart our cultural heritage are being described in chapter fourteen. The basic features of Bharatiya culture according to Dr. Syama Prasad Mookerjee are being talked here.

Chapter fifteen talks about the first general elections with the Jan Sangh in electoral arena. Although Jan Sangh received the sound blow in the term of electoral debacle he managed to carry this political party through the crisis. He was also successful in removing odds against Jan Sangh as it was widely dubbed as communal by its political detractors and media. His difference with Nehru is much talked about in this chapter on the important issues of the time.

Chapter sixteen is about the historic speeches which Dr. Mookerjee delivered in the Parliament on different burning issues of the time. He was painfully aware of the temper of Pt. Nehru and his tendency to regard all criticism as malicious. In his very first speech in the new Parliament on the address of the President on the 21st of May, 1952, he made a sincere and passionate plea for a correct approach towards the position.

Last three chapters of this book, i.e., from seventeen to nineteen deal with the famous Kashmir Movement initiated by Dr. Mookerjee. He had to put in much efforts to garner the public support by travelling in almost all parts of India. During the crisis time he indulged in a plenty of protracted correspondence with Pt. Nehru and Sheikh Abdullah in vain. He got arrested during the protest march held in Delhi. Protest meetings and strikes were observed against his arrest throughout the nation. After being released from jail he garnered support from several sections of society. Thereafter he determined to go to Kashmir where he got arrested and mysteriously died in the jail marking historical national lose and the vaccum created by him is yet to be filled.

1

Life of Dr. Syama Prasad Mookerjee: An Outline

Early Life

Dr. Syama Prasad Mookerjee, one of the founding fathers of independent sovereign India, was a great patriot, educationist, parliamentarian, statesman, humanitarian and above all, a campaigner for national unity and integrity. Born on 6 July, 1901 in Calcutta, he inherited a rich tradition of erudite scholarship, fervent nationalism and fearlessness from his father, Sir Ashutosh Mookerjee, who as the Vice-Chancellor of Calcutta University and a Judge of Calcutta High Court having occupied a unique position in the life of Bengal. His mother, Jogamaya Devi, was a devout Hindu lady, devoted entirely to her husband, family and Dharma. Being an upper-class Brahmin family with a high social status, the Mookerjee house in Bhowanipur, Calcutta, was known as much for its poojas as for its being an abode of Saraswati. Young Syama Prasad grew in an atmosphere where he could watch poojas, religious ceremonies and rituals and also listen to discussions on the most modern and scientific subjects between his father and great scholars coming from all parts of India and abroad. This, in fact, created in him, deep respect for India's age-old culture and close attachment to western thought and learning. A happy blending of Hindu spirituality, tolerance and humanity with scientific outlook and broad understanding, characterised the life of Syama Prasad throughout, both as an academician and as a parliamentarian.

Syama Prasad Mookerjee, had his schooling at the Mitter Institute, Bhowanipur which was specially instituted by Bisheshwar Mitter on the inspiration of his father Sir Ashutosh. The hard training at home and school, coupled with filial care of

Ashutosh, enabled the inborn qualities and brilliance of Syama Prasad to shine forth. While still at school, he would read books prescribed for F.A. and B.A. His father often used to take him to Calcutta University, which gave him an opportunity to exchange views with professors.

Syama Prasad, at the age of sixteen, passed his matriculation from Mitter Institute with a scholarship and joined the Presidency College, Calcutta. He stood first in the University in Inter Arts in 1919 and passed B.A. with Honours in English in 1921, securing first class first. But the nationalist in Syama Prasad never allowed him to take up English for M.A. He, therefore, took Indian vernacular—Bengali and another Indian language—instead of English for his M.A. which he passed with a first class in 1923. The taking up of an Indian vernacular for his M.A. was in keeping with his father's policy of according Bengali and other Indian languages their rightful place in the University education which, till then was dominated by English alone. In 1923 he passed his M.A. with first class first position in the University and next year passed his B.L., again a first class first, from the same University. Two years later he proceeded to England for higher studies in law and was called to the English bar in 1927. In 1938 University of Calcutta conferred on him the degree of D. Litt and Banaras Hindu University repeated the honour by conferring the degree of L.L.D. (*Honoris Causa*) the same year. In April, 1922, when he was the student of M.A., he was married to Sudha Devi, who became mother of his four children (two sons and two daughters) before she died in 1933. Syama Prasad, at that time a youngman of only 33, however, decides not to remarry. The brilliant record that he had at the University establish his reputation as a student and he was appointed General Secretary of the Presidency College Magazine which was a great honour for young Syama Prasad. The editorship of the College magazine provided him the first opportunity for self-expression and, for some time, drew him to the field of journalism. He started *Bang Wani* a Bengali journal, and also wrote in 1923-24, a regular feature for 'Capital', edited by Pat Lovell under the pen name "Ditch". This lure of journalism was a passing phase though he took to it again in forties when he started his own daily from Calcutta called *The Nationalist*.

Mookerjee passed his B.L. in 1924, once again standing first in the University. He also had to his credit the degrees of D. Litt. and LL.D. In 1927, he was called to the English Bar from Lincoln's Inn (England), which he had joined in 1926. He did not, however, practise law. While in England, he ably presented Calcutta University at the Conference of the universities of the British Empire and from then on, began to be counted as one of the leading educationists of India.

In 1923, the death of his father, whom he had been assisting in running the Calcutta University from his student days, brought him into the educational field even while he was still a student. He was known to have the closest insight into the educational plans and policies of his Vice-Chancellor father. He was elected to the University Senate and Syndicate in 1924 and represented the Calcutta University as a Congress candidate in the Bengal Legislative Council. In 1930 when the Congress decided to boycott the legislatures, he resigned his seat in the Legislative Council, but soon re-entered the Council as an independent candidate, with a view to safeguard the interests of his university. His main occupation, however, continued to be service to the cause of education.

Syama Prasad in 1934, became the youngest Vice-Chancellor of Calcutta University, which gave him the opportunity to put his aims and ideals regarding education of his people in practice. It was under his Vice-Chancellorship that Rabindra Nath Tagore delivered his convocation address in Bengali which marked the beginning of the end of the era of English superiority over Bengali and other Indian languages.

The great turn came in 1937, when, the introduction of the Provincial part of the Government of India Act of 1935 and the elections to the Provincial Legislatures gave a new twist to the situation in the country. He was again returned from the University constituency of the Bengal Legislature which afforded him an opportunity to study the working of provincial autonomy from very close quarters. In a house of 250 members, Hindus had been given only eighty seats for which mostly Congressmen were returned. The rest were divided between the Muslims and the British interests. The Muslim members were divided between the

Muslim League and the Krishak Praja Party. Had the Congress party formed a coalition with Krishak Praja Party, Bengal could have got a non-Muslim League stable Government. The Congress handling of the situation in and outside the legislature soon provoked him to think afresh about its policies and political conceptions.

The Muslim League, on Ministry, decided to strike at the educational structure, which his father and he himself had so assiduously built. The Indian National Congress policy of compromise with the Muslim League even at the cost of clear and vital national interest was repugnant to his innate nationalism which roused the man of action in him. Having failed to persuade the Congress leadership to change its policy of allowing the Muslim League a safe spell of power, he decided to go ahead all alone to topple the Muslim League Ministry. He mustered together all the non-Congress Hindu forces in the Legislature and formed the Progressive Coalition with Krishak Praja Party under the leadership of Fazal-ul-haq, with himself as the Finance Minister in the coalition ministry, this established his position as a practical and far-sighted political leader.

Under the influence of Veer Savarkar, he joined Hindu Maha Sabha and made it an instrument for check-mating the anti-national forces. Soon after, in 1939 he became its acting President and declared complete independence of India as the political goal of Hindu Maha Sabha. His joining the Hindu Maha Sabha was welcomed by Mahatma Gandhi who accepted that "somebody was needed to lead the Hindus after Malviyaji". Gandhiji was greatly impressed by the broad and thoroughly nationalistic outlook of Syama Prasad and is understood to have told him that "Patel is a Congressman with a Hindu mind, you be a Hindu Sabhaite with a Congress mind."

Syama Prasad Mookerjee in 1943, resigned from the Bengal Cabinet protesting against the interference of the Governor and the bureaucracy in the ministerial discharge of the affairs of the police and the general administration and characterising the much advertised provincial autonomy as a mere farce. The way he kicked the ministership made it clear to all that here was a man whom no temptation could deflect from the path of duty. His correspondence with Lord Linlithgow, in which he urged upon him to release the detained leaders, trust the people and permit the raising of a National Defence Force to meet the Japanese threat, was ample evidence of his persuasive firmness for the national cause.

In 1943, the Bengal famine brought the humanitarian in Syama Prasad to the forefront which the people of Bengal can never forget even though some of them may not have liked his politics. In order to draw the attention of the country to the distress in Bengal and organise large-scale relief for the famine-stricken people, he invited leading politicians, businessmen and philanthropists to devise ways and means to provide relief to the needy and the distressed. In response, Bengal Relief Committee was formed and the Hindu Maha Sabha Relief Committee was also organised. Syama Prasad was the moving spirit behind both the organisations. His appeals for fund evoked positive response from all over the country and large sums of money started pouring in. It was mainly because of him that the whole country rose like one man in providing relief, thereby saving lakhs of lives from the clutches of sure death.

In fact his sympathy had never been merely verbal, he made suggestions which were practical and which revealed his truely human heart that cried out for relieving human sufferings. After independence, he once suggested in Parliament:

> "We get, now Rs 40 per day. I do not know what the allowance of the members of the House of People will be hereafter. Let us agree to a voluntary cut of Rs 10 per day and let us set apart this sum for the purpose of opening homes where these women and children (of famine affected areas) may be housed and fed".

Most of the leaders of the Congress being detained, after the rejection of Cripps Proposals, which conceded, for the first time, the principle of partition of India on the basis of religion, had left the field open for the Muslim League to win over the waivering Muslims and establish its position as the mouthpiece of the Indian Muslims. The Muslim League, firm on its demand for partition, had decided to fight elections to the provincial legislatures on this very issue. The elections gave clear majority to the Muslim League in Sindh, Punjab and Bengal which did encourage the Muslim League to stress its demand for partition.

Later, the plan put forth by Shri Rajagopalachari known as 'C.R. Formula' practically accepted the partition of the Motherland. This, Syama Prasad considered, a very dangerous and dis-quieting development. He organised a countrywide campaign against the partition of the motherland. He was shocked to find when the British Cabinet Mission, before which he was arguing against partition, confronted him with the Poona Resolution of the Congress Working Committee which said that the Congress would not coerce any unwilling party to remain in India. He had supported the Congress in 1946 elections because he was assured by Sardar Patel that the Congress would never accept partition. He never knew till then that the Congress Working Committee had already conceded the right of the Muslim Provinces to opt out of India. Subsequently, Syama Prasad put all his energies to safeguard the interest of India. His well reasoned and forceful advocacy of the scheme for partition of Bengal soon became the universal demand of Bengali, Hindus. In spite of the opposition from some quarters the move for partition of Bengal, in the event of the demand for Pakistan being conceded, became so popular and powerful that it became impossible for the British Government, the Congress and the Muslim League to resist it. Thus, it was due to his efforts that half of Punjab and half of Bengal was saved for India. That explains his famous retort; "Congress partitioned India and I partitioned Pakistan".

Following the independence, Syama Prasad was invited by Gandhiji to join the first National Government. He accepted the invitation in the hope that he would be able to influence the policies of free India in its formative period and safeguard the interests of crores of Hindus who had been left back in Pakistan much against their will. The fact that he was given charge of the Ministry of Industry and Supply showed the faith reposed in his integrity and understanding of vital industrial and economic problems of the country.

In Union Cabinet, as Minister for Industries and Supplies, he laid the firm foundation of the industrial development of the country by setting up the three most successful gigantic industrial undertakings viz. the Chitranjan Locomotive Factory, the Sindhri Fertilizer Corporation and the Hindustan Aircrafts Factory, Bangalore. He judged every scheme and policy by the criterion of its practicability and usefulness to the people and was not wedded to any dogma or concept.

Gradually, on broad matters of policy, particularly regarding Pakistan, his differences with Pandit Nehru came to the surface. His heart bled so much for the refugees that he visibly became very weak during the massacre indulged in by the Pakistanis against the peace loving Hindus of East Bengal. When he found that Pandit Nehru was unwilling to accept his advice to back Sardar Patel's demand to Pakistan for transfer of land from East Pakistan to India in proportion to that occupied by Hindus forcibly ejected from Pakistan, and to provide adequate rehabilitation facilities for those unfortunate refugees and for satisfactory compensation for their properties lost to Pakistan, his disenchantment with Nehru's policies also grew. He did not hesitate to press his differences with Nehru to the point of controversy. The Nehru-Liaqat Pact of 1950 brought those differences to a climax. Having failed to prevent that pact being signed, he decided to leave the Cabinet and organise opposition to Nehru's policies from outside the government. This had its impact and the original draft of the Nehru-Liaqat Agreement, which committed Government of India to reservation of seats for Muslims in legislatures and services, was modified to eliminate these provisions.

In fact, the statement he made in Parliament about his resignation on 19 April, 1950 is a dignified but pathetic document of Indo-Pak relations. The reasons, he enumerated as to why the Nehru-Liaqat Pact would not solve any problem, are as valid today as they were in 1950.

Following his resignation from the Cabinet, Syama Prasad concentrated his energies on creating a political platform through which the ideology and policies he stood for, could be projected. He had already left the Hindu Maha Sabha which refused to accept his suggestion to open its door to all Indians, irrespective of caste and creed. Syama Prasad decided to give shape to a new national leadership in opposition. As a result of his efforts, the All

India Bharatiya Jana Sangh was formally launched in October, 1950. He was elected to lead the new organisation as its first All-India President. He visualised Jana Sangh as the spearhead of the nationalist forces in the country and wanted it to be so broad-based as to be able to comprehend and consolidate all of them into an effective political organisation. It was to be open to all citizens who owed unflinching allegiance to India and her great culture and heritage. Explaining the need for the new party he had said: "One of the chief reasons for the manifestation of dictatorship in Congress rule is the absence of well-organised opposition parties which alone can act as a healthy check on the majority party and can hold out before the country the prospect of an alternative government." Syama Prasad spent the rest of his life in building up this organisation as an alternative to the party then in power.

In 1952, Syama Prasad was returned to the Lok Sabha in the first general elections. However, the Jana Sangh, the party that he launched, could return only two more members. But he was not the man to despair. The one man in the Opposition, who stood head and shoulders above all others, was Dr. Syama Prasad Mookerjee. His pre-eminence was recognised by all and it was accepted by his friends and opponents alike that he was to be the chief spokesman of the Opposition in the first elected Parliament of India. He brought together a number of small parties including the Ganatantra Parishad of Orissa, the Akali Dal of Punjab, the Hindu Maha Sabha and a number of independents to form the National Democratic Party in Parliament, of which he was the elected leader. They all considered him to be their chief spokesman and conceded to him, by implication, the right to reply, on behalf of the Opposition, on all major questions. Even the party in power looked upon him as the unofficial leader of Opposition.

With his stature and acumen as a statesman, his parliamentary skill and eloquence, his deep understanding and constructive approach to the problems facing the country and his following outside the Parliament, he appeared to be the only real opponent of the Government. The Treasury Benches respected him for his deep understanding and appreciation of the issues and problems that came up before Parliament. His searching and penetrating probe into their policies and affairs and the ease and cogency, with which he countered their arguments were only to be seen to believe.

The most remarkable tribute came from the *Times of India* which commented that the "mantle of Sardar Patel had fallen on Dr. Syama Prasad Mookerjee". It was a most befitting tribute because Dr. Mookerjee had been exercising the same sort of sobering and restraining influence on the Nehru Government from outside which Sardar Patel as long as he lived had been doing from within.

His constructive and nationalistic attitude together with his enlightened but determined resistance to all anti-national and totalitarian policies and trends, made him the bulwark of freedom and democracy in the country. His role in Parliament as Leader of the Opposition earned him the title: "The Lion of Parliament".

The final act in the parliamentary life of this great statesman and parliamentarian occurred in 1953. By this time, his mind was fully engrossed with the problem of Jammu and Kashmir with a view to curb the then prevalent seccessionist activities. He decided to take up the cause of Jammu and Kashmir Praja Parishad which had been demanding that the State be fully integrated with the rest of India and should have the same Constitution. During his visit to Jammu in August 1952, he once told a mammoth meeting: "I will get you the Indian Constitution or lay down my life for it." His words proved prophetic. He decided to visit Jammu again in May 1953 to study, on the spot, the situation prevailing there. He was not in good health. His love of Hindus was so great and his passion for keeping the State of Jammu & Kashmir within the Indian Union was so irresistible that he rushed to Jammu where he was arrested. He fell seriously ill in prison and died a martyr's death to the cause of Indian Unity.

On his sad demise, the Parliament, the State Legislatures, the press and the leaders of public opinion irrespective of party affiliations, as also the leaders and rulers of the Buddhist countries of South-East Asia mourned his death as a great loss and paid glowing tributes and homage to his dedicated life devoted entirely to the service of his motherland. In Lok Sabha, mourning the unexpected demise of Dr. Syama Prasad Mookerjee, the then Speaker, Shri G.V. Mavalankar observed:

> . . . He was one of our great patriots and his services to the national cause have been equally great. The situation in which he passed away is tragic. It was God's will and who could help otherwise? . . . His ability, sincerity, the masterly manner of handling his subject, his eloquence and above all, his patriotism and love for his countrymen, entitled him to our respect.

The then Prime Minister Jawaharlal Nehru referred to the circumstances of his death as "peculiarly unfortunate". He described Dr. Syama Prasad Mookerjee as one of the leading figures of the House and a Leader of the Opposition, who played a very important part in the work of the House.

2

Family, Ideals and Heritage

Father: Sir Ashutosh Mookerjee

India, at the turn of the nineteenth century, was passing through a ferment—social, cultural, political and above all intellectual. Many factors, seen and unseen, had been at work since the advent of the British rule and consequent impact of the West on the placid mind of India. They had varied reactions on the different sections of Indians. Some were swept away by them from their ancient moorings and were tending to become a class of de-nationalised Indians as Macaulay had wanted them to be. Others determinedly reacted against this de-nationalising aspect of the Western education and influence and sought to save the ancient heritage of their land by reviving and idolising her past. And there was another comparatively small group of people who, in keeping with the best in Indian tradition, sought to create a synthesis of the old and the new, of the Indian culture and Western thought and scientific outlook. This class of people mainly consisted of such intellectuals, well immersed in Indian life and culture while having taken to the study of Western thought and literature with an open and balanced mind to assimilate the best in it without losing the best of their own heritage. Such people were naturally few in number. But their influence on the contemporary life and events was tremendous. They set the pattern for the making of new India.

Great Father of the Great Son

The most representative of this class of pioneers was Sir Ashutosh Mookerjee. Born in an orthodox high class Brahmin family in Calcutta on 29th June, 1864, Ashutosh got full grounding in the ancient lore and culture of the land of his birth. His father

Shri Ganga Prasad Mookerjee, M.B., was one of the best known physicians of Calcutta of his time. He commanded great respect not only for his professional skill but also for his scrupulously religious life in the best tradition of Brahmins.

Shri Ganga Prasad gave the best available guidance and education to Ashutosh. He brought him up in the stern discipline of an orthodox but enlightened Hindu home. At the same time he gave him the best of Western education then available in Calcutta.

Ashutosh was known to have worked from 15 to 18 hours a day even during his school days. To keep off drowsiness while reading, Ganga Prasad got prepared a breast-high table at which Ashutosh had to read while standing. He strictly regulated his diet also towards the same end. This hard training coupled with his inborn brilliance soon made Ashutosh the pride of his school. He became a member of the London Mathematical Society while yet a school boy and solved a large number of geometrical problems. Some of his solutions were found to be so excellent that they were accepted in England as original contribution to mathematical studies and were named "Mookerjee Theorems" after their inventor.

No wonder that Ashutosh turned out to be an intellectual giant of his age. His mastery over physical sciences, Sanskrit and law besides mathematics was so great that he came to be regarded as incarnate 'Saraswati' by his contemporaries.

The impress of Sir Ashutosh is writ large over modern Bengal. He had in him the makings of a great political leader and administrator. He made a start on that path in 1899 when he was elected to the Bengal Legislative Council as representative of the University of Calcutta, of which he had been elected a Fellow in 1889. He was re-elected to the Bengal Council in 1903 as representative of Calcutta Corporation and was elected to Imperial Legislative Council the same year as representative of the non-official members of the Bengal Council.

But in the meanwhile he had distinguished himself as an educationist and Lord Curzon had been so impressed by his work as a member of the Indian Universities Commission that he considered him to be the one man who could put the recommendations of the Commission, as embodied in the Indian

Universities Act of 1904, into operation. He therefore decided to appoint him Vice-Chancellor of the Premier University of Calcutta. That necessitated his elevation to the Calcutta High Court Bench because till then no non-official could be the Vice-Chancellor of Calcutta University.

The appointment of Sir Ashutosh as a judge of the Calcutta High Court in 1904 deprived the country of his active service in the political field. But the loss of politics was the gain of education. As Vice-Chancellor of Calcutta University; Sir Ashutosh moulded a whole generation of educated Indians after his own pattern more so, his second son, Syama Prasad Mookerjee. The most noteworthy of the qualities, which had made Sir Ashutosh the idol of his people, were his robust uncompromising nationalism and his fearlessness.

The nationalism of Sir Ashutosh was not a superficial feeling born out of Western education. It swelled from his orthodoxy, from his pride in Indian heritage and tradition. He made it a point all his life not to wear European dress except where his official duties strictly demanded it. He refused to visit England to attend the coronation of King Edward VII in spite of repeated requests of Lord Curzon. He knew, as his biographer Bipin Pal has put it, that:

> "once a Hindu is tempted to cross the barrier, he loses his claim to real social equality with his political masters and practically concedes to alien ideals and customs, the right to sit in judgment upon national ideals and institutions".

It was this pride in his own heritage and ideals which enabled him to stand up against the current of Westernisation which was then sweeping over Bengal. He was quick to realise that development of national language as distinct from English was essential to create appreciation and love in the new generation for their national life and culture. So he introduced Bengali as a subject in Calcutta University in 1906 and followed it up by instituting the M.A. degree in Indian vernacular, in 1914. Every student for this degree had to study one other regional language of India besides Bengali. His aim was to revive cultural unity of India through the building up of an All India literature in the Indian languages breathing same thought and ideals. It was a farsighted act of constructive statesmanship. It has been well expressed in the pithy sentence "He gave to the mother-tongue a place in step-mother's hall" inscribed on the pedestal of his bust in Darbhanga Hall of Calcutta University.

He was very much alive to the weaknesses that had crept into the social fabric of Indian life at the same time, and he never allowed his orthodoxy to stand in defence of them. He allowed his young widow-daughter to re-marry in spite of his orthodoxy and hue and cry of other people. He thus proved that his orthodoxy was not incompatible with modernism.

Later, this spirit of robust nationalism of his father and the truly Hindu atmosphere of the house of Sir Ashutosh had a deep influence on Syama Prasad. His pristine nationalism which later distinguished him from his contemporary politicians was a valuable patrimony that he received from his father.

But the quality of Sir Ashutosh which seems to have impressed young Syama Prasad most was his fearlessness and ardent love of freedom. Ashutosh was perhaps the most fearless of the public figures of India of his time. At a time when public men and politicians vied with one another in paying tributes to the blessings of the British rule and flattering the British Viceroys, Sir Ashutosh roared like a lion in the Provincial and Imperial Councils putting forth his point of view untrammelled by any considerations of fear or favour. His reply to Lord Curzon when he insisted upon his visiting England has been often quoted as a classic example of his fearlessness. On his telling the Viceroy about his inability to go because his mother did not approve of it, Lord Curzon told him in a commanding tone: "Then tell your mother that the Viceroy and Governor-General of India commands her son to go". Without a moment's hesitation Sir Ashutosh replied: "Then I will tell the Viceroy of India on her behalf that the mother of Ashutosh refuses to let her son be commanded by anybody excepting herself, be he the Viceroy of India or be he anybody greater".

This fearlessness was a natural concomitant of his independence of character and the spirit of freedom which brought him in clash with the highest dignitaries of the British rule in India at every step of his public career. "Freedom first, freedom second, freedom always" was his guiding principle of life.

Sir Ashutosh Mookerjee, the maker of modern Bengal, gave much to Bengal and India during his dedicated public life of about half a century. Modern Bengal bears an indelible impress of that towering personality and versatile genius, who had come to be regarded by his contemporaries as an incarnation of Saraswati, the goddess of learning — Eastern and Western — in all spheres of collective life; particularly the educational and the cultural. His understanding and love for Indian ideals and traditions enabled him to make them a living reality in his own life. He combined in himself all that is best in Eastern Culture and Western thought and he aspired to create in the lives that he was moulding an ideal and natural blending of the Indian spiritual and moral values and idealism and the Western scientific and matter of fact approached to the problems of life.

The senior Mookerjee picked up the talent from wherever he found, gave it a direction and scope under his protecting and paternal wings so that it may grow after the pattern he had set for himself. Shri Sarvapalli Radhakrishnan, Shri C.V. Raman and a number of other living Indian savants and scientists are his gifts to the nation. But his greatest gift, the perfect model of natural but intelligent blending of the two strains, the Eastern and the Western, was his son, Dr. Syama Prasad Mookerjee.

Ancestral Home

Syama Prasad spent his childhood in Bhawanipur, then a northern suburb of Calcutta, where his ancestral home still stands. This large but moderately built three-storeyed house, better known as 77, Ashutosh Mookerjee Road, had been a rendezvous of great intellectuals, jurists, politicians and statesmen of Bengal and India for over half a century. The first thing that catches the eye as one enters the long and dark porch of his old style house is a large wooden name plate.

It reads:	Sir Ashutosh Mookerjee	Out
	Rama Prasad Mookerjee	In
	Syama Prasad Mookerjee	Out
	Bama Prasad Mookerjee	In

followed by a number of other names of the younger members of the Ashutosh family.

To a casual visitor this continuance of the names of the members who are dead and gone on the name-plate looks rather unusual. But to those who know about the noble tradition of this house and its contributions towards the making of modern Bengal and India, this preservation of the names of Sir Ashutosh and Syama Prasad on the name-plate is a fit reminder of the heritage of this house.

Passion for Books

Known all over Calcutta as an abode of Saraswati, Sir Ashutosh had filled it with books on all subjects. The books were his one obsession, his ever lasting friends, with whom he conversed day after day, year after year, till the whole house became a vast library of rare books. Every room, every corridor had shelves of books piled up to the ceiling along the walls. The valuable treasure of knowledge, 85,000 books in all, some of them not available anywhere else, were given as a gift to the nation by Dr. Syama Prasad just a year before his death on behalf of the Mookerjee family. This treasure now makes up the Ashutosh Wing of the National Library of Calcutta. A look at the variety and quality of the books gives an idea of the versatility and rare understanding of sciences and humanities alike which distinguished Sir Ashutosh and his son Syama Prasad.

Childhood Impressions

This house is also well known to the people around for the pomp and show, devotion and piety, with which *poojas* had been celebrated there year after year. The most modern of men who have been living in it have continued to be most orthodox also in the matter of *poojas* and other celebrations, public and private, that enliven and variegate the humdrum life of a Hindu householder. It was at once the most modern and the most orthodox of the great houses of Calcutta.

Young Syama Prasad saw and imbibed with reverence the spirit of both these aspects of the life of his family. He watched *poojas*, the strict observance of the religious ceremonies, rituals and discipline by his father and other members of the family. He also listened to discussions on the most modern and scientific subjects between his father and great scholars who came there from all parts of India and abroad. This created in him a reverence for India's age old culture and thought together with deep attachment to Western thought and learning born out of intellectual understanding. He inherited from his devout mother Shrimati Jogmaya Devi and his erudite and fearless father a long tradition of devotion to learning and *Dharma* in the true sense of the term. Like William Pitt the younger he was trained up from his very childhood by his discerning father with assiduous care to play great role in the affairs of his motherland. A foundation was thus laid of a happy blending of Hindu spirituality, tolerance and humanity together with the scientific outlook and broad understanding of all that is best in the life and ideals of the West. This characterised the life of Syama Prasad throughout, both as an academician and a parliamentarian.

The Bengal of those Days
Nationalism Ideals and British Policy

The general atmosphere in the country, particularly in Bengal, in the early years of the twentieth century, was another potent influence in moulding the life and outlook of young Syama Prasad. He was born at a time when Lokmanya Tilak's firm assertion that "Freedom is my birth right and I will have it" and Bankim Chandra Chatterji's ecstatic hymn to the motherland — *Vande Mataram*— had begun a revolution in the minds of all patriotic Indians. The British plan to divide Bengal in order to weaken the nationalists, who mainly happened to be Hindus, was put into operation in 1904. This provoked the dormant national spirit and gave birth to a new phase of national struggle for freedom.

The reaction against the British Policy of divide and rule manifested itself in two forms. The more ardent among the younger generation took to the cult of the bullet and the bomb in supreme disregard of its hazards. The gospel of action as preached in the *Bhagawad Gita* and as practised by Shivaji, whose memory was revived by Lokmanya Tilak through organised celebration of Shivaji Utsav, became the inspiration for this young and determined group. The association of such great names as that of Lokmanya Tilak, Bipin Chandra Pal, Veer Savarkar, Lala Lajpat Rai, Aurobindo

Ghosh and Bhai Parmanand gave a new importance and halo to this cult of do or die.

Those who could not take to this extremist and dangerous path, took to the weapon of Swadeshi to break the economic hold of the British over India. Boycott of foreign ways of life was a natural concomitant boycott of foreign goods. The cult of Swadeshi revived and intensified the latent national feeling of the people, and lead to a rediscovery of their soul by educated Indians. It gave a crushing blow to the growing Westernisation that was then corroding the life of educated India. It made easy to task of nationalising the life and outlook of the new generation set before Syama Prasad by Sir Ashutosh. Therefore, it is no wonder that it had a lasting effect on the receptive mind of Syama Prasad. His inborn nationalism was sharpened and strengthened by this atmosphere around him.

Reaction to Separatist Tendencies of Muslims

The partition of Bengal and the movement for its annulment also brought to light the separatist tendencies of Muslims which could be played upon by the British. By playing the game of the British, the Muslim intelligentsia shook the faith of nationalist India in their patriotism and loyalty to the motherland. It also gave the first inkling of the future of British policy in India. But unfortunately, few Indian politicians of the day could then visualise the deadly significance of this British policy in winning over the Muslims to weaken the nationalist India. Syama Prasad was too young at that time to raise his finger against this subtle policy of the British which directly led to partition of India in August 1947. But he was destined to carry on the most determined fight against this policy after he entered politics to save them from its evil effects.

3

Educational Career of Dr. Mookerjee

Early Schooling Days

While the influences, of home and outside, were moulding imperceptibly the mind and outlook of young Syama Prasad, his father was also planning for a suitable type of education and training for his promising son. He could easily afford to send him to any of the public school run by Englishmen in Calcutta and elsewhere on the lines of public schools in Britain. Most Indians of his status did that then as now. But Ashutosh's nationalism, grounded as it was on Indian culture and ideals, would not allow him to send his son to public school. He was well aware of the fact that they could de-nationalise even the best and most promising of Indian boys.

The ordinary schools run by the municipality or the government were too neglected and mismanaged to develop the faculties of the children entrusted to them on right lines. They did not come up to Sir Ashutosh's standards. He therefore inspired his friend Shri Bisheshwar Mitter to open his Mitter Institute where Syama Prasad and his brothers got their early schooling.

Sir Ashutosh thereafter became a regular visitor of Mitter Institute. A great educationist that he was, he personally supervised the arrangements of the school and kept a vigilant eye on the progress of his sons.

He even took personal care in selecting the companions for his sons. He persuaded some of his close friends to send their sons of the same age-group to Mitter Institute, so that Syama Prasad and his brothers could have companions of his choice.

The hard training of home and school coupled with vigilance and paternal care of Sir Ashutosh enabled the inborn qualities and brilliance of Syama Prasad to shine forth. His precocity amazed his teachers and parents alike. He was always far ahead of his class.

At the same time he began to develop that idealism, that detachment from purely material things of life, which became the strongest feature of his public life. The notebooks of his school days contain many stray remarks which give an indication of the working of his mind. On one of them it was found written: "I want to be great. I do not want money". He did live up to this early idealism. He never allowed money or material comforts of life to motivate his actions and activities.

As Syama Prasad grew up in school, Sir Ashutosh began to take work of his private secretary from him. He would often dictate him letters which Syama Prasad wrote in long hand to be typed by him later.

This not only provided an outlet for his extraordinary energies, but also enabled him to study from close quarters his father, his way of working and dealing with men and matters. Sir Ashutosh believed in the age old Indian dictum: "I behoves the great to be ever active".

He never idled away his time. The manifold activities that he carried on simultaneously was a miracle for his contemporaries. This practical training that Syama Prasad had through his close practical association with his father in work, enabled him to imbibe these qualities in himself and develop a spirit of self-confidence which proved to be his greatest asset in later life.

From School to College

Having passed his matriculation from Mitter Institute at the age of sixteen with a scholarship, Syama Prasad joined Presidency College in 1917. This change over from school to college marked the beginning of new and very formative period of his life. It brought him into direct domain of his father. He could now feel the touch of his father in shaping of the educational life of Bengal. It provided him new opportunities of assisting Sir Ashutosh in his educational work, and get that insight into the affairs of Calcutta University which fitted so well for carrying on his father's work in the sphere of the University when the mantle, as architect of Calcutta University, fell upon him.

Syama Prasad was blessed at this stage of his life with a robust health which coupled with his simple living and intellectual brilliance, at once made him a favourite of his teachers and fellow-students. Like his father, he deliberately chose *Dhoti* and *Kurta* in preference to the European dress as his normal wear.

He passed his Inter-Arts examination in 1919, standing first in the University. This established his reputation as a student and he was appointed General Secretary of the Presidency College Magazine in 1920. It was a great honour for young Syama Prasad. The editorship of the college magazine provided him the first opportunity for self-expression. His writings of the time bristle with a young aspirant's vision of life indicative of his great future. Most remarkable among them from the point of view of understanding the man in Syama Prasad are his letters to Prof. Percival, a great scholar and teacher, who had helped mould a whole generation of Bengali intellectuals and men of action, including Sir Ashutosh, who had studied with him in the Presidency College. Syama Prasad had heard much about him from his father and he had a keen desire to get introduced to him. His appointment as editor of the Presidency College Magazine gave him the opportunity to fulfil his desire. He wrote to Prof. Percival his first letter on September 2, 1920, introducing himself and praying him for an article for the magazine. The acquaintance thus begun grew into deep personal affection between the young student and the great teacher who was then enjoying his well-earned rest in England. The most remarkable of the series of letters that passed between them is the one written by Syama Prasad on 20th of November, 1920. It give us an insight into the noble idealism that had taken hold of Syama Prasad and which continued to shape his actions all through the crowded life. The letter reads:

> My Dear Sir,
>
> I was away to Banaras during the Pooja Holidays and returned to Calcutta only a week ago.
>
> I have got your letter. I cannot say how proud I do feel. Such a letter his indeed worthy of you and you alone. From its very beginning to its end, it is couched in such terms,

which I cannot but describe as affectionate. They say — the writing shows the man – it is really so, sir, in your case.

We all deeply regret to find you are unable to write something for our magazine. May I request you to accept the copy of the first issue of the magazine for this session which I am sending to you in a separate cover.

I deem myself fortunate for having been able to get myself acquainted with you and I cannot but express the hope that you will bless me from your inmost heart that I may live a pure and manly life.

I beg to remain sir, with profound respects.

Yours affectionately,
Syama Prasad Mookerjee

"Pure and manly life" was the ideal he set before himself while still in his teens. He lived up to it. He aspired to be pure and he did remain pure — pure of character, pure of heart, pure in body and soul to the end of his life. He aspired to be manly and he did live a manly life. Manliness was in fact the dominant trait of his character. His fearlessness, his supreme disregard of self and his readiness to fight and suffer for all just causes were but manifestations of his manliness.

He did his B.L., once again standing first class in the University in 1924, and was enrolled as an advocate of the Calcutta High Court. The flare for writing that he had developed as editor of the Presidency College Magazine drew him to journalism also for some time. He started "Bang Wani" a Bengali journal in 1922. He also wrote a regular feature for "Capital" edited by Pat Lovell under the pen name "Ditch" during 1923-24. The Calcutta Review was also purchased by his father from Thacker Spink during the same period. By writing for these journals, he developed a fascinating style both in Bengali and English. But this lure for journalism was only a passing phase. He again took to it sometime in the forties when he started his own daily "The Nationalist" from Calcutta. But this too was short lived.

With his mastery over language, keen intellect, devastating logic and great gift of eloquence he could have easily risen to the top of the legal profession had he paid it the attention it demanded.

But that was not to be. Circumstances beyond his control coupled with his own inborn idealism drove him to a much wider and useful field from the broader national point of view. Instead of remaining content with only pleading for justice for his clients, he was destined to make justice to the whole of India his special concern.

Death of Father

The most unexpected of these circumstances was the untimely death of his father in May, 1924. Sir Ashutosh had retired from judgeship of Calcutta High Court in 1923. By the end of the same year he resigned the Vice-Chancellorship of Calcutta University after a heated controversy with Lord Lytton, the then Governor of Bengal, over financial support by the Government to the University. Sir Ashutosh was then planning to enter active politics. Had he done so, he would have surely come to the top not only in Bengal but also in All-India politics in no time. But his sudden death in Patna, where he had gone on a professional visit, cut short all plans. It also created a void in the public life of Bengal, particularly in the sphere of the Calcutta University, which was not easy to fill.

The one man who was known to have the closest insight into the educational plans and policies of Sir Ashutosh and the intricacies of the University administration which he controlled as its supreme arbitrator was young Syama Prasad.

So all well-wishers of the University considered his continued association with the University administration as essential for its healthy growth on the lines laid down by Sir Ashutosh.

It was this consciousness which prompted his old teacher and later Governor of West Bengal, Shri H.C. Mookerjee, to vacate his seat in the University senate early in 1924, so that young Syama Prasad could be elected to it. In June of the same year he was appointed a member of the Syndicate to fill the place of Sir Ashutosh on it. The mantle of Sir Ashutosh in the sphere of the Calcutta University, thus fell upon Syama Prasad, his natural and spiritual heir, at the young age of 23. He took upon himself to carry on his great tradition and complete his unfinished work of reconstruction of Calcutta University as a fit instrument for national rejuvenation.

Very soon he got so much engrossed in public duties that he could find little time for his professional work. He got elected to the Bengal Legislative Council as a Congress candidate representing Calcutta University in 1929 but had to resign his seat the next year when the Congress decided to boycott the Legislatures. But his sense of duty towards the University that had been literally built up by his father impelled him to seek re-election and get into the Legislative Council once again in 1931 as an independent candidate from the same constituency. Thus his life had become quite crowded while he was just thirty years.

Death of Wife: Abrupt End to Married Life

A new chapter in his life opened in 1933 when he lost his wife, Sudha Devi, whom he had married in 1922 and who had bore him four children. Syama Prasad was then in the prime of his life. Had he belonged to the common run, he could have re-married and carried on his domestic and professional life side by side with his public duties. But, steeped in Indian ideals, as he was, he took the death of his wife as a signal for renunciation of his personal life and dedication of his time and energies for the good of the society as a whole. He lived like a *Sanyasi* thereafter till his death. The blessings of his mother were with him in this noble resolve:

> "I had long dedicated my son for selfless service to the country and my son sacrificed his life for the cause of the motherland", she proudly declared after his martyrdom.

Taking over as Vice-Chancellor of Calcutta University

The first task he took in hand after his renunciation was that of completing the work of his father in re-constructing Calcutta University. As the youngest Vice-Chancellor of the biggest Indian University from 1934-38 and as President, Post Graduate Councils in Arts and Science for successive years, he not only completed the work his father had inaugurated for the development of Postgraduate teaching in the University but also made new and bold experiment of introducing Bengali as the medium of instruction for the college studies as well.

His fame as a devoted educationist, intellectual and orator

had by this time begun to spread beyond the boundaries of Bengal. He was elected a member of the Court and Council of the Indian Institute of Science, Bangalore, in 1935 and also became a member and then Chairman of the Inter University Board in the creation of which he had played a leading role. He wanted the experiments and developments in the field of education as undertaken by different Universities of the country to be correlated and coordinated so that a common pattern could be evolved by them for the educational life of the country as a whole. He was also nominated by the Government of India to the Committee of Intellectual Co-operation of the League of Nations as India's representative in 1938. In 1943 he was elected President of the Royal Asiatic Society of Bengal.

4

Debut as Educationist of Prominence

For fifteen years of his life, Syama Prasad concentrated his attention on Calcutta University. He literally made it his own as his father had done before him. He reconstructed it on the foundations laid by his father and established his reputation as an original thinker and brilliant educationist. Even after he took to active politics in 1939, education in general and Calcutta University in particular continued to be an absorbing interest of his life. As a result he continued to be regarded and respected as one of the foremost educationists of the country upto the end of his life, even by those who differed with his politics.

During this period, he served Calcutta University with single minded devotion in various capacities such as President of the Councils of Post-Graduate studies in art and science, Dean of the Faculty of Arts and Vice-Chancellor. Even though he was the youngest ever fellow and syndic of the premier University of the country, his intimate knowledge of the mind of its master architect who was no more there to guide its destinies, gave him an unprecedented position and say in its affairs. He began to be looked upon as a dependable guide in all intricate matters about which the knowledge of the original plan of Sir Ashutosh was deemed necessary. He became the interpreter of his plans and policies about the reconstruction of the University.

Days in England

It was yet a time of studentship for Syama Prasad. He was only 24 and had a keen desire to complete his legal studies in England. He went there in March 1926 and joined the Lincoln's Inn and was called to the English Bar in 1927. While in England he ably represented Calcutta University at the Conference of the

Universities of the British Empire. He began to be counted from then onwards as one of the leading educationists of India.

It was in England that Syama Prasad came in close touch with Dr. S. Radhakrishnan, whom Sir Ashutosh had put on the road to greatness by bringing him to Calcutta University from Mysore; and Sir Evan Greaves who remained his life-long friend. He was known to be a quiet and unostentatious type of student by his contemporaries in England. But his amiable nature won him a large number of friends. His nurse in the nursing-home to which he had to shift in October, 1926, because of a carbuncle was amusingly annoyed by large number of friends who would come to meet him there posing as his cousins. "This is another cousin coming", she would exclaim whenever a new face peeped in for her permission to meet Syama Prasad.

A Hard Choice: Law or Education

After his return from England in 1927 he took to legal practice for some time. But his pre-occupation with the University soon forced him to choose between law, which is a jealous mistress, and public and educational work. He chose the latter and never turned back from it during the rest of his life. He was elected to the Bengal Legislative Council as a Congress candidate representing the Calcutta University in 1929. He resigned his seat in the Council in 1930 when the Congress decided to boycott the legislatures. But as a practical man he failed to see the utility of withdrawing from the legislatures leaving the field open to toadies, to play mischief. He felt it necessary that the interests of the University be safeguarded in the legislatures, particularly because education had become a transferred subject under the Montagu-Chelmsford Reforms of 1921. So he sought re-election and was returned once again in 1930 as an independent member representing the Calcutta University. His main occupation however continued to be service in the cause of education. He sat in the Council as a watch-dog of the interests of the University.

The Youngest Vice-Chancellor

The real opportunity to show his mettle as an educationist and an administrator came to Syama Prasad in 1934 when he was appointed Vice-Chancellor of the Calcutta University. He was only 33 at that time and as such was the youngest Vice-Chancellor of any university in the country. It was hailed as a fit recognition of his great capabilities.

He had already lost his wife a year earlier, in 1933, when he was just 32. His mother to whom he was devotedly attached tried her best to persuade him to marry again. But he refused. He decided to dedicate the rest of his life to the service of his motherland. He first chose to serve her through the spread of right education among her sons and daughters. Vice-Chancellorship of Calcutta University gave him the opportunity to put his aims and ideals regarding education of his people in practice.

Being fully conscious of the fact that university education in India had originated not in the desire for conservation and betterment of her traditional culture, her arts, crafts and industries but mainly for imparting her people Western ideas through the medium of foreign tongue and for ensuring a regular supply of an indigenous machinery for the smooth working of a powerful bureaucracy, he wanted to see the syllabus and courses of studies so remodelled, systems of training and examinations so reorganised that the learner may grow up not as a merchandised recorder of information and theories, not as a dry specialist, but one whose critical judgement is strengthened and whose capacity for broad thinking and wide application of knowledge to problems of life is developed to the fullest extent. He explained his ideal about the reorganisation of educational life more explicitly in his second convocation address delivered on February 12, 1936.

> "Our ideal" he said, "is to provide extensive facilities for education from the lowest grade to the highest, to mould our educational purpose and to draw out the best qualities that be hidden in our youth and to train them intellectually, physically for devoted service in all spheres of national activity, in villages, in towns and cities. Our ideal is to make widest provision for a sound liberal education, to find the correct synthesis between vocational and technical training, remembering always that no nation can achieve greatness by turning its youth into a mere machine-made product with nothing but a material end in view. Our ideal is to afford the amplest facilities and privileges to our teachers so that they may be endowed with learning and character and freedom

and may regard themselves as not only the torch bearers and interpreters of knowledge and conquerors of new realms of thought, but also as makers of men and women, of leaders and workers, true and brave, upright and patriotic. Our ideal is to link up education with the best elements of our culture and civilization drawing strength, wherever necessary, from the fountain of Western skill and knowledge. Our ideal is to make our universities and educational institutions the home of liberty and sane and progressive thought — generously assisted by the State and the public — where teachers and students will meet and work in an atmosphere of harmony and mutual understanding, where none will suffer on grounds of caste, sex, creed and religious or political belief."

Important Works as Vice-Chancellor

Giving Bengali its due position in University Curricula

He pursued this ideal in a systematic way during four years of his vice-chancellorship. He did not spare time, energy, health, convenience, or anything worth in life, where they stood in the way of performance of what he considered his duty even against the advice of his doctors. The first thing to engage his attention as Vice-Chancellor was the position of Bengali and other vernacular languages in the curricula of the University. He wanted Bengali to occupy its rightful place in the educational life of Bengal. He took a long stride in this direction when he made Bengali the medium of instruction upto the matriculation, and introduced Honours Course in Bengali, Hindi and Urdu. To prepare text-books in Bengali, he got prepared a collection of technical terms and expressions in Bengal to be used in various subjects of study. He visualised a day "when in this manner the University will be able to prepare a complete glossary of words in all subjects and for all standards. This will enrich Bengali language and literature and also make it possible for us to take steps for extending the use of vernaculars for the higher examinations of the University". To enrich Bengali literature and to develop taste of the people for it, the University under his inspiration undertook the publication of a special series of Bengali books on different branches of knowledge. Bengal spelling was also standardised on his initiative.

It was under his vice-chancellorship that Shri Rabindra Nath Tagore delivered his convocation address in Bengali in 1937. It was a new departure in the right direction in the annals of the University. It marked the beginning of the end of the era of English superiority over Bengali and other Indian languages.

Reform in Examination System

He next turned to the reform and reorganisation of the system of examinations and courses of study. He introduced the system of compartmental examinations and gave concession to students who had failed for appearing for examinations without getting themselves admittees into colleges. The whole scheme of high school education was re-oriented by him. A variety of courses, and choices were introduced for the boys and alternative subjects and courses of study were prescribed for the girls.

Teachers' Training Department

He realised that increasing flow of trained teachers was a necessary prerequisite for bringing about and sustaining any reforms in the school education. To that end he organised a Teachers' Training Department at Calcutta University and introduced a system of short-term training courses, including a vacation course — precursor of the present day refresher course - to provide trained teachers for schools.

He initiated military training courses in the scheme of college studies. To the same end he started annual celebration of the University Foundation day, which fell on January 24, at the Calcutta Maidan. All the students of Calcutta would assemble there on the day with their badges and banners and take part in the march-past and other physical displays. It helped in developing *esprit-de-corps* among the students and harmony between the teacher and the taught. Speaking at the first celebration he called upon the Government of the day to provide opportunities for the youth to grow.

> "I have abundant faith", he declared, "in the glory of youth and what I ask from authorities in the name of students of Bengal is that they be given a chance to live, an opportunity to enjoy life and the amplest facilities for the development of

their health and character so that in the days to come they may be assets in the furtherance of the highest interests of our motherland."

It was this solicitude for the genuine interests of the student community which gave him tremendous hold over their affection and loyalty.

Students' Welfare Department

While he wanted the authorities to do their duty towards the youth of the country he did not lay much store by them. He went ahead with his own plans for assisting the youth through the Students' Welfare Department and Students' Appointment Board. The Students' Welfare Department worked for the promotion of mental and physical health of the students. To create a feeling of brotherhood among them he reserved hostels for the students coming from the so called backward classes were abolished and all of them were provided accommodation in general hostels and messes attached to the colleges at reduced seat rates.

The Students' Appointment Board gave guidance to the students about choice of careers, contacted employers and recommended to them youth suited to their requirements. It also gave specialised training to the students intending to sit for competitive examination for the public services. While he thus took keen interest in finding employment for the educated youth among whom unemployment was growing fast, he was resolutely opposed to the policy of restricting higher education urged on the ground that "suitable appointments for work cannot be found for all university-trained men".

The society and state, he held, must provide useful employment for educated men. This task cannot be directly undertaken by any seat of learning whose duty will be mainly to provide society with men and women trained according to correct systems and ideals.

Schemes for Technical Education

On his part he tried to give greater attention to technical and scientific studies. Without any encouragement from the government of the day, he put into effect a scheme for agricultural education and introduced the diploma course in education. He also initiated a scheme for imparting training in the large scale production of certain industrial goods in the Applied Chemistry Department of the University. He paid special attention to the expansion and equipment of science departments which fulfilled in his time the dream of his father that these departments should win, as a matter of right, admiration of the world.

On the Arts side, introduction of Tibetan and Chinese studies as a part of ancient Indian history and culture, the foundation of Ashutosh Museum of Indian Arts and Culture and the work of archaeological excavations undertaken by the University were some of his specific contributions to the growth of Calcutta University as a seat of Indian learning. He also improved and enlarged the University Library. The next University Library Hall built in his time was decorated with frescoes illustrating the development of Indian culture and civilisation with special reference to contribution made by Bengal.

On Retirement as Vice-Chancellor

Last but not the least important work of Syama Prasad for the Calcutta University before he retired as its Vice-Chancellor in August, 1938, was the settlement of the arrangements of Government financial help to the University. It was a ticklish question which had brought Sir Ashutosh into head-long clash with Lord Lytton in 1923, and had been hanging fire since then. According to this settlement Calcutta University was assured of a block grant of Rs. 4,85,000 a year.

Honours Conferred

His services to Calcutta University and his eminence as an intellectual and educationist had now come to be universally recognised and appreciated. He had been elected a member of the Court and Council of the Indian Institute of Sciences, Bangalore, as a representative of the Universities of Eastern India and had also become Chairman of the Inter University Board in the creation of which he had played a leading role. Calcutta University gave expression to its gratitude and appreciation of his services by conferring on him the degree of Honorary Doctor of Laws at a special convocation held in November, 1938. Speaking on the occasion Lord Borbourne, the Chancellor of the University, paid a most befitting tribute to Syama Prasad when he said : "Nobody can say that Syama Prasad Mookerjee is being honoured by this Honorary degree because he is the son of a great father. It is because he is himself. He has earned every bit of it".

Retirement from Vice-Chancellorship did not mark the end of his association with Calcutta University. He continued to be the life and soul of it for many more years. Politics, however, began to engage his attention more and more after 1938. But even after he became fully engrossed in politics which latter took him to wider fields of activity in New Delhi, his interest in education in general and Calcutta University in particular continued unabated. The country began to look upon him as a foremost expert on educational problems and his advice on educational matters continued to be sought after with eagerness till the last days of his life. Banaras University also conferred on him the honorary degree of Doctor of Laws in 1938. The Government of India also gave recognition to his intellectual eminence by nominating him as its representative on the Committee of Intellectual Co-operation of the League of Nations in the same year. The Royal Asiatic Society of Bengal, the premier organisation for Asiatic studies in India, honoured him by electing him its President in 1943.

Education his First Love

Dr. Syama Prasad Mookerjee always held education and its cause quite close to his heart. He missed no chance to be in an educational institution or among the academics on one pretext or the other.

His interest in and attachment with Calcutta University, which began when he was just a student of that University, was life long. He can well be called the joint maker, other being his father, of that Premier University of the country. Organisation of the Teachers' Training Department, establishment of Fine Arts Gallery and Museum, known as the Ashutosh Museum, as a wing of the Post-Graduate studies in Ancient Indian History and Culture; the introduction of Science teaching as a part of the Matriculation course and introduction of Vernacular as the medium of instruction and examination; the introduction of Military Studies as a subject for examination and the introduction of the system of examination by compartment were some of his contributions to the Calcutta University during his two terms as its Vice-Chancellor. He continued to be associated with that University in various capacities even after politics began to absorb most of his time and energies

He was also the moving spirit behind the Aurobindo University at Pondicherry in the creation of which he had a big hand. He wanted it to grow as an international centre of the spiritual culture of India.

Authority on University Education

Because of this long association with the educational life of the country and his deep understanding of the education problems, he had begun to be looked upon as one of the top most educationists and an expert in matters relating to University education.

The last public recognition of his status and stature as an educationist came in December, 1952, when he was invited to address the thirtieth annual convocation of the University of Delhi. The address he delivered on the occasion proved to be the last public expression of his views on education and, therefore, has a special importance for the understanding of his approach to the problems of education.

Like his father who zealously and successfully guarded the academic freedom and autonomy of Calcutta University against official encroachment, even when it came from such stalwarts of Pax Britannica as Lord Lytton, Dr. Mookerjee was very anxious to preserve the autonomy of the Indian Universities. He was particularly disturbed by the growing interference of the Education Ministry of the Government of India, presided over as it was by a man utterly ignorant of the problems and ideals of University education, in the Universities directly under its control. He, therefore, warned the Delhi University that "Proximity of a University to the seat of Central Government is sometimes fraught with the danger of unnecessary and irritating state interference which it is to be earnestly hoped will be avoided."

All necessary reforms in the Universities, he held, should be primarily carried out by the respective Universities themselves who should balance regional requirements with national progress. The Inter-university Board and the Universities Grant Committee could also guide the Universities by developing healthy conventions under which their considered opinions could not be easily flouted by the University concerned. Well informed deliberations in the State Legislatures and Parliament at the time of voting for grants could also, he held, help the Universities in the matter.

Stress on a National System

He stresses the need for developing a comprehensive national system to cater to the needs of all stages of education.

> "There need not be", he said, "any conflict amongst primary, secondary and university stages nor amongst literary, scientific, technical, vocational and agricultural courses of study. A national system of education", he pleaded, "must conceive of a balanced structure where due and proper emphasis will be laid on every section so as to maintain its harmony, its strength and solidarity".

Views on Medium of Instruction

Regarding the medium of instruction he advocated the use of mother tongue, and where it was not developed enough, of the regional language upto higher secondary stage. "But while Indian languages", he said, "must be fostered and developed in the widest possible manner, they must not take a hostile attitude towards English."

He also advocated publication under State patronage of selected works from different Indian languages in the Nagri script to facilitate comparative study of the different regional languages and to enable the people to comprehend the essential unity between the different languages of India.

Planned exchange of visits of University teachers and teams of students between different universities, he held, could go a long way towards developing unity of outlook and proper understanding of problem and peculiarities of different regions.

He suggested re-orientation of the policy of awarding scholarships for studies abroad. Such scholarships, he held, should be given for those subjects only in which specialised study was not possible in India.

To provide facilities for higher training in science and technology within the country speedily, he suggested, that different universities should specialise in particular branches of science and they must be open to advanced students in those sciences from all over the country.

He laid special emphasis on the education given to the youth of the country being purposeful. "It is a supreme task for university administrators and teachers," he said, "to read into the minds of the youth of re-awakened India and to place before them not only well regulated courses of study and well thought out programmes for extra-curricular activities but also rousing in them a true scientific spirit and a deep impulse for devoted service to the cause of national well being. A compulsory provision for three months of intensive social work for at least every intending graduate may narrow the gulf that divides the so called educated class from the illiterate masses."

Views on Free Elementary Education

It was his considered opinion that the ideal to be achieved in the educational sphere should be free elementary education for all and higher education for those who deserve it, and not for those who can afford but do not deserve to have it. It was, he held, the duty of the State to arrange for the higher education of brilliant but poor students. For the ordinary students, avenues of technical education and training must be provided after a minimum basic education. The number of students for different trades and profession should be related to the need of hands in the respective trades to avoid glut and unemployment.

A week later he was called upon to give his views on the important question of language and literature as President of All India Bengali Literary Conference — Nikhil Bharat Banga Sahitya Sammelan — which was held at Cuttack on the 24th and 25th of December.

Vernacular languages of India, particularly Bengali language and its literature, had always had special fascination for him. It was to demonstrate the importance he attached to these languages of the country that he had taken up Indian vernacular for his M.A. His interest in Bengali literature continued all his life. It was in recognition of his deep understanding of the literary trends in the Indian languages and the services he had rendered to Bengali language that he was elected to preside over the Twenty Eighth Annual Session of the Sammelan.

In the course of his Presidential address to the Sammelan he dwelt upon the role and position of regional languages of India *vis a vis* Hindi, the national language of the country. He stood for paying full attention to the development of all the regional languages. He was opposed to any kind of imposed uniformity and considered it contrary to the Indian tradition, "Achievement of unity amidst adversity", he said, "has always been India's aim. Bearing this cardinal fact in mind, we should give full scope to the different regional languages to further enrich themselves and discountenance any more to further the cause of one language at the cost of the other".

Dev Nagri being the script of Sanskrit, he held, should be adopted as the script for all Indian languages. He attached greater importance to unity of script as a factor for national unity than the unity of language itself.

Development of Hindi as a Language

He regarded Hindi as the natural lingua franca of the country and he wanted it to be developed and encouraged to such an extent that it could become an effective medium of expression in all provinces of the country. But to give Hindi a really Indian character and make it easily understandable by all, he thought it desirable that appropriate words and expressions used in different languages should be incorporated in it. He thought that an authoritative Hindi dictionary which should contain special words and phrases of all regional languages could go a long way in developing a common vocabulary and bringing all the regional languages nearer to one another and to Hindi.

His own experience of speaking in Hindi proved the practicability of the above suggestion. His Hindi was none too good when he became President of Bhartiya Jan Sangh. But realising that he will have to address common people in Hindi, he thought of learning Hindi with the help of an English-Hindi dictionary. But he had not the leisure for it. Pt. Mauli Chandra Sharma, thereupon, advised him not to bother about learning Hindi words and expressions. "Use your Bengali words and expressions whenever you cannot remember an appropriate Hindi word or expression", he told him, " and you will be perfectly understood by Hindi speaking audiences". He tried it and found it a marvellous success. Within a year he became as effective speaker in Hindi as he was in English and Bengali.

This deep insight into the cultural and educational life of the country coupled with his academic attainments and literary taste gave a quality and tone to his politics which was lacking in most other politicians of the day. He would never take anything on its face value. He had developed a historical perspective and analytical mind which made him go into the origin and development of all problems before the country with an open mind and rare objectivity.

From Education to Politics

From education to politics was not a long way during the period of Indian struggle for independence. Education awakened the mind, created political consciousness and aroused the desire for emancipation from the foreign strangle-hold. That is why most political workers and leaders came from the educated and professional classes like lawyers, doctors and teachers.

Factors leading to the shift

For a man like Dr. Syama Prasad, this movement from educational to politics sphere was as natural as it was inevitable. His innate nationalism, dauntless courage, power of elocution and family tradition could not but bring him into the political arena for serving his motherland and securing justice for his people in a wider sphere. His father Sir Ashutosh had also planned to enter politics after his retirement from the High Court. But providence did not spare him to enter the political field and take the political leadership of the country, for which he was so eminently fitted, in his hands. The unfulfilled aspirations of his great father might also have been a factor that drove Syama Prasad into politics. But the major factor was the political situation as it developed itself, particularly after the inauguration of the Government of India Act of 1935. Syama Prasad had to enter active politics to save the life work of his father and his own in educational spheres from the Islamic vandalism of the Muslim League and the lack of realism and pusillanimity of the Indian National Congress.

He had began his political career in a small way as early as 1929 when he was elected to the Bengal Legislative Council as a Congress candidate from the University constituency. It was in a way a necessary adjunct to his educational work. He was supposed to act as a watch-dog of the interests of the Calcutta University in the legislature.

The Congress call for boycott of councils a few months later put him in a fix. As an honest and conscientious man he felt it his duty to obey that call. But as a result he realised that some one must remain in the Council to keep watch over and safeguard the interests of the University which had come to be looked upon by the British bureaucracy as a breeding ground of seditious ideas. He, therefore, resigned his seat in the Council to honour the call of the Congress and sought re-election to it as an independent candidate from the same University constituency. He was re-elected. He got his early training as a speaker and a parliamentarian during this period. He also got insight into the working of the Congress and the Muslim League mind. The Congress attitude towards the Communal Award came as a great shock to him. It shook his faith in that organisation. But his main work continued to be in and for the University outside the Legislature.

Congress-Muslim League Compromise: A Blow to Educational Fabric of Bengal

The introduction in 1937 of the Provincial part of the Government of India Act of 1935 and the elections to the Provincial Legislatures in the same year created a new situation. He was again elected to the Bengal Assembly from the University constituency and so had the opportunity to study the working of provincial autonomy from very close quarters.

The new assembly elected on the basis of Communal Award

had 250 members out of which only 80 were Hindus most of whom had been returned on the Congress ticket. The Muslims were divided between Muslim League led by S.H. Suhrawardy and Krishak Praja Party of A.K. Fazal-ul-Haq. The Congress handling of the situation in and outside the legislature soon provoked him to think afresh about its policies and political conceptions. He saw how bankruptcy of statesmanship on its part was driving all the Muslim members into the fold of the Muslim League. The Muslim League was jeopardising the social, educational and cultural life of Bengal and the very existence of Hindus as equal and self-respecting sons of the soil by pushing through the legislature the Bengal Secondary Education Bill, the University Bill and the Calcutta Corporation Bill. These bills struck at the very foundation of the educational fabric of Bengal through the life-long labours of Sir Ashutosh with the co-operation and help of Hindu philanthropists and scholars and which Syama Prasad had been trying to further improve and fortify. The situation was a challenge to his manliness. He could not see his life work being destroyed by upstart and reckless political adventurers. The man of action in him was roused. The retirement from the vice-chancellorship freed him from the responsibilities of that office. He was free to take up the challenge of politics.

Politics demanded his alignment with one or the other recognised political parties of the country which might provide him with a popular base. Indian National Congress, the most powerful political organisation in the country, with which he had been passively associated since his entry into public life would have been his natural choice but for the experience that he had gained of its mind and its philosophy both in theory and practice, in and outside the legislatures. He had become thoroughly disillusioned with it. Its policy of compromise with the Muslim League even at the cost of clear and vital national interests was repugnant to his innate nationalism.

V.D. Savarkar (Hindu Maha Sabha): Guide and Mentor

He was, therefore, in a fix. As a seeker after truth, he was in search of light. His tormented soul wanted a guide. This he found in Sir Vinayak Damodar Savarkar, the renowned revolutionary and close companion of Lokmanya Tilak, who was then on a visit to Calcutta. Savarkar had just then been freed from his internment in Ratnagiri District by the Congress Government of Bombay. He had spurned the offer to join the Congress, which was then prepared to offer him the highest position in the organisation, because he felt that the Congress had departed from the aims and ideals which inspired it when he had served it with his life blood. According to Veer Savarkar, the Congress had fallen from the high pedestal of nationalism. He was convinced that Congress policy of appeasement of Muslim League at the cost of the national interests for which Hindus in general stood would destroy Indian unity and the main springs of its national life. He had raised a hornet's nest by joining the Hindu Maha Sabha, which he wanted to build as a true instrument of the national will based on the ideal of Hindu and on the love of the country and its age old culture. He had put a new life in Hindu Maha Sabha within a few months and had come to Calcutta to reorganise the Maha Sabha movement in Bengal.

Meeting with Savarkar

Shri N.C. Chatterji, the Calcutta host of Veer Savarkar, invited a number of leading citizens of the city to meet him. Dr. Syama Prasad was one of them. He was deeply impressed by Veer Savarkar. His analysis of the Indian political situation and his gospel of unalloyed nationalism as the only effective antidote to Muslim separatism and divide-and-rule policy of the alien rulers appealed to him as a practical and realistic approach to the problems posed by Muslim League in Bengal and elsewhere. He, therefore, decided to join Hindu Maha Sabha and make it an effective instrument for check-mating the anti-national policies of the Muslim League and the cowardly passivity of the Congress. He took a leading part in the Annual Session of the All India Hindu Maha Sabha held in Calcutta, in December of the same year and became one of its vice-presidents. Soon after he became its Acting President due to the continued ill health of Veer Savarkar, the President.

Joining the Hindu Maha Sabha

Dr. Mookerjee's decision to join the Hindu Maha Sabha instead of the Congress, in which he could have surely reached the top in no time, has been subjected to some ill informed criticism by some if his friends and critics alike. But the answer to their criticism is to be found in Dr. Mookerjee's writings and speeches. Speaking at the Amritsar session of the Hindu Maha Sabha in December 1943, he posed the question "why Hindu Maha Sabha?" and answered:

> "So long as communal considerations loom large in the field of Indian administration and sinister Anglo-Muslim conspiracy continues, the Hindu Maha Sabha must function as an active and fearless political organisation which can both defend the rights of the Hindus and of India as a whole. So long as a third party remains in India and an aggressive anti-national and anti-Hindu Muslim League party holds its sway over the Muslim masses, enjoying the favours of the British Government, and planning to veto the elementary rights of the majority, Hindus for their sheer existence must have their own political organisation to fight for their own rights and liberties. The political goal of Hindu Maha Sabha is complete independence of India. It stands for joint electorates, if necessary with reservation of seats. It asks for no special favours for Hindus in any part of the country. Its aim and policy are consistent with welfare and advancement of India as a whole."

Meeting with Mahatma Gandhi

His joining the Hindu Maha Sabha in 1939 was welcomed even by a man like Mahatma Gandhi, whom he met at Calcutta for the first time on the 26th of February, 1940. Gandhiji had just returned from Malikanda, near Dacca, where he had gone to attend the meeting of Nikhil Bharat Charkha Sangh. There he had received the reports of anti-Hindu riots in Noakhali and other places known to be engineered by the Muslims with the connivance of the Muslim League Ministry, and was perturbed over the lot of the Hindus.

He asked Gandhiji why Congress was not opposing separate electorates which he thought would lead to partition of India at some stage. He referred Lady Minto's Diary to Gandhiji in support of his contention. Gandhiji expressed his ignorance about the diary and requested him to send him selected passages from it.

When told about Dr. Syama Prasad's entry into Maha Sabha, Gandhiji said "Somebody was needed to lead the Hindus after Malviyaji". Thereupon Dr. Mookerjee commented, "But then you will dub me as communal". Gandhiji's reply was, "Like Shiva who drank the poison after churning the sea, somebody must be there to drink the poison of the Indian politics. It can be you". Gandhiji was greatly impressed by the broad and thoroughly nationalistic outlook of Dr. Mookerjee. Before parting, he told him: "Patel is a Congressman with a Hindu mind, you be a Hindu Sabhaite with a Congress mind".

The entry of Dr. Mookerjee into Hindu Maha Sabha and his quick rise to the position of its Acting President marked the beginning of his active political career.

His entry into active politics was hailed by his admirers and critics alike. His intellectual attainments, dauntless spirit, moral fibre and power of elocution made him look a welcome addition to the political stage of the country. Some, who knew by experience how all absorbing the political field was, felt that the gain to political life would be a loss to the educational and cultural life of the country in which he had already made a mark. The homely remark of a top Congress leader who wrote to him "active politics is like riding a tiger, you can ride it all right but it becomes impossible to climb down from it," was often recalled by Dr. Mookerjee in later years when he had come to realise the truth of that friendly advice.

5

Joining the Political Arena

Dr. Mookerjee was not going to see the destruction of national interests sitting quietly. He therefore decided to oppose all such moves openly. He worked against the Congress and Muslim League's Plans to Muslimise Bengal.

His Mentors and Guides

Two men influenced him during the decisive phase of his political life where he had to choose between Congress and the Hindu Maha Sabha, and helped him to decide his line of action. They were late Dr. Keshav Bali Ram Hedgewar, the founder of the Rashtriya Swayamsevak Sangh, and Swatantriya Veer V.D. Savarkar who had just then been freed from his internment in his home district of Ratnagiri. Both of them were patriots of very high order who had made extreme sacrifices for the cause of the country. They had shown the rare courage of publicly exposing the hollowness of Congress approach to the national problems and had placed before the country a programme for creating national solidarity on the basis of the concept of Hindutva or Hindu Rashtra, which laid stress on love of the country and its age old culture as the mainspring of patriotism and national consciousness and not merely on anti-Britishism. It appealed to the reason of Dr. Mookerjee. He, therefore, began to take an active interest in Hindu Maha Sabha, which was then being re-organised, and took a prominent part in its annual session which was held at Calcutta in 1939 under the Presidentship of Veer Savarkar. Next year he was nominated to act as Working President of the Maha Sabha owing to continuous ill health of Veer Savarkar.

The story of Dr. Mookerjee's life from 1940 to 1947, when the mistaken policies of the Congress bore their deadly fruit of partition and the misery and problems that came in the wake of it, is truly the story of the nationalist India. During this period he interpreted the mind and presented the case of nationalist India before the Congress leaders and the British rulers with relentless logic and force. He made himself one with the suffering humanity of Bengal and India and served it with single minded devotion and fearless determination.

Confrontation with Subhash Chander Bose

Bengal first saw his mettle as a political leader in 1940. Late Subhash Chander Bose had just then been driven out of the Congress. But he had his hold on Calcutta. He wanted to demonstrate his strength and popularity to his opponents in the Congress by capturing the Calcutta Corporation and himself becoming its Mayor. Dr. Mookerjee had also planned to put up Hindu Maha Sabha candidates to contest all seats. Subhash Bose realised that in a triangular contest between Hindu Maha Sabha, Muslim League and his group, Muslim League might secure a majority. So he proposed a deal to Dr. Mookerjee. Hindu Maha Sabha and his party, he suggested, should contest an agreed number of constituencies to be determined by mutual consultation. Dr. Mookerjee agreed. Constituencies were accordingly selected and candidates approved. But they could not arrive at any agreed decision about the candidates to be set up for two particular constituencies. Dr. Mookerjee suggested a way out. A panel was to be submitted by each party to the other out of which the other party should select a candidate who should thereafter be treated as common candidate of both the parties. The suggestion was accepted. Subhash Bose selected one from the panel submitted by Dr. Mookerjee. But the man selected by Dr. Mookerjee out of the panel submitted by Subhash Bose was not acceptable to the latter. He wanted a supporter of his, a strong man who was neither a Congressman nor a Hindu Sabhaite, but whose physical support was very much valued by him, to be nominated for the seat and not the one selected by Dr. Mookerjee in accordance with the agreement. Dr. Mookerjee argued with him to abide by the pact and not to insist upon the selection of his particular favourite. But Subhash Bose would not agree. He told Dr. Mookerjee that force was the ultimate argument in all matters and he would not accept any other candidate even if it meant failure of the pact, and contest for every seat, which was sure to result in victory of third party, viz., the Muslim League. Dr. Mookerjee's appeal to avoid placing the Calcutta Corporation in the hands of Leaguers who were already doing havoc with the administration of Bengal had no effect on him. Dr. Mookerjee therefore reluctantly decided to accept the challenge. The two great men of Bengal were thus pitted against each other.

Subhash Bose with the help of his favourite decided to intimidate the Maha Sabha candidates by the use of force. His men would break up all Maha Sabha meetings and beat up its candidate. As a result the Maha Sabha candidates got so much terrified and demoralised that they would not hold any meeting at all. Dr. Mookerjee could not tolerate it. He got a meeting announced to be addressed by himself. As soon as he rose to speak a stone hit him in his head which began to bleed profusely. This infuriated the audience that adored him. It fell upon the goondas, including the strong man of Subhash Bose, and gave them a thorough beating. That put an end to their hooliganism. Soon after Subhash Bose met Dr. Mookerjee and suggested that there should be no interference or attempt at disturbing the meetings of the rival parties.

He was equally successful in foiling the League plans to Muslimise and dominate the secondary education through legislation. Mr. A.K. Fazal-ul-Haque as Chief Minister in the League-Krishak Praja Party coalition was determined to put the Secondary Education Bill, which sought to take away control of secondary education from the University, which was controlled by non-Muslims, and entrust it to a nominated Board with a majority of Muslims on it. Speaking in the Assembly early in 1940 he declared: "The members of the Coalition party we also determined to show the world that they would be untrue to Islam and untrue to their heritage if they do not place this bill permanently on the Statute Book".

But the man who led the opposition to the bill inside and outside the legislature had not only determination but also reason on his side. Dr. Mookerjee attacked the bill with such force of logic coupled with persuasive eloquence that he won the hearts of Fazal-ul-Haque's own supporters. His sweet reasonableness, his deep insight into the educational needs and problems of the province and his burning faith in the justice of his cause won over many an erstwhile supporters of the bill, including the Chief Minister himself, to his side. He finally turned the tables on the Muslim Leaguers with a great speech on the 4th of September, 1941, in the course which he said:

> "I shall ask the government and its supporters to hold their hands and not to proceed with the present bill. Nothing will be more welcome to the Hon'ble Chief Minister and to the general public in the province than an agreed measure on educational reform. We the elders may fight our battle in other spheres of differences, but if both of us are anxious that our children should receive better education than what we have ourselves received, why should we not put our hands together and be determined to come to an honourable agreement acceptable to both parties".

Progressive Coalition with Fazal-ul-Haque

His appeal proved to be very timely. Differences had already arisen between Mr. Fazal-ul-Haque and his Muslim League partners. He was not prepared to bow to the dictates of Mr. Jinnah. This was putting a severe strain on his coalition with Muslim League. The indictment of Muslim League and its tactics by Syama Prasad brought many a waverer to his side. He therefore decided to break with the League. He submitted the resignation of his coalition ministry on the 7th of December, 1941. Obviously, it created a new situation. Fazal-ul-Haque, with his Krishak Praja Party was a force in the legislature. But he could not form a ministry of his own because he did not command absolute majority. He needed the support of some Hindu members at least to be able to form a ministry.

The Congress leadership, if it had a grain of realism in it, should have rushed to support him to keep the Muslim League out of office. Such a step might have changed the whole course of Bengal politics, may even the politics of India as a whole, by weaning away Fazal-ul-Haque from the communal politics of the

League. But that was not to be. The Congress leaders seemed to be determined to force Fazal-ul-Haque into the lap of the Muslim League by persistently refusing to form a coalition with him.

Dr. Syama Prasad was however fully conscious of the dangers inherent in such an eventually. He considered it to be a catastrophe for Bengal. He therefore thought it necessary, in the wider interests of Bengal and India, that the Muslim League should be kept out of power by befriending and strengthening Fazal-ul-Haque. To that end he mustered together all the non-Congress Hindu forces in the legislature and formed what is known as the Progressive Coalition with Krishak Praja Party under the leadership of Fazal-ul-Haque. This gave Fazal-ul-Haque absolute majority in the Assembly which forced the British Governor, Sir John Herbert, to invite him, much against his wishes, to form the Government. Mr. Fazal-ul-Haque accepted the invitation and his new cabinet was sworn in on the 17th of December, 1941. Dr. Syama Prasad Mookerjee became Finance Minister of Bengal in this Coalition Ministry. And with this began a new chapter of his political life.

This incident proved the mettle of Dr. Mookerjee as a politician of the people of Calcutta and created a salutary effect on his opponents. Subhas Bose earned to respect him and they became good friends though their paths remained different.

All India Tours

Dr. Mookerjee toured the whole of India in the capacity of Acting President of the All India Hindu Maha Sabha due to ill health of its President, Veer Savarkar.

On one of his visits to Lahore in 1940 he spoke so forcefully and convincingly that he set all his audience thinking. Hindu Maha Sabha was becoming the hope of the people as the organization which could meet the challenges of the time over ruling the Congress.

Addressing a rally at Lahore of R.S.S. he said : "I see in this organization the one silver lining in the cloudy sky of India". It was this admiration for the R.S.S. which continued to draw him closer and closer to it in his later years.

He toured the whole of India addressing mammoth rallies and left his impression on all those who came in contact with him.

His whirlwind tour took the country by storm. It was felt everywhere that a new and powerful star was rising on the Indian horizon. His personality gave to the Maha Sabha a new status and prestige in the political life of the country, and he himself became an All-India figure. But Bengal was to continue to be his main field of activity for some time more. It was the situation in Bengal, the miserable plight of the Hindus who were being systematically humiliated and despoiled by the Muslim League with the connivance of the British for the great sin of patriotism, which had impelled him to leave the temple of Saraswati and enter the political arena. He therefore naturally felt that Bengal had the first claim on his attention. The task that faced him in Bengal was twofold. He had to meet the challenge of the Muslim League. He had also to establish his position *vis-a-vis* the Congress leadership which had come to regard the Hindus as their own flock which could be fleeced by them at will.

The main figure on the Congress side in Bengal at that time was Shri Subhash Chandra Bose. His stand against Gandhiji at the Tripuri Congress and his subsequent retreat from the Congress Presidency had made him a hero in Bengal. He was planning to hold Bengal, and particularly Calcutta, as his own citadel. He wanted to demonstrate his strength to the Congress high command by standing in the Corporation elections pitted against the Hindu Maha Sabha and the Muslim League, which finally resulted in a compromise with the Maha Sabha at the behest of Dr. Syama Prasad Mookerjee.

This incident proved the mettle of Dr. Mookerjee as a political leader of the people of Calcutta and created a salutary effect on his opponents. Subhash Bose learned to respect him and they became good friends though their paths remained different.

This friendship slowly grew into mutual admiration. Both were patriots of the purest hue and were fearless men of action. So they could understand and appreciate each other. Both ultimately laid down their lives for the glory and freedom of the motherland as martyrs.

Checkmating the Muslim League's Plans

The problem presented by the Muslim League was of a different kind. With the connivance of the British bureaucracy the

League Ministry of Bengal was making a planned effort to Muslimise the life of Bengal. There were two main planks in its programme. One was to engineer riots, particularly in East Bengal, to demoralise the Hindus so that they may flee from their homes and hearths or get converted to Islam. The second was to Muslimise the administration and sap the sources of Hindus' pre-eminence in educational and cultural spheres by depriving them of their hold over the University and the secondary education.

Dr. Mookerjee successfully checkmated their plans. He was always first to visit the riot affected areas to inspire confidence in the Hindus by his personal courage and by systematic exposure of the League designs. The way he dashed to Dacca early in 1940 when that city was in the grips of worst riots, has become a classic example of his supreme courage, fearlessness and solicitude for the common people.

6

Confronting the Hostile British Government

Joining the Ministry in Coalition Government

Entry into Bengal Government marked the beginning of a new and very significant chapter in the crowded life of Syama Prasad. Bengal had so far known him as an educationist who had entered politics more under compulsion of circumstances than as a matter of choice. His association with the Hindu Maha Sabha was frowned upon by many of the Congress-brand nationalists. They doubted his wisdom in joining hands with Fazal-ul-Haque and some took even more uncharitable view of the step he had taken.

But the way Syama Prasad conducted himself as a Minister, the determined fight he put up against the hostile British Governor and unsympathetic bureaucracy, not only silenced his critics but also raised his stature as a practical and far-seeing politician, a capable administrator and above all as an arch-nationalist.

The position of the coalition ministry was anything but easy. Shri Sarat Chandra Bose who was to join it along with Syama Prasad and who would have brought a good deal of prestige and strength to the new government was arrested just on the eve of the formation of the ministry following the disappearance of Shri Subhas Chandra Bose from him house-prison. The governor and the British bureaucracy were openly hostile to the new ministry. They were chagrined at their failure to have a Muslim League ministry and wanted the coalition government to fall. The Defence of India Rules had made the position of the Governor, who had direct access to the secretaries and district officers over the heads of the ministry, exceptionally strong *vis-a-vis* the ministry. The powers of the ministry were circumscribed in many ways and it had little voice in the matter of all important questions of defence of the province against the impending Japanese invasion. But Syama Prasad was not the man to be daunted by such difficulties. The more hurdles the governor put in the way of the ministry the more determined Syama Prasad became to assert the rights of the ministry to be heard and obeyed. His stature as an educationist and leader of the intellectual elite of Bengal forced the Governor to show him deference whether he liked it or not. Fazal-ul-Haque had the highest regard for Syama Prasad not only for his abilities but also because he looked upon him as his "Guru Bhai". He held Sir Ashutosh, at whose feet he had received his education, in the highest esteem. As a result, Syama Prasad soon began to be looked upon as the brain and guiding spirit of the coalition ministry.

Courting Arrest

Within a few days of his becoming a minister, there arose an occasion which demonstrated to the world, as perhaps nothing else could, the dauntless spirit and the courage of conviction of Dr. Mookerjee. The annual session of the Hindu Maha Sabha was scheduled to be held at Bhagalpur in December end. But the Bihar Government imposed ban on it against which the Maha Sabha decided to launch a *Satyagraha*. Dr. Mookerjee dashed to Bhagalpur and courted arrest along with other Maha Sabha leaders. That remains the solitary case in the annals of British rule in India when a minister of the Crown in one province courted arrest in another province under the same Crown.

Confronting the British

The first task before the new ministry was to prepare Bengal to meet the danger of Japanese invasion which was becoming more threatening day by day. The British government of India was then thinking of withdrawing and following a scorched earth policy instead of preparing the people, whom they distrusted, to fight the enemy. The ministry which was prevented by the existing army laws from doing anything to mobilise and train the people for the defence of their homeland, felt very helpless in the matter. Dr. Mookerjee, therefore, decided to take up the matter directly with the Governor on a personal plane.

Resignation as Minister

When the Congress leaders were under detention in jail after the Quit India Movement of August 1942 and the British Government had started a policy of heartless repression all over the country, Dr. Mookerjee took up the cudgels on behalf of the people of India while he was still serving as a minister in the Government of Bengal. Having come to know that the Governor was going to New Delhi for consultation, with the Governor-General and the C-in-C, he addressed to him on March 7, 1942, a long letter drawing his attention to the pressing need for raising a Home Army in Bengal to meet the impending danger. The letter, which along with some other letters of Dr. Mookerjee addressed to the governor, Sir John Herbert, and the Governor-General, Lord Linlithgow, including his letter of resignation from the cabinet ranks among the most forceful political writings of the period.

Excerpts from Letter to Sir John Herbert (Governor)

In a thundering language he told the Governor that:

> "Britain's vaunted doctrine of benevolent trusteeship stands exploded and you can no more throw dust into our eyes. India cannot be held against her will merely on the point of bayonet."

To fling such bitter truth in the face of the foreign Governor when he was still a minister in his Government showed the highest type of moral strength that he possessed. He presented the case of the Congress as no Congressman might have dared and exposed the Government so thoroughly that it had to proscribe that correspondence which was published in a book from under the title *A Phase of Indian Struggle*.

> "You should impress upon the viceroy", he wrote to Sir John Herbett, "that even at this late hour there should be an immediate settlement between England and India so that Indians may spontaneously feel that it is really a people's war. A strong representative national government with power to direct the defence policy of India in India's paramount interest has to be set up immediately, if we are to win the war".

"It is only a Chinese Generalissimo", he added, "that has inspired the Chinese people to fight the enemy to the last man. It is a Churchill, your own man, that gives you the clarion call at the hour of crisis .... Here, on the other hand, real power is in the hands of an irresponsible bureaucracy whom we cannot remove if we consider such removal to be imperative in our national interest".

Referring to his plan of Home Army he wrote, "I have placed before you a number of times my proposal that we should be given the power to raise a Home Army for the defence of Bengal, ... Your objection," he went on, "to raise a Home Army for Bengal even at a critical time like the present, is that this is entirely against the Indian Army Policy. My reply is that today that policy must be determined first and foremost in the interest of India. Let India's interests be the supreme factor today and let Indians themselves decide how best to tackle the great peril into which you have thrown us."

He concluded his letter with an appeal. "There will be many objections, as I have said before, from routine standpoint. But my appeal to you and through you to the viceroy is that you must be bold enough today to discard red tape and rusty bureaucratic notions of administration. As I have told you repeatedly there are many Indians who do not like that British Administration be perpetuated in India. But there is no sensible well-wisher of India who desires that India should start on a fresh career of foreign subjugation under Japan. We have almost reached the end of our journey so far as our relationship with England is concerned. What is required now is a broad statesmanship based on a full recognition of the fact that India must in future be controlled by Indians themselves".

Stafford Cripps Proposals

He next addressed a long letter to Lord Linlithgow, the then Governor-General of India, outlining some tentative proposals for an Indo-British settlement. He also sought permission for interviewing Mahatma Gandhi in jail. But the British Government was so much scared by his trenchant and convincing criticism of their policies and his realistic approach to the problem of Indo-British Settlement that it thought it impolitic to allow the Congress leaders to come in touch with him. He refused permission to meet Gandhiji.

All his appeals fell on deaf ears and the situation in Bengal and elsewhere continued to deteriorate. In the meanwhile, the British government sent Sir Stafford Cripps to India to bring about an interim settlement between the people of India and the British government for the efficient and effective execution of the war policies. He met the top leaders of the Congress, the Muslim League and other political parties including Dr. Syama Prasad and tried to sell to them what is known as Cripps Proposal. While discussing his proposal with Syama Prasad, Sir Stafford found to his surprise that he was pressing the Congress viewpoint with the vehemence of a Congress leader. He therefore slyly asked him, "But are not your party and the Congress constantly at logger-hands?"

"True" replied, Syama Prasad "but that is a quarrel as between a brother and brother. Our goal is the same."

The reply came like a slap on the face of that champion of the divide and rule policy.

While Sir Stafford Cripps was carrying on his negotiations with the Indian leaders about his proposals, which specifically conceded the principle of partition of India on the basis of religion by conceding the right to Muslim majority provinces to secede from India if they so wished, the British governor of Bengal and his agents were busy in torpedoing the coalition ministry of Fazal-ul-Haque which included the leading spokesmen of both the Hindus and Muslims, which thereby gave a direct lie to the British assertion that Hindus and Muslims could not work together. The Governor, and the permanent services, particularly the British and pro-Muslim League personnel of it, were doing everything possible to discredit the ministry, by putting hindrances in the way of its smooth sailing and encouraging the Muslim League opposition to kick up communal trouble. A campaign of vilification was set on foot against Mr. Fazal-ul-Haque and pressure was being put on him that he must relinquish the post of chief minister to enable the Muslim League party to join the coalition. At the same time the Congress, after having rejected the Cripps proposals, was thinking of launching a direct action.

Realising that the ministry would be expected to fight the Congress agitation and handle situations arising out of it, Dr. Syama Prasad addressed another letter to the Governor on the 12th of July, in which he made detailed suggestions about easing the political situation in the country in general and Bengal in particular. He also deprecated the Governor's efforts to play down the ministry and boost the Muslim League opposition.

> "We are often told," he wrote to the Governor, "that India's future political advancement was being retarded because of the failure of leaders of Hindus and Muslims to work together in the sphere of state administration. For the first time in the history of British India, whatever democratic constitution has been handed over to us, in spite of its manifold defects, was sought to be worked in Bengal by Hindu and Muslim representatives who wielded considerable influence over their own community. The success of this experiment would naturally give a direct lie to the plea of communal disharmony standing in the way of India's political advancement."

He then charged the Governor and his agents with trying to discredit the ministry. After recounting an example of governor's partiality for the Muslim League opposition he wrote

> "this special pleading for the League which in fact made us look upon you at times not as an impartial constitutional head of the province but as a loyal and distinguished whip of the Muslim League party itself was indeed a mystery to all of us".
>
> He once again appealed to the Governor "to take the ministry in his confidence and enable it to serve Bengal and win the co-operation of the people to meet the impending danger of foreign invasion."

But this, like his earlier appeal, had no effect on the Governor who was following a calculated policy of bringing down the ministry ruthlessly and suppressing the rights and liberties of the people so that they should be completely demoralised.

In the meanwhile the failure of the Cripps Mission had made the prospects of a negotiated settlement between the government and the people of India remote and the talk of direct action was in the air. The Working Committee of the Hindu Maha Sabha met at Lucknow on the 7th of August. Dr. Mookerjee wanted the Maha Sabha to plunge in any movement that might be launched by the Congress for wresting freedom from the unwilling hands of the British. But Veer Savarkar and other leaders of Maha Sabha were opposed to this policy. Savarkar stressed the need of militarisation of the country by maximum recruitment to the armed forces.

Meeting with Gandhiji

Before returning to Calcutta, Dr. Mookerjee met Mahatma Gandhi, who was proceeding to Bombay, at Allahabad station. Mahatma Gandhi advised Dr. Mookerjee not to join the movement that he was then planning on the plea that somebody must remain behind to lead the country when the Congress leaders would be in jail.

Arrest of Congress Leaders

The Government of India had got the clue about the proposed "Quit India" move of the Congress and had completed preparations for arresting all the Congress leaders on the 9th of August, the day on which the resolution was passed by the Congress Working Committee, at Bombay. Detailed instructions had been sent to the provincial governors about the steps to be taken to suppress the movement. The Governor of Bengal had shown the letter of the Government of India to the Chief Minister but had refused to take the rest of the ministers in confidence before the policy outlined in it had been executed.

On the 9th of August, after the Congress leaders had been arrested, the Governor called Dr. Syama Prasad Mookerjee and other ministers and asked them either to accept the policy of the Government of India or to resign.

Letter to Lord Linlithgow (Governor-General)

Dr. Mookerjee told him frankly that he could not approve that policy and decided not to resign till he had made an appeal to the Governor-General to change that policy. Accordingly he wrote his historic letter to Lord Linlithgow on the 12th of August in which he put forth the view-point of nationalist India with commandable fearlessness and logic together with concrete and constructive suggestions for an immediate settlement between England and India.

"The demand of the Congress" he wrote to Lord Linlithgow, as embodied in its last resolution virtually constitutes the national demand of India as a whole. "It is regrettable", he added, "that a campaign of misrepresentation is now being carried on in some sections of the foreign press characterising the Congress demand as a virtual invitation to Japan and a surrender to chaos and confusion. No one desires that India should be plunged into a mass movement resulting in disorder and anarchy. At the same time a refusal on the part of the British Government to deal with the real demand of the people in a spirit of statesmanship will be an even greater disaster; for by this unwise decision it is they and not the Congress who will precipitate a crisis."

After recounting the possible effects of repression he appealed to the Governor-General to take a realistic view of the Indian situation which must be examined in the light of rapidly changing world movements.

Proposals for Indo-British Settlement

He then put forth certain tentative proposals "which may well form the basis of an honourable Indo-British settlement".

His proposals were:

- The British Government should declare that India's freedom is formally recognised.
- The viceroy or any one deputed by the British Government will be authorised to negotiate with the Indian political parties regarding the formation of an Indian National Government to whom power will be transferred.
- The Indian National Congress will declare its determination to fight the Axis powers and it will not conclude a separate peace with the enemy.
- The war policy of India will be in accord with the policy as determined by the Allied War Council on which India will be represented.

- The C-in-C will remain in charge of the operational control of war in India and will carry out the common policy of the Allied War Council.
- The Indian National Government will be able to raise an Indian army whose aim will be to help in the maintenance of internal security and also to defend the country against foreign aggression.
- The National Government will be composite in character and will include representatives of important groups and parties in the country. It will set up provincial governments also on a similar basis.
- The membership of the central and provincial cabinets will not be confined to members of the legislatures but may include outsiders who may wield influence in the country and may be of special assistance during the period of the war.
- The Indian National Government will concentrate on an active policy of industrialisation and economic uplift of India so that India may effectively prosecute the war.
- The India Office will be abolished.
- As regards the future constitution, the Indian National Government in due course will take necessary steps for the formation of a Constituents Assembly for the purpose. There will be a treaty between Great Britain and India which will specially deal with minority rights. In any case any minority will have the right to refer proposal regarding the future constitution to the arbitration of an international tribunal in case it considers such a step necessary for the protection of its just rights. The decision of such tribunal will be binding on the Indian Government and on the minority concerned.

"You as the representative of the British Crown," he concluded, "should be authorised to deal with the Indian problem with a definite mandate from the British Government. Other proposals", he added "may also be made. But the principal factor is that the British Government must make up its mind to transfer power before negotiations can at all be started".

He ended this letter on a personal note. "I have intimated to the Governor of Bengal," he informed the Governor-General "that I disapprove of the policy that has been launched by the British Government and their representatives at the present juncture. I am making this appeal to you in the hope that you will not allow false prestige to stand in the way but take immediate action for solving the deadlock. In case, however, you feel that British Government should not move further but allow the present impasse to continue. I must regretfully ask my Governor to relieve me of my duties as a minister so that I may have full freedom to help to mobilise public opinion in demanding a settlement".

He requested the Governor-General to forward his letter copies to the British Prime Minister, Sir Stafford Cripps and the Secretary of State for India "so that whatever the British Government may do, it may appreciate our attitude towards the present crisis".

Dr. Mookerjee did not receive a reply to his letter from the Governor-General till September. But in the meantime the engine of repression let loose by the central and provincial governments to put down any kind of manifestation of resentment against the British policy left no doubt in his mind as to what the reply would be. The refusal of the viceroy to permit him to meet Mahatma Gandhi in jail and secure his approval for his plan of settlement also pointed to the same conclusion. He therefore began to do his duty by the fighters for freedom in his own way. It is well known that the financed Shri J.P. Narain and many other revolutionaries during these hectic days. He arranged to provide books and other facilities to large number of students who had been imprisoned so that they might be able to pursue their studies from within the jails. But all his efforts to effect any material change in the policy of repression which was being directed by the Governor himself through the permanent officials over the heads of the ministry proved abortive.

Midnapore Disaster: The Final Straw

The helplessness of the ministry, in whose name the administration was being run to serve the people and alleviate their suffering was, however, finally and most painfully exposed by the Midnapore disaster. On October 10, Midnapore district was hit by a severe cyclone which resulted in the destruction of thousands of lives and brought untold misery to the people. The unsympathetic bureaucracy, presumably under the instructions of the Governor, thought the time fit for wreaking vengeance on the people for their active participation in the freedom movement. Not only the relief was withheld from the victims of cyclone but, what was worse, a veritable reign of terror was let loose by N.M. Khan, the notorious District Magistrate, through police and army personnel which were supposed to render assistance to the people. Thousands of houses were wantonly burnt down, women were assaulted and raped, the cattle were slaughtered and outraged people were hounded down like wild animals.

On getting news of the ghastly tragedy, Dr. Mookerjee rushed to Midnapore. What he saw there brought tears to his eyes and he began to tremble with rage. He had sharp exchanges with N.M. Khan, who refused to obey his instructions and persisted in the policy of repression. He even refused to allow private relief to be given to the victims of nature's wrath and bureaucratic repression.

Midnapore proved to be the last straw. Dr. Mookerjee felt convinced that the time had come when he should come out of the government and lead the opposition to the policy being pursued by the British Government and its agents in India and Bengal as a free man and expose the mockery to which the provincial autonomy had been reduced by those who claimed to be fighting to save the world for democracy.

Letter of Resignation

His letter of resignation, which he addressed to the Governor, Sir John Herbert, on the November 16, 1942, is a remarkable document. It reveals the fearless spirit of Dr. Mookerjee, his solicitude for the welfare of the common man and his righteous anger at the methods adopted by the British agents as perhaps nothing else could.

"My reasons for resignation," he wrote to the Governor "are two-fold. First as I intimated to you at the earliest opportunity, on 9th August last, I disapprove of the policy adopted by the British Government of India with regard to the present political situation in the country. I am aware that you, as provincial Governor, have hardly any responsibility for the formulation of this policy. But my second reason mainly concerns you. And that is connected with the manner, in my opinion unwarranted, in which you have interfered with the work of the ministry and have rendered the so-called provincial autonomy into a meaningless farce".

Dr. Mookerjee was not the man to be daunted or deflected from the path of duty by fear or favour. He dominated the cabinet so long as he remained in it and checkmated the evil designs of the Anglo-Muslims. He quit it with deep disdain when he found that he could no longer serve his people and country by continuing in it.

Riots at Dacca

Soon after his resignation from the Bengal cabinet there began the terrible riots at Dacca which were directly engineered by Muslim League with the connivance of the British Governor and administrators. The Anglo-Muslim conspired not to let the country even hear of this holocaust. Press was forbidden to publish any news about it under the Defence of India Rules. But as soon as Syama Prasad came to know of it he decided to visit Dacca. The British Chief Secretary at first would not permit him to do so. But when he insisted he was allowed to go. But there was no conveyance. A chartered plane was going to carry Kh. Nazimuddin and other Muslim ministers there. Dr. Mookerjee requested the Governor for a seat in it. But just before he reached the aerodrome, the plane took off to avoid him. But he was not the man to be daunted by such tactics. He got into a tiny private monoplane and risked his life in that ricketty thing. When he landed safely at Dacca, the British Deputy Commissioner would not let him enter the city on grounds of safety. He would not give him police escort either. But Dr. Mookerjee was determined to be amidst his suffering brethren. He dashed to the city and directly went to the palace of Nawab of Dacca, the President of Bengal Muslim League from where the whole carnage was being planned and organised. The whole of Dacca was amazed at his boldness and courage. The Hindus came to adore him; even the Muslims came to respect him.

After his return to Calcutta he wanted the public to know

what had happened in Dacca. But the Press was forbidden by Defence of India Rules. The only way to get the news published was to first have the matter raised in the Assembly. The Press could then give publicity to the news in the form of proceedings of the Assembly. But he needed some minimum support in the Assembly for moving the Adjournment Motion. He wired to Maulana Azad, the then Congress President, to instruct Congress legislators to support him. But Azad refused to do anything in the matter just then. Thereupon Dr. Mookerjee wrote to Gandhiji who admonished Azad and directed him to wire to Bengal legislators to support Syama Prasad's move. Thus, he was able to tell the country what had happened in Dacca. It was as a result of his exposures in the Assembly that the Government was forced to restore calm and punish the guilty.

Famine in Bengal

The year 1943 saw Bengal in the terrible grip of a man-made famine. Men and women, mostly Muslims, began to die like rats and dogs. But the Muslim League Ministry uttered not a word about the murderous bungle that had created the famine. The Press was forbidden even to publish any news about it which took a toll of 35 lakh lives. It was again Dr. Mookerjee who broke the news of it to the startled nation by issuing a statement which was published by a monthly magazine. The Government warned him and the magazine for it. But he refused to keep quiet and dared them to do their worst. He made a national issue of it. The way he organised relief for the famine stricken and the cooperation he secured from all sections of society in all parts of the country revealed his great organising capacity and his deep humanity which was not shackled by any consideration of caste and creed or by provincialism.

The Amritsar Session Surrender

After that the whole of nationalist India began to look to him and the organisation he represented for guidance. Hindu Maha Sabha could then have surely filled the political vaccum created by the suicide of the Congress. But Hindu Maha Sabha, with all its ideological strength, was organisationally too weak and ramshackle to take advantage of the situation. It threw away its chance of becoming a force in Indian politics. When its top leaders in Punjab made an object surrender at Amritsar, where Maha Sabha Session was held in 1943 under the presidentship of Dr. Mookerjee. The last minute bar on taking out the President elect in procession was a challenge to Maha Sabha. Dr. Mookerjee wanted the Reception Committee to take up the challenge and defy the ban. The people also wanted a bold policy and were prepared to suffer. But the Chairman of the Reception Committee and other Maha Sabha leaders, who had to take the decision, happened to be arm-chair politician. They failed to rise to the occasion. This weakness not only brought Hindu Maha Sabha in disrepute but also enabled the misinformed critics to accuse Dr. Mookerjee, the most fearless of Indian political leaders of the day, also of weakness and cowardice. But Dr. Mookerjee continued to carry Maha Sabha on his strong shoulders. His personal achievements continued to bring credit and strength to that organisation.

An Impatient Congress

Release of Congress leaders in 1945 created a new situation in the country. They were thoroughly frustrated and many of them had become impatient for power. The Muslim League ideology in the meanwhile has taken roots among the Muslim masses with the direct help and encouragement of the British. The demand for Pakistan had gained force and momentum and the Muslim League had come to be recognised by the Government as the sole representative organisation of the Indian Muslims.

The Congress leaders got unnerved by this situation.

Shri C. Rajgopalachari had in the meanwhile put forth his formula which virtually conceded Pakistan to Muslim League. It was for sometime subjected to bitter criticism by a section of Congressmen. But C.R. had come to be recognised as the brain trust of the Congress and his pull with Gandhiji was well known. It therefore created the feeling in Muslim League circles that Congress was giving in. What had been put forth merely as a bargaining counter appeared to be coming within their grasp. They decided to take advantage of the situation and raised the tempo of their agitation.

Call to Unite against British

It did not take Dr. Mookerjee long to grasp the new situation. He warned the country about the coming catastrophe and gave all nationalist forces a call to unite and assert themselves against the Congress policy to surrender.

The response to his appeal was tremendous. Congress leadership felt the ground slipping from under its feet. It, therefore, decided to reassure the country about its bona-fides. Sardar Patel met Dr. Mookerjee in Calcutta and assured him that Congress would not accept Pakistan. Mahatma Gandhi also gave him similar assurances and requested him not to organise a separate front. Dr. Mookerjee took them on their word. But the Congress Working Committee threw away the case for United India in its Poona Resolution which, while making pious prophecies of faith in the unity of India, declared towards the end that it will not coerce unwilling parts of the country to remain within India. But for winning the election of 1946 it publicised only the first portion of this resolution which dealt with untenability of partition and expressed Congress desire for keeping the unity of the country unimpaired.

It was the biggest hoax played on the people of India in pre-independence days. The Hindus were taken in. They voted Congress into power wherever they happened to be in majority. Almost all the Muslim seats went to the Muslim League except in the N.W.F.P. A Muslim League ministry was installed in power in Bengal and the Muslim League leaders became more emphatic in their demand for partition.

In August 1946, they launched the Direct Action and started large-scale violence to cow down the Congress leaders. Dr. Mookerjee who had again been returned to Bengal Legislative Assembly from the Calcutta University constituency stood by the people in that catastrophe and helped them to stand up in self-defence. They gave a creditable account of themselves against the organised Muslim League goondas who had the backing of Muslim League ministry as well. Though Direct Action failed in clearing Calcutta of all the Hindus yet it had the desired effect on the Congress leaders. They got thoroughly demoralised.

The Cabinet Mission

The British Cabinet Mission that came to India soon after, even though it was convinced of the impracticability of Pakistan, was struck by the imbecility of Congress leaders. Dr. Mookerjee pleaded with them to take a firm stand against any scheme of partition. But he was silenced by the Mission which declared that the Congress had already committed itself to Partition by its resolution about noncoercion of any unwilling part to remain within India.

Partition: The Inevitable Course

That convinced Dr. Mookerjee that Partition of the country was inevitable. Thereafter he bent his energies to saving as much as he could from going to Pakistan because he know that Congress leaders in their impatience for power would not mind giving the whole of Bengal and even Assam in the bargain to Pakistan. It was mainly due to his efforts that half of Bengal was saved for India.

Later, when the Constituent Assembly of India was formed by the close of 1946 he was elected to it from Bengal. His qualities of head and heart, his skill as a parliamentarian and above all his deep application and devotion to duty, soon marked him out as the coming man and made him the subject of adoration of all in the Assembly. He began to be recognised as a national figure.

7

Fighting the Tide of Partition

Dr. Syama Prasad's main purpose in getting out of the government was to be free to mobilise public opinion in support of his plan for a negotiated Indo-British settlement on the basis of the tentative plan submitted by him to Lord Linlithgow. But he did not get much time for that. The food situation in Bengal soon forced the humanitarian in him to concentrate all his attention on devising ways and means for relieving the distress of the famine-stricken people.

Famine Relief Work: Fighting Indifference of Government

Food situation in Bengal had begun to deteriorate by the beginning of 1943. There were many reasons for it. The cyclone that hit Midnapore district in October had completely destroyed the paddy crop in some other districts as well. The stoppage of supplies of rice from Burma after it fell before the Japanese and the denial policy of the British in East Bengal, as a precautionary measure against the Japanese invasion, had further aggravated the situation.

Fazal-ul-Haque's ministry drew the attention of the people and the Central Government to this deteriorating food situation in Bengal through a statement made on the floor of the legislative council towards the end of February, 1943. The statement said that there was a deficit of about 25 per cent in rice supply and that steps must be taken to meet this deficit. But this ministry was dismissed by the Governor in March and in April a Muslim League ministry was put in the saddle. The new ministry thought it fit to repudiate the February statement of the previous ministry about food scarcity and instead began to issue statement after statement assuring the people that there was no actual scarcity and that the rise in the prices of rice was due to hoarders who would be forced to release the stocks. This criminal indifference of the ministry to the actual situation was matched by most irksome restrictions imposed by the British bureaucracy and military authorities on plying of vehicles and boats in pursuit of the denial policy. Their aim was to demoralise and emaciate the people so that they should not be able to render affective help to Indian National Army of Netaji Subhash Chandra Bose if it succeeded in penetrating into Bengal through Burma.

By the beginning of July the food situation had become so grave that thousands of people from the village began to trek to cities after disposing of all their cattle and chattels in search of food. Even in cities the price of rice had risen so high that most of the middle-class families with fixed incomes were finding it difficult to get two square meals. But in spite of all this, the ministry and the bureaucracy went on merrily with their exploded notion that there was no actual deficit and nothing tangible was done to relieve the growing distress of the people.

Setting up of Relief Committees

Dr. Mookerjee who had already seen the distress of the people of Midnapore, for whom he had organised large-scale relief through private efforts, could not remain indifferent to the calamity which appeared to be engulfing the whole of Bengal. He decided to draw the attention of the country at large to the distress in Bengal and organise large-scale relief for the famine-stricken people. To this end he invited some leading politicians, businessmen and philanthropists to a meeting on the 29th of July, to think over the situation and devise ways and means to face it. As a result Bengal Relief Committee was formed with Sir Badri Das Goenka as president and Dr. Syama Prasad Mookerjee as vice-president.

Soon after Bengal provincial Hindu Maha Sabha, of which Dr. Mookerjee was the president, organised the Hindu Maha Sabha Relief Committee in response to the express wish of some donors who wanted their money to be spent through the Hindu Maha Sabha. Dr. Mookerjee was the moving spirit behind both the organisations. His appeals for funds found a ready response all over the country. The people had such trust and faith in Dr. Mookerjee that large sums of money began to be sent to him to be spent as he thought fit.

After sometime the Arya Samaj, the Marwari Society and the Ramakrishna Mission also plunged into the relief work. They had their separate centres and separate funds for the purpose. This created danger of duplication and consequent wastage of efforts and money. Dr. Mookerjee thereupon took steps to co-ordinate the activities of the different relief societies by setting up a Relief Co-ordination Committee with Shri Badri Das Goenka as president and himself as vice-president.

The response to his appeal for help was tremendous. The whole country from Assam to Kanyakumari responded magnificently to his call. The Bengal Relief Committee alone received cash donations amounting to Rs. 27,55,502 and commodities such as clothes and grain, etc., valued approximately at rupees ten lakhs. The Hindu Maha Sabha Committee received donations amounting to Rs. 8,54,582 in cash besides thousands of maunds of food grains.

As a result of these large-scale relief measures of Bengal Relief Committee and other relief organisations under the guidance of Dr. Mookerjee, the distress, particulary in cities, was relieved to some extent. But in spite of these herculean efforts of Dr. Mookerjee this man-made famine took toll of more than 30 lakh lives.

The Bengal famine threw lurid light on the *bona fides* and motives of the British government and its Muslim allies in India. The attitude of the British bureaucracy throughout was openly hostile. It tried to minimise the disaster in every possible way. The demand for forming an all party national coalition ministry, in the place of purely Muslim League ministry, to meet the situation was persistently turned down. The Muslim League in the turn refused to budge from its stand about no scarcity till the situation had completely gone out of its hands. Even then it took no steps to organise relief till after private agencies through their unaided efforts shamed it into action.

Dr. Syama Prasad was, on one hand, busy with famine relief in Bengal, the Muslim League under the leadership of Mr. Jinnah and with the active connivance of the British, was busy consolidating its position in different parts of the country. The arrest of most of the leaders of the Congress after the rejection of Cripps Proposals, which for the first time conceded, so far as the British were concerned, the principle of partition of India on the basis of religion, had left the field open for the Muslim League to win over the wavering Muslims, and establish its position as the mouth-piece of the Indian Islam.

The CR Formula: Taking up Cudgel Againt

As the noise made by the Muslim League for partition of India, backed as it was by the entire Muslim and Anglo-Indian Press in the country, grew louder, some Congress leaders like Shri C. Rajagopalachari, who happened to be out of jail began to be unnerved. And in keeping with the tradition developed by the Congress since it came under the influence of Mahatma Gandhi, their inclination to appease the Muslim League even at the cost of vivisection of the motherland began to manifest itself in different ways. The plan put forth by Shri C. Rajagopalachari, better known as C.R. formula, which practically accepted partition, was the most notorious of such appeasement gestures.

Dr. Syama Prasad Mookerjee considered this to be a very dangerous and disqueting development. He therefore decided to take up the cudgels on behalf of the nationalist India against the nefarious Anglo-Muslim game of destroying the age old unity of the country, whose consolidation in the political sense had been the one positive contribution of the British rule over India.

The Amritsar Session

The 25th Annual Session of the Hindu Maha Sabha which was held at Amritsar in December, 1943, gave him the opportunity to call the attention of his countrymen to this new danger and sound a note of warning to all concerned. In the absence of Shri V.D. Savarkar, the president who could not be present due to illness, Syama Prasad was called upon to preside over the historic session of the Maha Sabha. It was historic firstly because it was being held at a time when political life of nationalist India had been almost brought to a standstill by the British repression and secondly because it marked the highest water-mark of the Hindu Maha

Sabha popularity in the country. Under the able leadership of Veer Savarkar and Dr. Syama Prasad Mookerjee, the Hindu Maha Sabha was then making a successful bid to fill the vacuum created by the expulsion of the Congress from the political arena of India.

The Presidential address delivered by Dr. Mookerjee on the occasion gave a clear exposition of his political philosophy and his stand about the demand for partition. "The only solution of the Indian problem," he declared, "is rigidly to exclude all extraneous considerations based on caste and religion from the field of politics. We stand for equal political citizenship of all without any distinction. I admit that there are classes and communities which are backward and which have to be give special protection for educational and economic advancement. The constitution itself should guarantee the preservation of religious, social and cultural rights of different classes". It was thus clear that he did not want any special advantages for the Hindus. His approach to communal problem was absolutely rational and national. But he was not prepared to offer bribes which might cut at the roots of the national unity to win the cooperation of certain communities for the common national cause. "Patriotism" he declared "can never be purchased at the market place by an open bidding. If the Indian National Congress, as the mouth-piece of progressive Indian public opinion, was prepared to concede, even on fundamental issues affecting national solidarity and self-respect for the sake of winning the support of Muslim leaders, the British representatives were always ready at hand to offer a higher price at every stage and thus frustrate a combination between the two great communities of India. Today the Muslim League, which is acknowledged by the government as perhaps the only spokesman of Muslim view-point in India, has raised the cry of breaking India into fragments as a condition precedent to political settlement. None knows better than the British government itself that Pakistan is a sheer impossibility. We oppose it not merely because Hindus cannot tolerate the idea of vivisection of their motherland but because both economically and politically such a decision will be dangerous to the welfare of India as a whole . . . Let it be clearly understood" he added "that there can be no settlement with the Muslim League on the basis of Pakistan".

Dwelling on the need and the role of the Hindu Maha Sabha he declared,

> "If a time comes when religious and communal considerations disappear from the field of Indian administration and all parties are swayed by one common national ideal, there may be no need for a separate political organisation for Hindus as such. But let us not forget what we really are today. Politics detached from realities is not only meaningless but dangerous".

This stress on realism, on walking on hard earth instead of soaring into sky, was the special contribution of Dr. Mookerjee to the Indian political thinking at a time when utopian idealism of Mahatma Gandhi was swaying the minds of Indian intelligentsia. It was this way of thinking which brought him so close to late Sardar Patel in his later days.

Lapse by Maha Sabha Leaders at Session: A Setback

The effect of Amritsar session and his great speech was, however, marred to a good extent by an unfortunate lapse of the local Maha Sabha leaders. The District Magistrate of Amritsar, probably in pursuit of a set policy not to allow Maha Sabha to gain popularity and prestige, imposed a ban on the taking out of the Presidential procession just at the eleventh hour when all preparations for it had been completed. The feelings of the people who had thronged to Amritsar in lakhs for the session ran high. They wanted the procession to be taken out in spite of the ban. Dr. Mookerjee was also of the same opinion and wanted that the ban should be broken. But the Reception Committee lacked the courage and guts demanded by the occasion. It decided to drop the procession. This had a demoralising effect on the people who expected the Maha Sabha leaders to rise to the occasion give a practical proof of their preparedness to suffer for a just cause. The Hindu Maha Sabha never recovered from this setback it got at Amritsar in 1943. It fell in popular estimation and thus failed to take advantage of the halo Dr. Mookerjee had created for it. Some people even began to doubt the courage and fearlessness of Dr. Mookerjee. They failed to realise that he could not override the decision of the Reception Committee in the matter.

Aryan Congress Session (Delhi)

A couple of months later, Dr. Mookerjee presided over the Fifth Session of All-India Aryan Congress held in Delhi from the 20th to 22nd of February, 1944. In the course of his Presidential speech he paid a glowing tribute to late Swami Dayananda Saraswati and the Arya Samaj:

> "The greatest service of the Arya Samaj" he said "is that it has roused amongst the people a profound sense of individual and national self-respect, a virility of mind and a love of the country's culture and civilisation, destroying the poisonous sense of inferiority complex which turns man into a crowd".

He also strongly condemned the decision of the Muslim League ministry of Sind to ban certain parts of 'Satyarth Prakash' — the monumental work of Swami Dayanand. He appealed to Arya Samajists to work in cooperation with other parties for the consolidation of the Hindu forces and freedom of Hindustan. He dwelt at length on the Muslim League's demand for Pakistan and declared that "any one who seeks to disturb India's unity or to foment disruption is guilty of the highest act of treachery and must be resisted at any cost".

The Calcutta Press, then as now, was controlled either by Anglo-Indians or by the Congress. It avoided giving proper publicity to the views of Dr. Mookerjee on the question of partition and other pressing national problems. He herefore started an English daily of his own — *The Nationalist* — in 1944. It soon became a powerful organ for moulding public opinion. But the financial strain of running an English daily soon proved to much for him and it had to be closed down after a year.

For a United India

The stiff opposition of Dr. Mookerjee to the idea of partition, and his forceful advocacy for united India coupled with the rebuffs that Mr. Jinnah got at the hand of Sir Sikandar Hayat Khan and Sir Chhotu Ram in Punjab, the key province of Pakistan of his conception, went a long way in nipping the mischief that Cripps Proposals had set on foot.

Gandhi's Support Blessings to C.R. Formula

Mr. Jinnah's stock stood pretty low and the idea of Pakistan began to be scoffed at, even by prominent Muslims.

Just at that time, Dr. Mookerjee learnt to his great dismay that Mahatma Gandhi, who had been lately released from prison, had blessed the C.R. Formula for partition and had sought a meeting with the crest-fallen Mr. Jinnah at the latter's residence at Bombay. Nothing could have been more impolitic and inopportune. Dr. Mookerjee was deeply distressed at this misconceived move which, he was quick to realise, would bolster up the tottering image of Mr. Jinnah. He therefore immediately decided to do everything possible to prevail upon Mahatma Gandhi to desist from meeting Mr. Jinnah. To that end he sent his trusted secretary, Shri Manoranjan Choudhury, with a personal letter to Mahatma Gandhi imploring him not to lend his support to C.R. Formula and not to meet Mr. Jinnah for a settlement on that basis. This letter dated 19th of July, 1944, is a historic document and deserves to be quoted in full for it gives an index of Dr. Mookerjee's burning patriotism, his passionate faith in the unity of India and his realistic assessment of the results of the appeasement policy of the Congress towards Mr. Jinnah and the Muslim League.

77, Ashutosh Mookerjee Road,
Calcutta.
19th July, 1944.

Dear Mahatmaji,

Srijut Manoranjan Choudhury is going to see you with this letter and some notes and papers regarding the Bengal situation. He will explain to you how events have developed in Bengal, both as regards politics and food since August, 1942. All available literature are being sent through him for your perusal.

Frankly speaking, we feel greatly perturbed at the terms offered by Mr. Rajagopalachari to Mr. Jinnah. We are most anxious for a proper Hindu-Muslem settlement. But we do not believe that the way in which Shri Rajagopalachari is proceeding will ever secure that end. Your own past experience must have convinced you that Mr. Jinnah has no intention of playing the game. He does not regard himself as an Indian and has no concern, whatsoever, for the freedom of India as a whole, for which generations of Indians have lived and died. A possible partition of Bengal and of India is abhorrent to us. In any case, we feel deeply cut that you should have identified yourself with this proposal without hearing different points of view. We regard you as something above the Congress and any commitment made by you places all of us in a position of a great embarrassment. Manoranjan Babu will explain to you how many people in Bengal belonging to different political organisations are feeling on this matter. Our fear is that Mr. Jinnah will treat this offer as a mere spring-board in order to demand further concessions both within Hindustan area and in the so-called Pakistan area. The result will be further chaos and confusion. The British government will not move by what you have said, because it has no intention to part with power. Mr. Jinnah will not move, because he does not want that deadlock should be ended. But your concession will remain and will add to our future difficulties. I do implore you to reconsider the step you have taken. If Mr. Jinnah and the Muslim League refuse to respond to the terms, you should categorically withdraw your support and stand for an undivided India. Only in 1942, in *Harijan* you expressed yourself in the clearest terms against any scheme of partition of India and you rightly stated that such a proposal would only give rise to new quarrels amongst ourselves.

I feel that you should lay down your scheme for the attainment of Indian freedom with the cooperation of all parties and communities. Those who want freedom for the whole of India with interests of the minorities fully protected should be asked to cooperate with you in popularising such a scheme. Many Moslems today are realising that Pakistan is an impossibility and a hoax. The British government itself is withdrawing its support to Mr. Jinnah wherever it suits government to do so. Just at this psychological moment you raise him up as the only man who can deliver the goods for the Moslem stand-point. This is a great blow to many

Moslems outside the League who imbued by national sentiments have been fighting for the bigger cause of Indian freedom.

I do hope you will realise the serious condition of Hindus in provinces where they are in a minority. You have stated that while approving of the terms you regarded yourself as an Indian and not as a Hindu. Surely, if you as an Indian can specially think of Moslem demands and are prepared to appease Mr. Jinnah on this account, why should I not as a Hindu ask you as an Indian, to stand by the just and legitimate rights of Hindus as well. If you are an Indian and do not concern yourself with Hindu or Moslem questions at all, you should shun the Moslim League completely and only offer to cooperate with all those who are only Indians and nothing else.

I am coming to Poona on 1st August to attend the Tilak Anniversary and hope to stay there for three days. Meanwhile, Manoranjan Babu will meet you and bring to me any message that you may be good enough to send to me. I hope you are feeling stronger.

With best wishes,

Yours sincerely,

Sd./- Syama Prasad Mookerjee

Dr. Mookerjee followed up his letter by a personal meeting with Mahatma Gandhi at Wardha on his way back from Poona early in August, 1944. Shri C. Rajagopalachari was also at Wardha at that time. Dr. Mookerjee placed before Mahatma Gandhi and C. Rajagopalachari the dangers inherent in any scheme of partition of India on the basis of religion. With a prophetic vision he told Gandhiji that Pakistan if created was bound to have a foreign policy opposite to that of India, which would endanger Indian security and create very many new unseen problems.

Gandhi's Assurance

Gandhiji, in reply, told him that he was committed to meet Mr. Jinnah and that he could not go back on it. But he assured him that he would never accept partition of India so long as he was alive.

The Bilaspur Session of Hindu Maha Sabha

This gave some consolation to Dr. Mookerjee. But his fear were not wholly allayed. He gave expression to his fear and anxiety in his presidential address to the 26th session of All India Hindu Maha Sabha held at Bilaspur in the last week of December, 1944.

> "Mr Jinnah's dream of Pakistan" he said "was fading away even from the minds of a section of his own followers. His prestige and that of the Muslim League were on the wane when Gandhiji came forward to give his blessing to what is called the C.R. Formula and thus gave the League a fresh lease of life. Mr Jinnah has rejected even this scheme and asks for further surrender. Gandhiji's commitment however remains. . . Once we allow religious considerations to determine the sovereignty of particular areas in India, which will by no means be confined to one single community following one religion, there will be no peace and progress for us. Again self-determination for provincial units will create warring zones within the country and completely shatter its central authority".
>
> "Pakistan," he went on "is no solution of the communal problems. It will rather make them more pronounced and can only end in civil war. Let us not delude ourselves by ignoring the fact that urge for Pakistan is to see Islam re-established in India as the sovereign power. To placate it is to let loose that worst type of fanatical zeal".

He suggested a cessation of hostilities between the Indian political parties and creation of a common platform for the formulation of a common demand on the most fundamental problems of India's liberation and re-construction.

> "It may be," he added, "that Muslim League will not join in such a demand, but there will be other Muslims who have been stabbed in the back by the C.R. Formula who are prepared to stand for Indian Nationalism with rights of minorities duly protected. It will be an act of the finest Indian statesmanship if today there can be a combination of all the nationalist elements in the public life of India for the preparation of an invulnerable national opposition to the continuance of the imperialistic designs of Britain".

British Bargain with Congress

But all his pleadings and exhortations fell on deaf years. The Congress lacked the will and the confidence to ignore the Muslim League and take a correct nationalistic stand. It talked of Indian nationalism and claimed to be the custodian of the right of all the Indian people as such. But in practice it treated the Muslim League as the sole spokesman of Indian Muslims and tried to gain its support by striking a bargain with it at the cost of the rights of the Hindus and the wider national interests.

The end of the Second World War in May, 1945, changed the situation. The British thought it fit to extend general amnesty to the Congress leaders and workers in jail and seek a settlement on the basis of Cripps Proposals. To that end the Lord Wavell, convened a conference of political leaders at Simla in August, 1945, to prepare ground for an Interim National Government on the basis of parity between the Congress and the Muslim League. The Hindu Maha Sabha was not invited to this conference. When the Congress decided to join the Interim Government, Mahatma Gandhi was known to have suggested the inclusion of Dr. Syama Prasad Mookerjee in the cabinet. Sardar Patel liked the idea. But Pandit Nehru would not agree and therefore the idea had to be dropped.

Dr. Mookerjee was touring South India at that time. Gandhiji wanted him to come to Delhi or Simla to meet him. But Dr. Mookerjee was so disgusted with the Congress surrender to Muslim League on the issue of parity that he did not think it worthwhile to change his programme.

Attempts Towards the Indian National Army

Soon, after, the Indian National Army question flared up. The British Indian government decided to try the top leaders of I.N.A. on charges of treason. This was too much for the Indian public opinion, which had come to regard the I.N.A. as the highest type of patriotic venture, to tolerate. Protest meetings and demonstrations began to be held throughout the country. Early in November, 1945, I.N.A. — Day was observed all over the country. In Calcutta students walked out of their classes *en-masse* and held a mighty rally. The police authorities wanted to break the demonstration by show of force. The students were not in a mood to submit. As a result, passions ran high and a violent clash between the students and the police with dangerous repercussions all over Bengal appeared to be inevitable. The situation was, however, saved by the timely intervention of Dr. Mookerjee who was held in high esteem by the students as their friend, philosopher and guide. His fearless but tactful handling of the situation won wide applause from all quarters.

In the meanwhile, the conservative government of Mr. Churchill had fallen and the Labour Party had come to power in Britain. The new government of Mr. Attlee decided to send of high-powered cabinet mission to negotiate on the spot a settlement with the Indian leaders on the basis of complete independence on some agreed basis. It suggested the convening of a Constituent Assembly for which provincial legislatures were to act as electoral colleges, to draw up a new constitution for the country on the basis of a weak centre with only four subjects and autonomous provinces with residuary powers and option to form groups within the Indian Union for specific common purposes.

The Idea of Partition

The Congress till then was officially pledged to partition. The All India Congress Committee at its Allahabad meeting held in 1942 had passed the resolution of Jagat Narain Lal which said that the Congress would not accept partition of India in any form or shape. But the C.R. Formula and Gandhiji's blessings to it had diluted the Congress stand on this vital question to a good extent since then. The Muslim League, on the other hand, was firm on its demand for partition and its position had definitely improved during the war years. It decided to fight the elections to the provincial legislatures on this very issue.

Elections to Provincial Legislatives

The nationalist opinion in the country was definitely hostile to any idea of vivisection of the motherland. It expected the Congress to take a bold stand in the matter and not submit to pressure tactics of the Muslim League. But the Congress leadership lacked the confidence and the courage of conviction that the situation demanded. Its Working Committee passed a resolution at Poona on the eve of the elections which said everything in support of united India but ended with a tame declaration that the Congress would not force any unwilling part to remain in India. By this Poona resolution the Congress virtually accepted the principle of partition much against the opposition of Sardar Patel. But in public it only harped upon the first part of the resolution and asserted that it would not compromise on the question of partition. It made unity of India the main plank of its election manifesto even though it had actually decided to accept division of the country if Muslim League was returned in majority in the Muslim majority provinces.

Dr. Syama Prasad Mookerjee saw through the Congress game and decided to put up his own candidates wherever possible. But just before the elections, he got his first serious heart attack which kept him confined to bed for a long time. Just then Sardar Patel visited him on his sick bed in Calcutta and assured him that in spite of the Poona resolution he would oppose the partition tooth and nail and appealed to him to strengthen his hands.

As a result the field was left open to the Congress which won most of the Hindu seats all over the country on the specific plank that it will not accept partition of Indian come what may. Dr. Mookerjee was returned unopposed to the Bengal Legislative Assembly from the Calcutta University constituency. Soon after, he was elected to the Constituent Assembly of India by the Bengal Legislature.

Muslim League Victory: The Ultimate Blow

The elections gave clear majority to the Muslim League in Sind, Punjab and Bengal. In North Western Frontier Province it failed to secure a majority but was returned as the second biggest party. In other provinces too the Muslim electorate solidly backed the Muslim League.

The success at the polls naturally encouraged the Muslim League. It became more aggressive and intransigent about its demand for partition. The Congress under the leadership of Mahatma Gandhi and Pandit Nehru began to betray signs of panic. The Poona resolution had already committed it to allow those areas which refused to remain with India to secede. Bengal, Punjab and Sind were now in a position to demand secession in terms of that resolution. The Cabinet Mission began to feel inclined in favour of partition and the Congress too began to think of partition as something inevitable. It had no Abraham Lincoln to give it the correct lead and courage to follow it.

As a last effort Dr. Mookerjee met the Cabinet Mission and pleaded with them with all his convincing logic and arguments, not to allow India to be partitioned. But the members of the Cabinet Mission silenced him by showing him the Poona resolution of the Congress which had got all the Hindu votes whereby it stood committed to partition.

It was only then that Dr. Syama Prasad Mookerjee realised that the game had been lost.

8

The Accession Question

Choice of Lahore versus Calcutta

The number of Hindus including Sikhs left behind in West Pakistan was near about one crore — about eighty lakhs in Punjab about fifteen lakhs in Sind and about five lakhs in N.W.F.P., Baluchistan and the States of Bahawalpur, Kalat, Dir and Swat. They owned much of the business and urban property in all these areas. A major part of agricultural lands was also owned by them in the districts of Lyalpur, Sheikhpura, Montgomery, Lahore and Gujranwala which constituted the backbone of united Punjab from the economic point of view. The city of Lahore proper had a majority of Hindus who owned more than 80 per cent of its business and property. It was directly contiguous to the Hindu majority districts of Amritsar and was situated on the east bank of the Ravi which could form a natural boundary between the two dominions of India and Pakistan. Most of the educational institutions which included the D.A.V. College, Lahore, whose campus was bigger than that of Aligarh Muslim University, were financed and run by them. According to the criteria laid down for the guidance of Radcliffe Commission, Lahore should have been surely awarded to India. But the Commission gave it to Pakistan on the plea that Calcutta was being awarded to India. Calcutta had to remain with India because it was surrounded on all sides by Hindu majority areas of Bengal.

Wrongful Accession of Hindu Majority Areas to Pakistan

Thanks to partisan-cum-political approach of Mr. Radcliffe and ineptitude of the Congress leadership, which failed to present its case effectively, the adjoining district of Khulna which had over 60 per cent Hindu population was given away to Pakistan.

What was worse, the district of Thar Parkar in Sind, which was directly continguous to Jodhpur and Kutch, which had acceded to India and which had over 80 per cent Hindu population was not given to India. Here the Congress leadership was alone to blame. It never put up a claim for it even though the Muslim League leaders claimed and got Sylhet district cut off from Assam even through it had only 51 per cent Muslim population.

Had Thar Parkar and the adjoining Hindu majority Talukas of Hyderabad district of Sind come to India, not only a truncated Sind like truncated Punjab and Bengal would have remained with India in which Sindhi Hindu refugees from Pak occupied Sind could have been resettled but also the problem of Kutch arising out of Pak claim on the Rann of Kutch would have never arisen.

Though in minority the Hindus dominated the economic and cultural life of East Bengal even more than West Punjab and Sind. They numbered over 13 millions and constituted 30 per cent of the total population of East Bengal at the time of partition. They were politically the most conscious section of the community in the whole of Bengal and they had made the greatest sacrifices for the freedom of India. They owned nearly 80 per cent of the national wealth of East Bengal. They owned most of the urban property and organised and financed 95 per cent of the 1,290 high schools and 47 colleges of East Bengal and 90 per cent of teachers from University to high schools came out of them. There were a number of centres of Sanskrit learning spread all over East Bengal. This population of 13 million included progressive middle class and a very active and virile rural population of Nam Sudras. Beside the Hindus there were half a million Buddhists who lived in the Chittagong hill tract. They too were, to a man, opposed to partition.

The two-nation theory on the basis of which partition was demanded and conceded had some logical though dangerous implications. It made Hindus aliens of Pakistan and Muslims aliens in India. The past history of Islam and the utterances and writing of the protagonists of Pakistan before the partition gave a clear indication that there would be no place for Hindus in Pakistan. Mr. Jinnah had himself admitted it and suggested complete exchange of population in an interview to a foreign correspondent. The late Dr. B.R. Ambedkar, a farsighted jurist, had also clearly pointed out in his famous book *Thoughts on Partition* that exchange of population will be the logical corollary of Partition and had given a detailed procedure to bring it about in five years. The Congress leadership accepted the partition but refused to accept its logical corollary of exchange of population. Dr. Mookerjee also did not think of it at that time. But Master Tara Singh and Hindu leaders of Punjab, who had a better insight into the Muslim mind and who had got a foretaste of what was in store for them in Pakistan in the Rawalpindi massacre of March, 1947, were wise enough not to depend upon the assurances of Congress leaders about their safety in Pakistan after they had accepted partition over their head. The massacre of Sheikhpura soon after the formation of Pakistan gave them a clear idea of what was in store for Hindus and Sikhs in the days to come. They, therefore, gave a call to Hindus and Sikhs to leave their hearths and homes and move towards East Punjab just as their ancestors had done when Afghanistan had come under the heels of Islam. As a result, within a few months of the partition virtual exchange of population took place between East Punjab and West Punjab. Sindhi Hindus followed suit after a few months. The loss in human lives and misery suffered by the people in this unprecedented upheaval was incalculable. The Hindus lost property worth hundreds of crores of rupees and about one million people lost their lives on both sides. But it saved the sufferings Hindus of West Pakistan from the process of slow annihilation like cats and dogs at the hands of the Muslim rulers of Pakistan.

The Hindus of East Bengal failed to see the writing on the wall at that time. Perhaps, they had no such experience to draw upon as their compatriots of West Pakistan had. They were also taken in by the assurances of Congress leaders including Mahatma Gandhi and Sardar Patel, Dr. Syama Prasad Mookerjee was a party to such assurances. They had in fact greater faith in him than in all the Congress leaders put together and looked upon his inclusion in the Indian cabinet as a guarantee for their own security and welfare. Dr. Mookerjee too was conscious of the faith they had reposed in him. He had hoped that the Congress leadership would learn the lessons of partition and adopt a reciprocal and firm policy towards Pakistan. He had joined the cabinet to influence the Government from within to honour the assurances and pledges he had given to the Hindus of East Bengal. He, therefore, considered the general policies of the Government, particularly those pertaining to Pakistan, as much his concern as those concerning departments specifically entrusted to his care.

But it did not take him long to realise that the Congress leaders, particularly Pandit Jawaharlal Nehru had learnt nothing and forgotten nothing. Aided and abetted by Maulana Azad, he seemed determined to pursue the same policy of appeasement towards Pakistan that the Congress had pursued towards the Muslim League of which the partition of the country was the result.

It did not take the rulers of Pakistan long to see through the mind of Nehru and Gandhi. They knew how their policy of bluff and bluster towards them had paid rich dividends in the past. They had been able to carve out the vast Islamic State of Pakistan out of India without much effort and were determined to bring the rest of India under the crescent flag through war. *Has ke liya Pakistan — lar ke lenge Hindustan* (we have got Pakistan in fun and we will acquire Hindustan by force) was their pet slogan and it well revealed their mind. They, therefore, decided to follow the same policy of bluff and bluster, of *goondaism* and aggression towards the Congress rulers of India which they had followed toward the Congress on behalf of the Muslim League before the partition. The way Hindu India had submitted to their blackmail and had accepted partition without a murmur encouraged them to persist in their belief that Muslims were destined to rule and that Hindustan could be bullied to submit to their dictates.

Kashmir's Accession to India

The Pakistani rulers first tried this policy on Kashmir. After having failed to pressurise Maharaja Hari Singh to accede to Pakistan through economic blockade, Pakistan launched an armed attack on Kashmir on October 22, 1947 in spite of the fact that it had entered into a standstill agreement with the Maharaja on August 15. The en-masse desertion of the Muslim soldiers of the

Maharaja's army to the invaders made their task easy. They reached the outskirts of Srinagar by October 24. There were two alternatives before the Maharaja. He could either surrender before the armed aggression and sign the instrument of accession acceding his State to Pakistan or fight back the aggressor with Indian help. Being a proud and patriotic ruler, Hari Singh chose the second alternative. He sent his Prime Minister, Shri Mehar Chand Mahajan, who later rose to be the Chief Justice of India, to Delhi to plead with the Indian leaders to accept the accession of Kashmir and send armed support to defend it against Pakistani hordes.

Nehru's Policy of Appeasement

Pandit Jawaharlal Nehru who claimed to be a Kashmiri and, therefore, had refused to allow Sardar Patel to handle Jammu and Kashmir State, now developed, cold feet. He was unwilling to accept the accession of Jammu and Kashmir lest it should result in Indo-Pak war. His procrastination irritated Justice Mahajan so much that he decided to fly to Karachi and formally surrender Kashmir to Jinnah on condition that safety be assured to the hundred thousand strong Hindu population of Srinagar which was sure to be butchered at the hands of the invaders. But the timely intervention of Sardar Patel and pleadings of Sheikh Abdullah, who had fled from Kashmir in the wake of Pak invasion saved the situation. Accession of Kashmir was accepted and Indian armed forces were rushed to Srinagar just in time to save it from falling into the hands of the enemy.

It was a victory for the viewpoint of Sardar Patel who had the backing of Dr. Mookerjee, Sardar Baldev Singh and Dr. N.V. Gadgil. But the coward in Pandit Nehru reasserted itself when he fell into the trap of Mr. Jinnah who decided to politicise the issue after he had failed to get a military decision in his favour. He made a mockery of the principle of joint responsibility of the cabinet when he made an offer of plebiscite in Kashmir after normalcy had been restored there, without the approval of the cabinet. Besides being *ultra vires* of the instrument of accession, which did not provide for any conditional accession, this offer betrayed the same policy of appeasement which had been the hallmark of Nehru's policy towards the Muslim League.

The bungling regarding Kashmir that was thus begun by Pandit Nehru has continued ever since. While Sardar Patel was able to tackle the problem of 600 odd Princely States, including Bhopal and Hyderabad in one year, Pandit Nehru failed to tackle one State which he considered to be his special domain. Dr. Mookerjee had to atone for the sins of Pandit Nehru by laying down his life in a Srinagar jail to save Kashmir from the machination of Sheikh Abdullah who had turned from a supplicant to a dictator because of the wrong approach and policies of Pandit Nehru.

The way Pakistan, even when it was militarily and economically very weak, was able to commit aggression on Kashmir and get away with 33,000 square miles of Indian territory including the strategic region of Gilgit in the bargain, set the pattern of Indo-Pak relations. The rulers of Pakistan learnt that aggression against India pays just as the leaders of Muslim League had learnt before partition that separatism and *goondaism* against Congress pays. Pakistan has been faithfully following the pattern in her relations with India ever since.

Accession of Hyderabad

Hyderabad too was treated by Pandit Nehru as his special domain for the simple reason that its ruler happened to be a bigoted Musalman. Nizam Usman Ali of Hyderabad knew the character of Pandit Nehru and was fortified by the tacit support of Maulana Azad who had been living on his doles for many years. He, therefore, adopted a very intransigent attitude. He not only refused to accede to India but what was worse began to conspire with the Portuguese to acquire Goa from them which would have given him an outlet to sea. At the same time he began to increase his army and tyrannise and suppress his Hindu subjects, who constituted 90 per cent of the population of his State, with the help of Razakars led by Kasim Razvi. He secured the services of the British Jurist, Sir Walter Monkton, to negotiate a settlement on his behalf with the Government of India. Pandit Nehru agreed to accept a semi-sovereign status for Hyderabad with a standing army of its own. Encouraged by this climb down by the Government of India, he decided to persist in his demand for recognition of full sovereignty and began preparations to move the U.N. in the matter.

Dr. Syama Prasad Mookerjee deeply felt this national humiliation. He realised the dangers inherent in such a policy of appeasement towards the enemy within. He knew from experience that Pandit Nehru was incapable of firm resolute policy where Muslims were concerned. Many of his other cabinet colleagues felt the same way. The only way to change this policy, they felt, was to entrust the handling of Hyderabad problem to Sardar Vallabhbhai Patel, who should have, even otherwise, dealt with it as the Minister of States. But it was no easy job to make Pandit Nehru, whose inveterate love of power and dictatorial temperament had become manifest by that time, to withdraw from the handling of this vital question. Dr. Mookerjee thereupon hit upon a clever stratagem to achieve this end.

At a meeting of the Cabinet he pointed out that the Hyderabad question was getting complicated and hence needed special attention. The Prime Minister, he added, was already overworked and therefore could not burdened with any more work. He, therefore, suggested that Sardar Patel be requested to handle the problem as his exclusive charge. A number of other ministers supported him. Sardar Patel, who had already been sounded on the matter, expressed his consent to the suggestion even before Pandit Nehru could comment on it. He could not reject the suggestion after Sardar Patel had expressed his acceptance. The handling of Hyderabad question thus passed into the hands of the right man.

It is a well known fact that even after the question had passed out of his hands, Pandit Nehru made many attempts to deflect Sardar Patel from his firm resolve to end the festering sore of Hyderabad once for all by a bold and timely stroke of Police Action. But secure in the support of Syama Prasad Mookerjee and a majority of his other Cabinet colleagues and conscious of the popular demand for bold action, Sardar Patel went ahead with his plans. The Police Action, boldly and efficiently executed, met little resistance. This integration of Hyderabad State with the rest of India was thus finally and irrevocably completed. The whole country remembers Sardar Patel with gratitude for his statesmanship and realism in tackling the Hyderabad problem. But few are aware of the part, mentioned above, played by Dr. Mookerjee in making it possible for Sardar Patel to tackle the problem as he did. How one wishes that the Kashmir problem had also passed into the hands of Sardar Patel through some similar stratagem.

9

The Final Division

In the wake of the growing demand for partition Punjab and Bengal were the two key provinces on which the edifice of Pakistan as conceived by the Muslim League rested. Both of them had slight Muslim majorities. The Communal Award had given the Muslim majority in both these provinces additional weightage which had put them in commanding position in both these provinces. The Zonal Scheme which had been put forth as an alternative to partition by the Cabinet Mission had put these provinces as a whole in the two Muslim majority zones to be constituted in the east and west of the country. The Muslim League therefore took it for granted that both of these provinces as a whole would be included in Pakistan. But the redeeming feature in the situation of these provinces was that the Hindu population in both of them was concentrated in districts adjoining the neighbouring Hindu majority provinces. These compact Hindu majority parts of Bengal and Punjab could logically demand their inclusion in India in the event of partition of the country on communal basis.

Riots in Calcutta

The Muslim League leadership was conscious of this fact. It therefore decided to take advantage of the situation created by its electoral success, the Congress nervousness and favourable change in British attitude, to terrify Hindus of these areas into submission to their will. The Muslim League leaders and their British patrons were particularly interested in annexing Calcutta to Pakistan. To that end a planned orgy of loot and massacre was let loose on Calcutta on the 16th of August, 1946. Thousands of innocent Hindus were butchered, their houses and shops looted and burnt in broad daylight with the direct connivance of the Muslim League administration. But the League plan to terrify Hindus out of Calcutta was foiled by the determined resistance put up by the Calcutta Hindus under the fearless leadership of Dr. Syama Prasad Mookerjee, to the organised goondaism of the Muslim League. The Hindustan National Guards — a volunteer organisation that had been started by Dr. Mookerjee to checkmate the goondaism of the Muslim National Guards of the Muslim League — gave a good account of itself in this crisis. Dr. Mookerjee himself moved about the riot-affected areas, with supreme indifference for his own safety, to give courage and consolation to the afflicted people.

Sometime later the same story was repeated in Noakhali and its surrounding villages. Dr. Mookerjee was again the first to rush to the affected areas at great personal risk to give succour to the victims of bestial persecution at the hands of soldiers of Islam.

These happening sent a wave of indignation all over the country. To the Hindus of Bengal they gave a taste of Pakistan. The prospect of utter humiliation and annihilation in their own land for the freedom of which they had made the greatest sacrifices began to assail their hearts. The Congress leaderships, in which they had put their faith, lacked both realism and courage to appreciate the situation and take up its challenge. The eyes of nationalist Bengal were, therefore, once again turned towards Dr. Syama Prasad Mookerjee.

Partition of Bengal

Dr. Mookerjee then decided upon a bold move which partitioned Pakistàn of Jinnah's conception and saved half of Bengal for India. He realised that the only way of saving Bengali Hindus from sure annihilation under perpetual Muslim domination was to divide Bengal so as to separate its Hindu majority. Western part from the Muslim majority Eastern part. It was a painful idea for a patriot of Bengal who was conscious of the great sacrifices his predecessors had made to annul the earlier partition of Bengal. It demanded exceptional courage to put forth a proposal which was sure to give in the first instance a great emotional shock to the patriotic Bengalis — none but Dr. Mookerjee could have done it.

Once he had made up his mind, he put in all his resources to educate and mobilise public opinion accordingly. He undertook a whirlwind tour of the whole of Bengal particularly of the East Bengal, addressed mass rallies wherein he boldly put forth his plan of partitioning Bengal to save the Hindu half from being lost to Pakistan.

This was followed by a two day conference of Hindu representatives from all parts of Bengal in the middle of March which unanimously resolved that a separate province must be created comprising the Hindu majority areas in Bengal.

Congress' onus of Partition on Mookerjee

As this move gained momentum and strength it began to be subjected to severe attack both by the Muslim League and the Congress. The Congress critics who were perturbed more by the growing influence of Dr. Mookerjee on the Hindu masses than by the move itself, began to shift the onus of accepting partition of the country on Dr. Mookerjee. They asserted that the creation of the new province as visualised by Dr. Mookerjee would support the cause of Pakistan.

Mookerjee's Reply

Dr. Mookerjee replied to the criticism through a detailed statement issued on March 9, 1947.

> "It is wrong" he said "that his move supported the cause of Pakistan. We are against Pakistan in any shape or form. It does not, however, depend on Bengali Hindus alone whether division of India will be prevented or not. If Hindus and other nationalist forces throughout India are really determined not to allow any portion of India to go out of the Indian Union, they will get the largest measure of support from Bengali Hindus. If on the other hand an attempt is made to place Bengal out of the Indian Union due to commitments with which the British Government, the Muslim League and the Congress are closely associated, we shall at any rate break the solidarity of Eastern Pakistan, save one area of Bengal and link it up with the Indian Union."

To those who criticised his scheme on the ground that division of Bengal on religious basis would be against the fundamental principle of nationalism he retorted, "No one desires religion to be introduced into politics. But why must we hide our head ostrich-like and ignore present realities? It is not we who want division of India or any part thereof merely on religious considerations. But if we find that the whole of Bengal is going to be dominated by communal frenzy and 45 per cent of its population reduced to a state of slavery only because they follow a particular religious faith, is it a crime on our part to demand that we must have our own territory where we can live as free men? And was not", he asked, "Sind carved out from Bombay only to placate communal whims and did not many of our present Congress opportunists quietly acquiesce in such division much to the detriment of the Hindus of Sind?"

Referring to the criticism that his scheme would be stoutly opposed by the Muslim League he said that he expected that because "if this scheme succeeds Eastern Pakistan would virtually finish". "It is all the more reason" he added, "why all Hindus in Bengal should sink their differences and stand united on this great issue in spite of all the isms that divide them". He urged upon his compatriots to look at the problems facing them with "complete realism" and not allow themselves to be carried away by emotions.

He concluded his momentous statement with an appeal to the Congress party in Bengal to rise to the occasion and support his move in the wider interests of nationalist Bengal and India.

His well reasoned and forceful advocacy of the scheme for partition of Bengal did succeed in winning a large number of Congressmen to his side and soon it became the universal demand of Bengali Hindus.

The Muslim League leadership in Bengal was naturally perturbed over it. It could not logically deny the right of the Hindu majority areas of Bengal to determine its own future when it was demanding the same right for Muslim majority areas. But it realised that success of Dr. Mookerji's move would truncate East Pakistan, deprive it of Calcutta and leave it "moth eaten".

Suharawardy Scheme

Mr. H.S. Suharawardy, the brain of Muslim League in Bengal, then put forth the scheme for United Sovereign Bengal mainly to counteract the move of Dr. Mookerjee. He feigned to be a Bengali first and appealed to the Bengali sentiment of the Congress-minded intelligentsia which had an emotional antipathy for any idea of partitioning Bengal once again. Some top Congress leaders like Shri Sarat Chandra Bose fell into his trap. He was reported to have obtained Mahatma Gandhi's blessings as well for his scheme.

Meeting with Gandhi

But Dr. Mookerjee was not the man to be deflected from his resolve by these manoeuvres. He met Mahatma Gandhi at Sadpur on 13th of May, 1947, to ascertain his views on the Suharawardy scheme of United Sovereign Bengal. Gandhiji told Dr. Mookerjee that he had not yet made up his mind but was trying to find out what the proposal really meant. He then asked Dr. Mookerjee about his own opinion about it. Dr. Mookerjee replied that though apparently Mr. Suharawardy was the author of this scheme, it was really being sponsored by the British commercial interests and that Lord Mountbatten had personally asked him to give the proposal careful consideration. But, Dr. Mookerjee asked, what was there to prevent this United Sovereign Bengal from seeking voluntary alliance with Pakistan. Mr. Suharawardy, he feared, could surely manipulates a decision of this kind with the help of the majority of Muslim votes. "Can you contemplate Bengal lying separate from the rest of India?" he asked Gandhiji, to which he had no reply.

In spite of the opposition of some top Congress leaders the move for partition of Bengal, in case the demand for Pakistan was to be conceded, became so popular and powerful that it became impossible for the British Government, the Congress and the Muslim League to resist it. The 3rd June announcement by the British Government which laid down the blue print for India's independence after its partition into two States of Bharat and Pakistan conceded the right of Hindu majority areas of Bengal and Punjab to opt out of Pakistan and a Boundary Commission under the Chairmanship of Mr. Radcliffe was appointed to demarcate such areas.

Radcliffe Commission on Partition

The terms of reference under which the Radcliffe Commission was to work gave it a large scope to play havoc with the boundary line that was to divide Hindu Bengal from the Muslim Bengal that was so to go to Pakistan. Dr. Mookerjee therefore took up the task of preparing and presenting the case of Hindu Bengal before the Boundary Commission. A Committee of leading jurists was set up for the purpose and a detailed plan showing the areas that should constitute West Bengal on the basis of their being Hindu majority was drawn up. According to it the whole of Khulna district which had over 60 per cent Hindu majority should have come to West Bengal. But the Congress spokesmen in their anxiety to see East Pakistan grow up as a viable unit were prepared to forgo Indian Bengal's claim to Khulna to appease their Pakistani counterparts. As a result the Radcliffe award proved to be very unfair to West Bengal. A large tract of land containing over two million Hindus which should have legitimately formed a part of West Bengal was awarded to Pakistan.

As the plan for partition began to be given effect the Hindu minority in East Bengal, which had already got a bitter taste of Muslim dominated administration, began to feel nervous. The leaders of East Bengal Hindus had supported the demand for partition of Bengal in the hope and on the understanding that their co-patriots of West Bengal and the rest of India will look to their welfare. They wanted to be assured that they would not be left at the sweet mercy of Pakistan. Dr. Mookerjee therefore undertook another tour of East Bengal. He persuaded the top Congress leaders like Gandhiji and Sardar Patel also to visit East Bengal and authoritatively reassure its Hindu population which had always remained in the forefront in the fight for India's independence. At numerous places he told large audiences that he was conscious of the great sacrifices they had made for the wider interests of India and their Hindu brethren of West Bengal and assured them that he would watch their interests and stand by them in all their difficulties. He remained dutifully conscious of this pledge ever after and did all he could to redeem it.

Role in the Constituent Assembly

At the same time his performance in the Constituent Assembly of India, his political acumen, oratorical skill and mastery of parliamentary procedure were winning new laurels for him. His position as one of the top most public figures whose record of service in the cause of the country's independence could be surpassed by few, was universally recognised.

So far as Bengal was concerned, he had become its undisputed leader and spokesman. No wonder therefore that his name readily occurred to the Congress leaders who were then engaged in selecting personnel for the national government to be formed on the 15th of August, 1947.

10

First Cabinet Amidst Aggression and Genocide

The First Governor of Free India

As the hour of independence came closer bringing with it the harsh reality of partition, 'even as, the heart of every patriotic Indian was bleeding. The people of West Punjab, North West Frontier Province, Sind and East Bengal were passing through an unprecedented orgy of violence against the body and soul of all those who had stood for the unity of India, Pandit Jawaharlal Nehru, the Prime Minister designate of independent India minus Pakistan was busy in planning the festivities which were to mark the dawn of freedom with partition and finalising his cabinet which was to be sworn in on August 15. Mookerjee was too disgusted with the way the Congress leadership had behaved at this crucial juncture of India's history to have any respect for them or expect any gesture of goodwill from them. He was devoting all his time and energies to salvage as much as possible for India through the partition of would be Pakistan. Pandit Nehru had no love lost for him. Left to himself he would have formed a cabinet of yesman in which even top Congressmen like N.V. Gadgil might have had no place. But fortunately Pandit Nehru did not have quite a free hand in the matter. The Congress organisation was controlled by Sardar Patel. But for Mahatma Gandhi's intervention Sardar Patel and not Pandit Nehru would have been elected President of the Indian National Congress in 1945 which would have *ipso facto* made him the first Prime Minister of the country. Mahatma Gandhi was conscious of the temperament mental weaknesses and ideological obsession of Pandit Nehru as also of the contradictions within the Congress Party, which he wanted to dissolve after freedom had been attained to pave the way for the formation of political parties on the basis of distinguishable social and political programme and ideology. He also realised that freedom had been achieved by the combined effort of all the nationalist forces in the country and not by Congress alone. He wanted the first Government of free India to be truly national Government capable of inspiring confidence and creating enthusiasm in the whole nation. He, therefore, insisted that the first cabinet should be broad based. It was on his insistence that a number of distinguished non-Congressmen were also invited to join the cabinet. They included Sir John Mathai, the noted economist and business magnate, Sir Shanmukham Chetty, the well known financial expert, Dr. B.R. Ambedkar, a celebrated jurist and leader of the Scheduled Castes. They were all invited in their individual capacity for their talents and eminence in different spheres of national life and not as representatives of any particular interests or parties.

Inclusion in Cabinet as Minister of Industry and Supply

Dr. Syama Prasad Mookerjee was not prepared for the invitation. He had developed a distrust and contempt for Congress leaders who had betrayed the faith put in them by the people in the General Election of 1946 which had been fought on the issue of Akhand Bharat versus Pakistan.

Dr. Mookerjee was given the important portfolio of Industry and Supply. He would have personally preferred Education which had been his special field since his early youth. That would have been in the best interests of the country as well. He could have laid a sound foundation for a really national education policy and moulded the new generation of the country on healthy lines and prepared them for an intellectual revolution which must precede any social and economic revolution worth its name. But that was not to be. Maulana Azad, who knew little about education, Indian culture and heritage, was determined to keep education ministry within his grip with a set purpose. The country has paid dearly for his stewardship of the Education Ministry for the first 15 years of the most formative period of India as a free nation.

The fact that Dr. Mookerjee was given charge of the Ministry of Industry and Supply showed the faith the Congress leaders had in his integrity and understanding of vital industrial and economic problems of the country. His experience as Finance Minister of undivided Bengal and his general grasp of things was also a factor on this choice. It gave Dr. Mookerjee an opportunity to lay the foundations of India's Industrial Policy and prepare the ground for industrial development of the country in years to come. The loss to education and cultural life was thus a gain on the economic and industrial side.

His record of work as Minister for Industry and Supply for the two and half years he remained in office amply justified the faith and trust that had been put in him. He brought his solid intellectual grasp and realistic understanding of the problems of industrialisation in a predominantly agricultural country, whose industrial growth had been deliberately checked by the unsympathetic foreign government, to bear upon the task entrusted to him. His experience first as Chief Executive of Calcutta University, the biggest employer of top intellectuals and scientists in the country and then as Finance Minister of undivided Bengal stood him in good stead. He suffered from no ideological inhibitions and therefore could handle the task entrusted to him with refreshing realism. His intellectuals eminence, mental alertness and rock-like integrity evoked spontaneous respect and fullest cooperation from British trained civilians. As a result he was able to make a fine job of his work. Even his political opponents have nothing but praise for the way he handled the industrial problems and formulated industrial policies in the most formative years of independent India.

Industrial Projects Initiated

The Chitranjan Locomotive Factory, the Sindri Fertilizers Corporation and the Hindustan Aircrafts Factory, Bangalore the three most successful and industrial undertakings of free India, were conceived and organised by him. The new model third class coaches of the Indian Railways manufactured by the Hindustan Aircrafts Factory are also the result of his deep personal interest in the matter. "I myself sat, slept and moved about in the first coach when it was manufactured to test whether it suited common Indian railway travellers" he told me with a legitimate pride when I was travelling in such a third class coach from Delhi to

Pathankot in his company in August, 1952. He also initiated talks with some leading German firms for setting up new steel plants to improve the quantity and quality of steel production in India.

Ideologies on Industrial Development

He had very clear ideas on the role of private capital in the industrial development of the country as also on relationship between capital and labour. He was convinced that in an industrially backward country like India which had just achieved freedom, the primary task was to mobilise all resources, private and government, for a cooperative effort to make the country self-sufficient in essential goods, particularly those needed for the defence of the country. He believed in giving full scope to private enterprise under suitable government regulation and control to play its part in the industrialisation of the country. He wanted the State to utilise its meagre resources for developing that sector of the industry whose development was essential for the defence of the country but for which private capital was not readily forthcoming. He thus wanted a rational co-ordination and adjustment, in the light of the actual conditions in the country, between the Private and the Public enterprise for speedy but orderly industrialisation of the country.

In formulating this policy he was solely guided by a realistic assessment of the needs and circumstances of the country and not by abstract theories or dogmas. He was, in fact, not wedded to any dogma. He kept his mind open and judged every scheme and policy by the criterion of its practicability and usefulness to the people.

Apart from the basic objections to total nationalisation, he was convinced that India had not the requisite resources, experience and trained personnel to nationalise all industries and run them efficiently. He was, therefore, opposed to loose talk about nationalisation of all industries which only scared the private capital.

He also knew by experience that State managed industries had been generally working less efficiently because of lack of incentive and initiative on the part of government employees who managed them, excessive use of or blind adherence to government rules and formalities and top-heavy administration. He, therefore, initiated the policy of managing the State controlled industries through corporations, organised on the lines of joint stock companies, with government supplying the major portion or the whole of the share capital and having some of its own nominees on the Board of Directors together with a number of private industrialists. This has now become the general pattern for running the public undertakings in India.

The same consideration of wider national good which prompted him to advocate a policy of co-operation and co-ordination between the private and the public sectors guided his approach to the question of industrial labour. He stood for cooperation between the labour and capital in the interest of increasing production. The theory of class struggle as a means of progress never appealed to his rational mind. But he did not want cooperation of labour on the terms of employers. He stood for profit sharing between capital and labour so as to enable labour to develop a genuine interest in the industry. It was this solicitude for the welfare of labour which inspired as much confidence in the labour as his realistic and practical approach to the problem of capital did amongst the employers. The workers of the Hindustan Ship-building Yard at Vishakapatnam demonstrated their confidence in him when they offered to abide by any decision he might give in regard to their dispute with the management just on the eve of his last tragic journey to Kashmir.

He not only laid down correct policies for his own Departments but also proved a tower of strength for the government as a whole by his able advocacy and defence of its policies and actions. He used to put his heart and soul into the task entrusted to him. His deep understanding of problems and ingenuity sometimes saved situations which his colleagues thought were hopeless.

Conflict with Nehru

The problem which brought him in direct conflict with Pandit Jawaharlal Nehru, was the problem of India's relations and dealings with Pakistan, particularly in regard to the condition of Hindu minority in East Bengal. The doting attitude adopted by the

Government of India towards Pakistan ever since its inception in the face of deliberate and determined acts of hostility on her part, never appealed to Dr. Mookerjee. The utter indifference of the Government of India towards the fate of millions of Hindus in Sind, Baluchistan and N.W.F.P., not to speak of those in West Punjab who had never asked for partition but who were all the same being victimised and squeezed out of their homelands simply because they happened to be Hindus; who adored undivided India as their mother and made sacrifice for its liberation, appeared to him criminal. The failure of the Government of India to name Pakistan as aggressor, even after the fact of her aggression in Kashmir had been fully established, and the forced payment of Rs. 55 crores to Pakistan under pressure of Gandhiji's fast, pained him and convinced him of the imbecility of the government of which he himself was a member. He instinctively felt that this policy would only encourage Pakistan, born as it was out of successful bullying of Congress leaders by the Muslim League fanatics, to persist in ruffian tactics towards free India and extermination of all non-Muslims from within its boundaries. Through no heed was paid to his pleadings and protests from within by the government just then, yet he observed with satisfaction that opinion within and without the government was growing against this weak-kneed attitude towards Pakistan. Moreover, Gandhiji and Pandit Nehru, the chief advocates of this policy, were getting isolated. He was, therefore, hopeful of reorientation of the policies of Government of India towards Pakistan and the problems its creation had created. Naturally he considered his continuance in the government useful for the national cause.

Assassination of Mahatma Gandhi

The assassination of Mahatma Gandhi on 30th January, 1948 changed the whole perspective. The unprincipled but clever exploitation of the event for their own ends by Pandit Nehru and his left wing supporters within and without the Congress created a strong public reaction against the advocates of a bold policy towards Pakistan. Gandhiji, whose popularity and influence on the people had reached the lowest ebb during the days preceding his assassination, overnight became a martyr in the eyes of even his worst critics. His assasination not only rehabilitated him in the hearts of his countrymen but also gave a new lease of life to those who used to shine in his reflected glory. As a result the tables were turned. The idealist Nehru emerged as the political heir of Gandhiji and rose in the people's estimation. On the other hand the realist and practical Sardar Patel and Dr. Mookerjee got isolated within and without the Government.

The succeeding months saw the policy of appeasement towards Muslims and Pakistan pursued with a vengeance. Pakistan was quick to take note of the changes in India. It decided to take advantage of the situation by starting a fresh offensive in Kashmir as also against the Hindus within Pakistan. West Pakistan had by that time been well nigh cleared of all the "undesirables" but more than 13 million Hindus still lived in East Bengal. Now came their turn.

Dr. Mookerjee was deeply concerned with the job of Hindus in East Pakistan. His position and his attitude towards them was well known. He summed it up in the following convincing passage in the statement he made in Indian Parliament on the 19th of April, 1950, after his resignation from the Cabinet.

> "When the partition of India became inevitable I played a very large part in creating public opinion in favour of the partition of Bengal, for I felt that if that was not done, the whole of Bengal and also perhaps Assam would fall in Pakistan. At that time little knowing that I would join the first Central cabinet, I along with others, gave assurances to the Hindus of East Bengal stating that if they suffered at the hands of the future Pakistan Government, if they were denied elementary rights of citizenship, if their lives and honour were jeopardised or attacked, Free India would not remain an idle spectator and their just cause would be boldly taken up by the Government and people of India."

Massacre of Hindus in East Bengal

As the Pakistan Government began to show its dragon's teeth to the Hindus of East Bengal, whose security and interests it had undertaken to safeguard according to the terms of the partition agreement, Dr. Mookerjee urged upon Pandit Nehru and his other colleagues to remember the pledges they had given to them and to do something for their safety. The result was the first Inter-Dominion Agreement signed at Calcutta in April, 1948, which dealt mainly with the question of minorities in the two Bengals. This agreement, however, failed to produce any lasting results. India on the whole observed its terms, but the exodus of Hindus from East Bengal continued unabated. It was a one way traffic. This is just what Pakistan wished for. There were numerous conferences of officials from both the sides and copious correspondence was exchanged between the two governments. But judged by actual results, Pakistan's attitude continued to remain unchanged.

The increasing exodus of Hindus from East Bengal and the news of their sad plight, in spite of the April, 1948 Agreement, created a stir in India once again. Dr. Mookerjee again pressed for some strong and determined action. But all the Nehru Government did was to sign another Inter-Dominion Agreement at Delhi in December, 1948. It was a virtual repetition of the first agreement. The same old platitudes about the treatment of Hindu and Muslim minorities in both the countries were solemnly repeated.

Pakistan had no intention to honour this agreement either, and the unending tale of woes of East Bengal Hindus continued. During the course of 1949, the situation in East Bengal deteriorated further and the exodus of a far larger number of Hindus from that province started. In spite of these two Inter-Dominion Agreements about 20 lakhs Hindus were forced to leave their hearth and homes in East Bengal during the first two years of Pakistan's existence, besides millions who were uprooted in Punjab and Sind.

But the worst came in early 1950 when a planned massacre of Hindus on a wide scale was started by the Muslims all over the province. According to the government figures, more than fifty thousand Hindus were butchered, thousands of Hindu women were abducted and raped and inhuman and most barbarous crimes were perpetrated against them. All the socially conscious Hindus began to be driven out of East Bengal. It was all done with the direct connivance and encouragement of the Pakistan Government.

Nehru's Policy of Appeasement of Aggressor and Oppressor

As the news of this devilish carnage began to seep through to India through the word of mouth of the uprooted humanity from East Bengal a wave of shock spread all over the country. It even stirred the conscience of many of the men in power, who began to realise the futility of paper agreements with Pakistan which were honoured only in their breach. A feeling of urgency about the problem began to grow and some bold and firm action to dissuade Pakistan from persisting in this game of exterminating or throwing out all the Hindus from East Bengal began to be advocated. It was realised that the problem was not communal but political, not provincial but national. But the one man who remained impervious to all this was Pandit Jawaharlal Nehru. His innate cowardice which he had been successfully hiding under high sounding slogans and winsome theatricals at mass meetings, would not allow him to take any bold and quick step. Everyone including some ministers of the Central Cabinet felt ashamed at the pusillanimity of the government.

Mookerjee's Revolt against Agreements and Declarations with Pakistan

Dr. Syama Prasad Mookerjee naturally felt the tragedy most. He led the opposition to Pandit Nehru's dilatory tactics from within. He had a number of passages-at-arms with him in the numerous Cabinet meetings held to discuss the situation. All his hopes were finally dashed to the ground when he learnt of the invitation to Mr. Liaquat Ali Khan, the Prime Minister of Pakistan, whose hands were dripping with blood of countless Hindus, for making another agreement and pious declarations about the welfare of the minorities. He protested against this course of action. He reminded the Prime Minister of the fate of the previous agreements and warned him against falling into the trap of Liaquat Ali Khan who wanted to avoid the nemesis which his satanic policies in Pakistan ought to have brought upon him.

But he was over-ruled by the Prime Minister who lost his temper when he could not meet his arguments. The things came to such a pass that Dr. Mookerjee had to rebuke him and tell him, on his face that he was flouting all traditions and conventions of joint responsibility and joint deliberations of the cabinet in respect of vital national problems such as the one created by the situation in East Bengal.

Resignation from Cabinet

From that time onwards, Dr. Mookerjee felt that he could neither do any good to the country, nor redeem his pledges to the people of East Bengal, by continuing in the Cabinet. The call of duty summoned him to walk out of the exalted position he had held in the Government of his country, which he had accepted for the service of the motherland two and a half years back. He sent in his resignation on the first of April 1950 and Pandit Nehru readily agreed to relieve him of the burden of office. But other Ministers, particularly Sardar Patel did not like Dr. Mookerjee going out of the Cabinet at that crucial time. He pressed him hard to withdraw his resignation. Even Pandit Nehru later requested Dr. Mookerjee to reconsider his decision and withdraw the resignation. A lesser man might have yielded to this pressure. But Dr. Mookerjee was a man made of sterner stuff. Name, fame and glamour of office had no attraction for him. Like a true sanyasi, he preferred the path of duty towards his people and his conscience to a world of comfort and position; and he thereby proved that he was a true *karma yogi* who had imbibed the spirit of the Lord's *Gita*.

Though the resignation of Dr. Mookerjee failed to deter Pandit Nehru from following the suicidal path of national humiliation and betrayal of the solemn pledges given to Hindu minority left in Pakistan, it did stir the conscience of the nation including some of his cabinet colleagues. Thanks to the determined opposition of Shri N.V. Gadgil and Sardar Patel, the original draft of the Nehru-Liaquat agreement which committed Government of India to reservation of seats for Muslims in legislatures and services, was modified to eliminate these provisions. This saved India from going back to the path which had directly led to partition of 1947, for the time being at least.

Revolt against Nehru-Liaquat Agreement

The statement that Dr. Mookerjee gave in the Parliament on April 19, 1950 regarding the causes of his resignation from the

Nehru cabinet is a dignified but pathetic document which deserves to be read and re-read by all those who want Indo-Pak relations to be put on a sound footing. It reveals that clear grasp of the true character of Pakistan and her rulers and the ideological and practical motivations of their attitude and policies towards India which made his approach to all Indo-Pak problems so refreshingly realistic and practical. It indicated prophetically the course of Indo-Pak relations and the fate of Hindu, Buddhist and Christian minorities left in Pakistan if the Government of India persisted in its policy of appeasement of the aggressor and the oppressor as typified by the Nehru-Liaquat Agreement and the events that preceded it.

> "There is nothing of a personal character," he declared, "which has prompted me to resign and I do hope that those with whom I have disagreed will appreciate the depth of my convictions just as I have unhesitatingly appreciated their own. My differences are fundamental and it is not fair or honourable for me to continue as a member of the Government whose policy I cannot approve of.
>
> "I have never felt happy about our attitude towards Pakistan. It has been weak, halting and inconsistent. Our goodness or inaction has been interpreted as weakness by Pakistan. It has made Pakistan more and more intransigent and has made us suffer all the greater and even lowered us in the estimation of our own people. On every important occasion we have remained on the defensive and failed to expose or counteract the designs of Pakistan aimed at us.
>
> "The recent Agreement, to my mind, offers no solution to the basic problem. The evil is far deeper and no patchwork can lead to peace. The establishment of a homogeneous Islamic State in Pakistan's creed and a planned extermination of Hindus and Sikhs and expropriation of their properties constitute its settled policy. As a result of this policy, life for the minorities in Pakistan has become 'nasty, brutish and short'. Let us not be forgetful of the lessons of history. We will do so at our own peril. I am not talking of by-gone times; but if anyone analyses the course of events in Pakistan since its creation, it will be manifest that there is no honourable

place for Hindus within that State. The problem is not communal. It is essentially political. The Agreement unfortunately tries to ignore the implications of an Islamic State. But anyone, who refers carefully to the Objectives Resolution passed by the Constituent Assembly of Pakistan and to the speech of its Prime Minister, will find that while talking in one place of protection of minority rights, the Resolution in another place emphatically declares "that the principles of democracy, freedom, equality, tolerance and social justice as enunciated by Islam shall be fully observed".

The Prime Minister of Pakistan while moving the Resolution spoke thus:

"You would also notice that the State is not to play the part of a neutral observer wherein the Muslims may be merely free to profess and practice their religion, because such an attitude on the part of the State would be the very negation of the ideals which promoted the demand of Pakistan and it is these ideals which should be the cornerstone of the State which we want to build. The State will create such conditions as are conducive to the building up of a truly Islamic Society which means that the State will have to play a positive part in this effort. You would remember that the Quaid-e-Azam and other leaders of the Muslim League always made unequivocal declarations that the Muslim demand for Pakistan was based upon the fact that the Muslim had their own way of life and a code of conduct. Indeed, Islam lays down specific directions for social behaviour and seeks to guide society in its attitude towards the problems which confront it day to day. Islam is not just a matter of private beliefs and conduct".

In such a society, let me ask in all seriousness, can any Hindu expect to live with any sense of security in respect of his cultural, religious, economic and political rights?

It is not the ideology preached by Pakistan that is the only disturbing factor. Its performance has been in full accord with its ideology and the minorities have had bitter experiences, times without number of the true character and functioning of an Islamic State. The Agreement has totally failed to deal with this basic problem.

Today there is a general impression that there has been failure both on the part of India and Pakistan to protect their minorities. The fact however is just the reverse of it. A hostile propaganda has been also carried out in some sections of the foreign press. This is a libel on India and truth must be made known to all who desire to know it. The Indian Government — both at the Centre and in the Provinces and States — generally maintained peace and security throughout the land after Punjab and Delhi disturbances had quietened down, in spite of grave and persistent provocations from Pakistan by reason of its failure to create conditions in Sind, and East Bengal whereby minorities could live there peacefully and honourably. It should not be forgotten here that the people who came away from East Bengal and Sind were not those who had decided to migrate to India out of imaginary fear at the time of partition. These were people who were bent on staying in Pakistan, if only they were given a chance to live decent and peaceful lives.

The supreme question of the hour is can the minorities continue to live with any sense of security in Pakistan? The test of any Agreement is not its reaction within India or in foreign lands, but on the minds of the unfortunate minorities living in Pakistan or those who have been forced to come away already. It is not how a few top-ranking individuals in Pakistan think or desire to act. It is the entire set-up of that State, the mentality of the official circles — high and low — the attitude of the people at large and the activities of organisations such as 'Ansars' which operate together and make it impossible for Hindus to live. It may be that for some months no major occurrences will take place. Meanwhile, we may on our generosity supply them with essential commodities which will give them added strength. That has been Pakistan's technique. Perhaps the next may come during the rainy season when communications are virtually cut off.

I have found myself unable to be a part of the Agreement for the following reasons :

Firstly — we had two such Agreements since Partition for

solving the Bengal problem and they were violated by Pakistan without any remedy open to us. Any agreement which has no sanction will not offer any solution.

Secondly — the crux of the problem is Pakistan's concept of an Islamic State and the ultra-communal administration based on it. The Agreement side-track this cardinal issue and we are today exactly where we were previous to the Agreement.

Thirdly— India and Pakistan are made to appear guilty, while Pakistan was clearly the aggressor. The Agreement provides that no propaganda will be permitted against the territorial integrity of the two countries and there will be no incitement to war between them. This almost sounds farcical so long as Pakistan troops occupy a portion of our territory of Kashmir and warlike preparations on its part are in active operation.

Fourthly— events have proved that Hindus cannot live in East Bengal on the assurance of security given by Pakistan. We should accept this as a basic proposition. The present Agreement on the other, hand calls upon minorities to look upon Pakistan Government for their safety and honour which is adding insult to injury and is contrary to assurances given by us previously.

Fifthly— there is no proposal to compensate those who have suffered nor will the guilty be ever punished, because no one will dare give evidence before a Pakistan Court. This is in accordance with bitter experience in the past.

Sixthly— Hindus will continue to come away in large numbers and those who have come will not be prepared to go back. On the other hand, Muslims who had gone away will now return and in our determination to implement the Agreement Muslims will not leave India. Our economy will thus be shattered and possible conflict within our country will be greater.

Seventhly— in the garb of protecting minorities in India, the Agreement has reopened the problem of Muslim minority in India, thus seeking to revive those disruptive forces that created Pakistan itself. This principle, carried to its logical conclusion, will create fresh problems for us which, strictly speaking, are against our very Constitution.

The course of India-Pak relations since then, culminating in the unprovoked aggression by Pakistan first in Kutch and then in

Kashmir, which resulted in full-fledged Indo-Pakistan war of 1965 and the subsequent developments in India and Pakistan have clearly proved that Dr. Mookerjee was a true statesman who could see ahead and was head and shoulder above the petty politicians of the time who could not see beyond their nose.

The genocide of Hindus and other non-Muslim minorities continued unabated in (the then) both wings of Pakistan, till the creation of Bangladesh. Pakistan has been cleared of all Hindus, the number of Hindus in Bangladesh has dwindled considerably instead of going up on the basis of the fast rate of growth of population in that country. On the other hand the number of Muslims in India has increased manifold. What is worse, the appeasement policy of the government has put them back into the lap of the Mullahs.

Dr. Mookerjee clearly visualised the dangerous potentialities of the India Government's policies towards Pakistan and her supporters and agents left behind in India. He therefore, began to work to create a political platform through which Indian nationalism might project and assert itself and checkmate the evil effects of the policies being pursued by Pandit Nehru in the name of the Indian National Congress.

Dr. Mookerji's ability as a parliamentarian was well known and no one doubted his capacity to handle the job entrusted to him efficiently and effectively. His main object in accepting the invitation to in the cabinet was to impart a touch of realism and firmness to the policies of the Government of free India towards Pakistan, which he was convinced would be India's born enemy, and her protagonists left behind in India. He hope to reinforce the government from within and redeem the pledges given by him to the Hindus left behind in Pakistan. He banked on the support of his senior colleagues like Sardar Vallabhbhai Patel and Shri N.V. Gadgil who shared his assessment of Pakistan and his deep concern and anxiety about the fate of Hindus left behind in the areas lost to her.

The performance of Dr. Syama Prasad Mookerjee as a Minister in the first National Government of free India, his record of service and achievements during the two and a half years he was in office and his exit from the cabinet by resignation in April, 1950, in spite of the best efforts of Sardar Patel and Pt. Nehru to retain him, are some of the most momentous events in his crowded public life. They give an insight into the working of his mind, his acumen as a statesman, skill, integrity and ability as an administrator and his deep sense of duty which enabled him to always keep the cause of the country and his people above his personal interests.

11

Hindu Minorities of Pakistan After Partition

For Dr. Syama Prasad Mookerjee the plight of the Hindu minority in East Pakistan and the indifferent attitude of the Government of India towards it, which had impelled him to kick his cabinet post in 1950, continued to be a matter of deep concern so long as he lived. His interest is the welfare and security of the Hindu compatriots of East Bengal, who had been thrown at the mercy of Pakistan much against their will, grew out of the highest patriotic and humanitarian considerations and not out of any narrow, parochial or communal considerations. The condition of Hindus in Pakistan was, he held, the acid test of that State's right to exist. Partition of the country had been accepted on clear understanding that the minority communities in both the new dominions will be guaranteed security of life and property and equal rights and treatment before law. This was the argument given by the Congress leaders like Mahatma Gandhi, Pt. Nehru and Sardar Patel against the case for exchange of population made by representative Hindus of East Bengal as also by Dr. Ambedkar, who had worked out a detailed scheme for the purpose, in his *Thoughts on Pakistan*. Dr. Mookerjee had also his doubts about the fate of Hindus in Pakistan and he supported the idea of planned exchange of population. But he changed his views after the assurances given by the Congress leaders and he had himself conveyed these assurance to the Hindus of East Bengal, which region he toured extensively on the eve of Partition.

Absolute Insincerity of Agreement by Pakistan

The subsequent developments had shown that Pakistan was not at all sincere about her professions regarding the treatment of minorities in Pakistan. The Government of India had tried to remind her of the obligations that Partition Agreement had put on her about minorities and had entered into a number of pacts for the purpose. The Delhi Pact between Pt. Nehru and Mr. Liaquat Ali of April, 1950, was the third of such agreements about the treatment of minorities in the two Dominions.

Dr. Mookerjee had lost all faith in the pious agreements with Pakistan which were honoured by her only in their breech. He had opposed Nehru-Liaquat Pact because he was convinced that its fate would be no better than those of the earlier agreements. In his statement on his resignation he had enumerated seven convincing reasons, based on irrefutable facts, why he thought the Pakistan would not honour the Agreement and that the process of exterminating or squeezing out the Hindus will continue unabated.

The actual happenings in Pakistan after the Delhi Pact proved his fears to be too true. Liaquat Ali had come down to Delhi in April, 1950, only to save Pakistan from the nemesis that his policy of extermination of Hindus was drawing upon her. Pt. Nehru then played his game and the only realistic way of setting the question once for all, for which Sardar Patel had prepared the country, was abandoned. Having thus outwitted Pt. Nehru, Liaquat returned to Karachi only to carry on his settled policy of squeezing out all Hindus from Pakistan by new and more subtle ways.

Secret Circulars on Treatment of Hindus

They included a secrete circular to all the thana officers to report on the "extent, nature and source of influence wielded by particular individuals of the minority (Hindu) community and the forces and parties that might work against them".

It was followed sometime later by another circular to all heads of commercial firms in East Pakistan to obtain the previous approval of the District Magistrate before giving employment to any non-Muslim. It was clear that no commercial firm would like to incur the displeasure of the government and undergo the botheration of securing permission from District Magistrate for giving employment to any Hindu.

Sometime later another fourteen page long secret circular to all the District Magistrates, which was later produced before the Pakistan Constituent Assembly by Shri Bhupendra Kumar Datt, a member of that Assembly from East Bengal, instructed them to not to return the lands and properties of the returning Hindu migrants but to distribute them among the Muslim refugees. A long list of Statutes and orders and the relevant legal bars were to be put forward in each case one after the other. In all other matters the District Magistrates were instructed to "talk sweetly to minorities and their representative, even with a smile on your lips". "You have", it significantly added, "earned the complements of persons like the honourable Mr. C.C. Biswas who have stated that it was only some subordinate officials who were responsible for the troubles; try by all means to maintain your reputation". It concluded with the advice, "Keep this instruction secret. Do not trust other officers. They sometimes mismanage and mishandle things".

Nehru-Liaquat Pact : A Dead Letter

No wonder, therefore, that Nehru-Liaquat Pact became a dead letter within a few weeks after it was signed so ceremoniously at Delhi. Pakistan continued its policy of squeezing out the Hindus. But it now saw to it that they were not driven out in very large numbers at one time because she had seen by experience that, besides creating sharp reaction in India which disturbed the equanimity of the mind of their friend Pt. Nehru, that could also lead to counter-action by the people of India even against the wishes of their government.

Assassination of Liaquat Ali Khan

Consequently the steady influx of refugees from East Bengal continued unabated throughout 1950 and 1951. But after the assassination of Liaquat Ali Khan at Rawalpindi by the end of 1951, which was exploited by Pakistani Press to malign the enemies of Pakistan by which they meant India and Hindus, attempts began to be made to repeat the performance of Feb-March, 1950. Killing and looting of Hindus and dishonouring of their womenfolk again began on a fairly large-scale in different parts of East Bengal. As a result the sense of insecurity in the minds of East Bengal Hindus, which Delhi Pact and failed to remove, became intense once again and they began to leave their hearths and homes in large numbers to save their life and honour.

Mass Exodus of Hindus

Dr. Mookerjee drew pointed attention of the Prime Minister to this increasing exodus from East Bengal in the course of his speech on the President's address in the opening session of the newly elected Parliament in May, 1952. But, as we have seen above, it not only failed to evoke and response from Pt. Nehru but, what was worse, led to some angry exchanges between the two. Pt. Nehru in his reply to the debate not only minimised the gravity of the situation but also gave a handle to Pakistan for counter propaganda against India by making the absolutely baseless statement that minorities were being ill-treated in India as well.

Pakistan was quick to exploit this attitude of India's Prime Minister towards the critics of their policy in India. The campaign of intimidation and humiliation of Hindus with a view to convert them to Islam or to squeeze them out of Pakistan was, therefore, intensified. It also helped the rulers of Pakistan to divert the attention of Bengal Muslims from the growing demand for autonomy for East Bengal. To make the humiliation of the Hindus complete and to prevent young Hindu girls from being sent away to West Bengal for the safety of their honour a "Girls Release Duty" was imposed on all Hindu girls leaving Pakistan. Their hopeless guardians had either to pay the tax or leave their sisters and daughters to the mercy of Pakistan goondas.

Passport System

To make things worse preparations were started for the introduction of passport and visa system for movements between East Pakistan and India. The idea of Pakistan in doing so was to avoid large-scale exodus all at once, which they feared would create sharp reaction in India. Its settled policy now was to squeeze and not to flood Hindus out of Pakistan. It also wanted to create a sense of helplessness among the lower classes of Hindus, mostly artisans, whose stay in Pakistan was considered necessary for the maintenance of already shattered economy of East Bengal, as a pre-requisite to their conversion to Islam. But to begin with it had the opposite effect. The Hindu in East Bengal felt that the passport system was being devised to seal them off and prevent their escape to India to save their life and honour. So many of them decided to escape to India before the passport system came into operation. Increased harassment by Ansars and other Pakistanis, with the active connivance of Pakistan Government, further aggravated the situation. As a result lakhs of Hindus left their hearths and homes and began to move towards the Indo-Pak border. The situation became similar to that created by the planned killings prior to Nehru-Liaquat Pact.

As these refugees began to arrive in Calcutta in large numbers and tell their tales of woe, a stir was created in West Bengal as also in the rest of India. Dr. Syama Prasad Mookerjee was naturally very much perturbed over the situation. He immediately took up the matter with the Government of India. He urged upon the Government to oppose the introduction of passport system and to adopt a definite and firm policy towards Pakistan to put effective pressure on her to behave as a civilised government towards the Hindu minority. He also appealed to Pt. Jawahar Lal Nehru to visit West Bengal and see the situation created by the exodus from East Pakistan for himself.

To begin with no heed was paid to his appeals and the Passport system came into operation on the 15th of October, 1952. This created a new problem. Lakhs of Hindus who had left their homes in distant parts of East Bengal and were on the move towards the border were completely stranded. Thousands of them lay helpless on rail and ferry heads on the Pakistan border not knowing what to do. They lay there not only exposed to rain and sun but also to the depredations of Pakistani *goondas* who preyed on their meagre possessions and their women-folk. The rules for the issue of passports were made so difficult and complicated that for the common man it became a problem to secure one. The price of post-card size photographs, needed to be appended to the application for Passport, shot up to Rs. 40 a piece.

This situation forced the Government of West Bengal also to reinforce the appeals of public leaders like Dr. Mookerjee to Pandit Nehru for paying a visit to West Bengal and taking some effective step against Pakistan.

Nehru's Visit to East Bengal

As a result Pt. Jawaharlal Nehru paid a hurried visit to Calcutta on his way to Assam on the 18th and 19th of October, 1952. Dr. Mookerjee submitted to him a memorandum detailing his analysis of the problem and suggesting that some effective pressure must be put on Pakistan if this problem of the Hindus of East Bengal was to settled. The gravity of the problem, he held, should be judged not from the number of refugees, though that in itself was a big and grave problem, but from the conditions in East Bengal which forced them to become refugees. He suggested that as a first step economic sanctions should be imposed against Pakistan and if that did not bear the desired result other plans and methods, earlier contemplated by Sardar Patel and Pt. Nehru himself, should be adopted. But all his reasoning and appeals went unheeded by Pt. Nehru. Dr. Mookerjee was not the man to lose heart. He immediately set himself to the task of awakening the country to the gravity of the situation and to mobilise public opinion in support of his stand. He had always looked upon this problem not as a provincial or communal problem but as a political problem of nationwide importance. It was, therefore, his endeavour that it should be treated as a national problem towards the solution of which all parties should cooperate.

The attitude adopted by Pt. Nehru towards his appeals convinced him that he was either not amenable to appeals and reason or was incapable of taking such initiative. So he decided to take the initiative himself.

Going Ahead in Face of Opposition

He approached the leaders of all the non-Congress and non-Communist parties working in West Bengal and held an all parties conference for evolving a joint front and a common policy about East Bengal Hindus. Congress as a party would not come into his joint front on the issue for obvious reasons. The Communists, true to their anti-national role in the past, adopted the opposite policy of defending Pakistan in the creation of which they also had a big hand. They suggested that a goodwill mission should be sent to Pakistan and started a campaign of vilification against Dr. Mookerjee and those who cooperated with him. But in spite of this opposition he was able to bring all the other Opposition parties on a common platform on this issue. Huge joint public meetings of the non-Communist and non-Congress parties were held at Calcutta Maidan on the 16th of October, and at Gandhi Grounds,

Delhi, on the 26th of October, in which Government of India's policy towards Pakistan and its indifference toward the lot of Hindu minority there was severely criticised by leaders like Acharya J.B. Kripalani, Chairman of the Praja Socialist Party, and Shri N.C. Chatterji besides Dr. Syama Prasad Mookerjee.

In the course of his speech at Calcutta meetings, which he presided, Dr. Mookerjee referred to the fundamental issues involved in the treatment of minorities in Pakistan. India, he said, was not partitioned as a result of a war. It was an agreed act, intended for solving communal bitterness; but the basic condition was that people belonging to all communities would continue to live in both countries and would receive the protection of their respective governments as indeed any civilised government would be willing to do.

He declared that Pakistan Government's persistent and deliberate failure in undertaking the responsibility for the safety and protection of the minority people entitled India to examine the whole problem of Partition *de-novo* and proceed to act as any self respecting nation would do. It was not the misery of the suffering migrants alone that called for redress; if this exodus was unchecked it would give a blow to the safety and security not only of North Eastern India but of the entire country.

Pakistan, he declared, had been emboldened to behave in this scandalous manner because of the weakness and vacillation of our own government. If only the Government of India took up a firm attitude and if Pakistan Government knew that its acts of omission and commission would lead to consequences which would hit the vital interests of that country economically and politically, the Pakistan Government would never act as at present.

Delhi Pact, he declared, was dead and gone. Pact after pact had been made between India and Pakistan only to be repudiated by the latter country in practice. He demanded that this policy of appeasement, of Pacts, of wait and see, must be reversed.

East Bengal Minorities Convention

Dr. Mookerjee followed up by organising an East Bengal Minorities convention on an all India level at Calcutta on the Ist and 2nd of November, 1952. The convention which was held at the University Institute Hall under the Presidentship of Smt. Sucheta Kripalani was an eloquent testimony to the statesmanship, constructive mind and organising ability of Dr. Syama Prasad Mookerjee. He was the moving spirit behind the whole thing. It was his stature as a national leader, the faith in his integrity and his constructive and realistic approach to the problem which had brought such different, and even mutually hostile, elements as the Praja Socialists, the Revolutionary Socialists and the Hindu Sabhaites on one common platform for a national purpose. It also demonstrated the growing strength and influence of his own party, the Bharatiya Jan Sangh, whose nationalistic and progressive approach to the problems of the country and capacity to act was slowly being recognised even by its erstwhile critics.

The all parties convention unanimously demanded that economic sanctions be imposed against Pakistan and supply of essential goods to her be stopped as a first step to put effective pressure on her to behave as a civilised government. It also demanded withdrawal of passport and visa system between the two Bengals which, it declared, had been causing incalculable hardship to the people on both sides of the border.

The convention also appointed a small sub-committee consisting among others of Dr. Mookerjee and :Smt. Sucheta Kripalani to draw plans and take action, about the implementation of the decisions and recommendations of the convention. .

The convention concluded its deliberations with a huge public meeting at Wellingdon Square, on the 2nd of November, where Dr. Mookerjee as also the spokesmen of other parties laid stress on the urgency of the problem and called upon the people to be prepared even for making sacrifice to secure justice to their compatriots of Pakistan.

Addressing another huge meeting a few days later at Park Circus Maidan, which was attended by a large number of Muslims, he appealed to the Muslims to support the stand taken by all parties convention. Pakistan government, he told them, had turned out to be an enemy of humanity and it was the duty of every man, be he a Hindu or a Muslim, to raise his voice of protest wherever humanity was oppressed.

To educate and mobilise public opinion all over the country

about the problem the Sub-Committee issued an appeal under the signatures of leaders of all the non-Congress and non-Communist Parties of the country including Dr. Mookerjee, Acharya and Mrs. Kirpalani, Shri N. C. Chatterji, Master Tara Singh, General Mohan Singh, Shri R. S. Ruiker of the Forward Bloc, Shri S. S. More of the Peasants and Workers Party and Shri Rajbhoj of the Scheduled Castes Federation to observe November 23 as the All India East Bengal Minority Rights Day all over the country under the combined auspices of all the parties.

Last Speech in Parliament

Before that Dr. S. P. Mookerjee once again presented the case of East Bengal Hindus before the Parliament on the 15th of November, in one of his most forceful speeches which was listened to with rapt attention by the Chief Justice, Mr. Patanjali Sastri and other judges of Supreme Court, Secretaries of the various departments of the central government and a number of foreign diplomats, including Shri Shuaib Qureshi, the High Commissioner of Pakistan in India, besides a full house and crowded visitors galleries.

In the course of that speech, which proved to be his last speech in the Parliament on the question of East Bengal which had been uppermost in his mind since the partition of India, he appealed to the Parliament, to the representatives of 360 millions of free Indians,

> "to make up their mind once for all whether under the existing circumstances it is possible for the minority to live in East Pakistan. That is the fundamental issue. And if they say that it is not, then to make up their minds whether it is possible for the free government of India to take any effective steps for their protection".

He reminded Pt. Jawaharlal Nehru of the pledges and assurances that he along with other Congress leaders had given to Hindus of East Bengal on the eve of partition and he also recalled his speech on the 15th of August, 1947; in the course of which he had said :

"We think also of our brothers and sisters who have been cut

> off from us by the political boundaries and who unhappily, cannot share at present in the freedom that has come. They are of us and will remain of us, whatever may happen in future, and we shall be sharers in good and ill fortune alike."

And then he called upon Pt. Nehru,

> "who is now Prime Minister of India, to fulfil this pledge which he had given in such noble words to those who had suffered with him and others like him for the liberation of their motherland".

He recalled his own experiences of conferences with Mr. Ghulam Mohammed and Khwaja Nazimuddin when he was a minister in the central cabinet. He described them as bitter and tragic experiences of failure which have continued all these five years and reminded Pt. Nehru of his own statement in Feb., 1950: "When peaceful methods fail other methods will be adopted by the Government", and asked him to "tell us whether time has not come to adopt other methods".

He put to the government the fundamental question: "Do you believe that you have any responsibility for the protection of the minorities"? "Pandit ji" he went on, "had said on that occasion (Feb. 1950) that they are our concern : the protection of minorities is a matter which we will have to take in hand. They will be rehabilitate in their homes, if possible, or elsewhere if necessary".

Referring to the question of rehabilitation of those who had come out of Pakistan he quoted some representative Harijans of East Bengal who had come over to India to save their honour and religion but had again gone back to Pakistan. They had told him, "We came to India for rehabilitation ; we have not got it. Our children have died. We are going back. What is the crime we have committed? We did not want Pakistan. You asked us to live there and it is only because we are Hindu we are facing this crisis. We will embrace Islam, we will surrender ourselves". And he asked :

"Will it bring credit to India? Will it be something of which India can be proud"?

Explaining his own approach to the problem he said : "I look at this problem, from two points of view. One rehabilitation and the other the future of people who are still in Pakistan. "Rehabilitation" he added, "must naturally be continued". But it is not an easy task. And if more continue to come, your rehabilitation plans will never be successful. Where will be your planning schemes. What are you going to do if another fifty or sixty lakhs of people are pushed out of Pakistan and they come over here."

This, he declared, went against the very basis of partition : "We accepted Pakistan under certain basic conditions. When that basic condition is not observed by Pakistan, then the very basis of partition disappears. From that point of view the Partition stands annulled and India is not bound by her commitments. It is not my wording alone. The Prime Minister himself has declared from that very place that the basic condition is that minorities must be protected by Pakistan".

"We" he continued, "have done our duty. India has protected its minorities".

He was opposed to any communal or parochial approach to the problem. "It is a national problem", he declared, "we must find a national solution for it." The killing of some innocent Muslims because Hindus are butchered in Pakistan will be a vicious circle and is most inhuman. The true interpretation of Hinduism is that if a man goes wrong you should punish him, but if a man is innocent and you go and cut throat that simply poisons the atmosphere. It does not save people".

He placed before the Parliament a few of the hundreds of cases of cold-blooded butchery of Hindus and barbarous crimes against their womenfolk that had been reported to him, which brought tears in the eyes of Congress members even, and he made a pathetic appeal to Pt. Nehru not to underestimate the woes of Hindus by making such statements as "everything is all right expect some insecurity." "He may declare his helplessness", he added, "but for heavens sake do not say things which are not true. That would be like throwing salt into the gaping wound. You may not be able to protect them, you may not be able to help them but do not minimise the gravity of the situation".

"Unfortunately", he continued, "the statements which the Prime Minister made during the last few days will form part of Pakistan propaganda" against India.

Coming to the remedies he made it clear that he wanted a solution of the problem and was prepared to give his fullest cooperation to the government for the purpose. "We do not want that people should be killed by inches. If they have to die let them die all at once" he declared. "This is a chain of terrible humiliation and misery which affects not individuals alone but which humiliates the status and stature of the nation".

"We have given some remedies," he added "other remedies may be suggested. Economic sanctions is one. Naturally demand for land is one. It was Sardar Patel's remedy. If one-third of the population who happen to be Hindus are pushed out, Pakistan must give one-third land. We cannot ruin the whole country of India for misdeeds of Pakistan. There must be a re-partition of the territory of Pakistan and these people must be settled there".

Then he referred to a remedy suggested by no less a man than Gandhiji with whom he had once discussed the problem along with Rajkumari Amrit Kaur. Gandhiji, he revealed, had told them, "Let India play her part; you protect the minorities, let not one man be turned out of here; then turn towards Pakistan and say: we have fulfilled our part, but you have not; it becomes a world problem, it becomes a moral problem. And if Pakistan fails to do so, if there is no other remedy, you must take charge of East Bengal, let the Government take charge and protect the people."

"I am not advocating war" he explained "but if there is no other way of protecting the minorities of East Pakistan except to take charge of the that territory, Government of India someday will have to consider it". He thought that such an eventuality could even be completely avoided if the Prime Minister were to declare that his Government would act firmly and not adopt a policy of weakness and appeasement" because, "goondaism does not wish to face war. They want to gain something without sacrifice."

He denounced the policy of appeasement adopted by Pt. Nehru towards Pakistan and ridiculed his defence for it. "I am amazed at it" he declared. "He (Pt. Nehru) may say, I cannot find a solution: I can sympathise with that. But he glorifies the appeasement and goes on appeasing. At whose cost? If he does it at his own cost, I do not mind, though I shall be sorry. But what right has he to appease at the cost of the nation? It is a question of the honour and self-respect of India. Something has to be done to prevent a major catastrophe."

"It was", he held, "primarily the task of the Government to find a remedy. Opposition could only suggest something and offer its cooperation." "Find out an effective solution", he therefore asked the government, "by which these people can be enabled to live exercising their elementary rights without being ruined as refugees or beggars or slaves."

Referring to the healing touch theory of Pt. Nehru he said: "The Prime Minister very often says he believes in a healing process. Undoubtedly. Healing by what means? Healing by curing the diseases? If there is a cancerous growth, will you put sandal oil on the cancer and heat it? You will have to go to the root of it. You will have to appreciate what the disease is".

What pained him most, he declared, was that "Government are running away from the real problem. They just say there is no problem, people are not coming. But coming or not coming the disease is there." And then he repeated the suggestion that he had made in, 1950. "Until you can go and settle there with your wives and daughters, you cannot realise the agony of millions".

Finally he appealed to the Government to not to talk of Gandhian ideology because "whatever Gandhiji was, cowardice was not within his ideology. Inaction was not within his ideology. He would have never sat quiet and helpless. Resist non-violently if possible, violently if necessary, but never submit to a wrong", was his philosophy. "I ask the Government", he placed, "to accept that as policy. Resist this national wrong."

He wound up this great oration, the most pathetic but eloquent and convincing advocacy of the cause of millions of Hindus of East Bengal, by an exhortation which needs to be harked today as never before:

"Peace undoubtedly is wanted, but peace with honour. Let us follow the path of peace. If we can lay out the scheme whereby we can finally solve this problem peacefully, then let us do it. But if not, do not submit to wrong things."

East Bengal Day

Twenty third of November was observed as East Bengal Day throughout India. As was expected Bharatiya Jan Sangh played the leading part in it. All other parties cooperated. Dr. Mookerjee himself addressed a mammoth meeting in Ramlila ground in New Delhi, which was presided over by General Mohan Singh and was addressed by all the leaders of the Opposition parties and groups in the Parliament except the Communist Party.

The mass enthusiasm for the cause of East Bengal Hindus created by the observance of this day had some effect on the minds of the rulers both at New Delhi and Karachi, Gods of Karachi realised that they had over-done themselves. So steps began to be taken by them to repeat the old tactics. Some reassuring speeches were made by Khwaja Nazimuddin, who also started correspondence with Pt. Nehru for another meeting, presumably to be followed by a Pact on the lines of Nehru-Liaquat Pact. But he was thrown over-board before he could come to Delhi and the drama of "friendly" talks with Nehru was performed by his successor, Mr. Mohammed Ali.

Continuously Drawing Nehru's Attention to Problems

In New Delhi, Pt. Nehru got restive over this unholy combination of nationalist parties like the P.S.P., the Revolutionary Socialist Party and the Forward Bloc with the "Communal" Parties like Jan Sangh under the leadership of communalist Mookerjee. This started the correspondence between Pt. Nehru and Shri J.P. Narain, the P.S.P. leader, for a Congress-P.S.P. coalition so that the latter could be weaned from the growing influence of Mookerjee.

But so far as the condition of Hindus in East Bengal was concerned it remained what it was. Pakistan continued to be as insincere as ever and Pt. Nehru's heart remained too full with the miseries of the people of Tunisia, Morocco and Korea to have any tears for his own compatriots of East Pakistan.

As a result the conviction began to grow in the mind of Dr. Mookerjee, a conviction that was to be confirmed by the failure of his efforts to persuade Pt. Nehru to, at least, meet Pt. Premnath Dogra to settle the Jammu issue, that the Prime Minister was not amenable to reason and that he had become too much puffed up by his unlimited power to take into consideration any viewpoint which was not backed by such power as he could feel. He was thus being driven to the path of Satyagraha much against his wishes as the only means of making the "democratic" Government to do anything in the matter.

Ironically before he could do anything for East Bengal, Kashmir issue came to a head and it assumed such urgency that he had to throw himself completely in it. But he never for a moment became oblivious of East Bengal. In his Presidential address at the Kanpur Session of the Bharatiya Jan Sangh, he drew pointed attention to the problem of East Bengal, along with that of Kashmir. It was his plan to take up the issue of East Bengal and do everything possible for forcing the hands of Government of India to settle it in a satisfactory manner as soon as his hands were free from Kashmir. But Kashmir freed him from his mortal bounds, bequeathing the great burden on his heart about East Bengal to his followers.

12

Emergence of Jan Sangh

Dr. Syama Prasad Mookerjee's exit from the Central Cabinet marked the beginning of a new, and as later events were to prove, the most momentous phase of his crowded life. He had entered the cabinet as a provincial leader of Bengal but he came out as a national leader. All the non-Congress nationalists had begun to look upon him as their tribune and spokesman. The Congress legislators and leaders who had watched his life and work from close quarters had also developed a new respect for him. They had begun to look upon him as the most effective critic and opponent of their policies, particularly those pertaining to relations with Pakistan.

His resignation created a stir in the country. The Congress circles felt uneasy and their controlled press tried to minimise the importance of the event. But the people in general hailed it as a brave and conscientious act. The people of the capital demonstrated their appreciation of the stand taken by Dr. Mookerjee by giving him a grand reception which was attended by over a thousand representative citizens drawn from all walks of life, to congratulate him on his bold decision. Some of the independent minded Congress-men like Shri H.V. Kamath M.P., who had been painfully watching democracy, being butchered in the one party Parliament, also hailed his exit from the cabinet as the beginning of a healthy Opposition within the Parliament. It was taken for granted by them that he will create and lead the Opposition in the Parliament.

Need for Opposition

The tragedy of the situation was that no organised opposition then existed within or outside the Parliament. The Parliament which was also the Constituent Assembly was elected indirectly by the Provincial legislatures in 1946, when the main problem before the country was the demand for Partition. Congress then presented itself as champion of Akhand Hindustan and, therefore, all the Hindu seats went to it. The Muslims sent in Muslim League nominees who, for sometime, formed the main opposition. Partition converted the Muslim opposition into Sovereign Parliament of Pakistan. The few Muslim members that remained in the Indian Parliament joined the Congress to cover their past sins. So the role of opposition in the debates had to be played by a few outspoken Congressmen and the liberals like Pt. Hirday Nath Kunzru. But for voting purposes they all belonged to the Congress party. This made the debates and deliberation of the Parliament very tame and unreal. Dr. Mookerjee after his resignation, therefore, found, himself a solitary member in the opposition. After some time his erstwhile colleagues in the cabinet, Shri K.C. Neogy and Shri John Mathhai also joined him. But they soon withdrew from the active Parliamentary field altogether leaving Dr. Mookerjee to fight the opposition battles against a steam roller majority single handedly.

Status of the then Opposition

Communist Party

But a greater handicap than the absence of any organised opposition within the Parliament was the absence of any effective and well knit organisation outside that could mobilise and organise the nationalist opinion in the country. The Communist Party was no doubt there. But it acted, as elsewhere, as the agent of Communist Russia and, therefore, could not appeal to the nationalist opinion in the country. Its cult of the bomb and the bullet whose worst demonstration it had been giving in Telengana had isolated it from the general Indian public for the time being at least.

Socialist Party

The Socialist Party of India under the leadership of Shri Jai Prakash Narain and Acharya Narendra Deva had begun to make some headway. But its basic approach to the problems of the country, political as well as economic and social, was very much the same as that of Pt. Nehru's Congress. It was more or less a wing of the Congress itself.

Ram Rajya Parishad

Ram Rajya Parishad was another organisation that was just then making some headway in erstwhile princely States like Rajasthan and Madhya Bharat. It drew its sustenance from feudal elements, and the social and economic policies it advocated were not only very conservative but too out of date to find acceptance with the people in general. A dynamic and progressive mind as that of Dr. Mookerjee could have little sympathy for its approach to national problems.

Hindu Maha Sabha

The Hindu Maha Sabha, the organisation whose destinies he had guided for many years as its President, was of course there in the field with the same outlook and pursuing the same policies which it had been doing before independence and partition of the country. But Dr. Mookerjee had outgrown it during the three years since independence.

He realised immediately after the dawn of Independence that Hindu Maha Sabha, if it was to play its rightful role of nationalist opposition to Congress, must re-orientate its policies and outlook. With the abolition of the separate electorates the Hindu Maha Sabha, he argued, must broaden its base-admit members of all religious communities into it and play its proper role of national organisation of all the Hindus, which term is and ought to be accepted as a synonym for Indian, both having been derived from Sindhu, which was pronounced Indus by the Greeks. He wanted Hindu Sabha to make the world realise the true import of the word Hindu and take up the task of Hinduising politically, socially as well as culturally those elements in the country which had been mislead by the British propaganda and Congress folly to detest their own national name and ideals and play the role of disruptionists. The Muslim problem, he was convinced, could be solved in free India once for all if their outlook on cultural, social and political problems of the country was Hinduised or nationalised while leaving them free, in keeping with the Hindu tradition of absolute tolerance, to carry on their religion and way of worship as they pleased. That, he thought was the only sure way of rooting out the poison of two nation theory and undoing the mischief that the

British and the Muslim League had done with the connivance of the Congress leaders, who had walked into their trap. Failing that, he suggested, the Maha Sabha should cease to be a political organisation and concentrate on the social and cultural uplift of the Hindu society in the religious sense of the term.

The Maha Sabha leaders were at that time very much embittered by the Congress betrayal of the trust put in it by the people and terrible massacres and carnage that had been going on in Pakistan to exterminate or squeeze out all the Hindus. They wanted to capitalise the anti-Congress and anti-Muslim feeling that it had generated in the Hindu masses in general throughout the country to make Maha Sabha an effective political force. They, therefore, did not think it worth-while to accept the advice of Dr. Mookerjee to reorientate the policy of the Maha Sabha.

But with the assassination of Gandhiji on the 30th January 1948, the tables were turned on Maha Sabha. The party in power exploited the situation to suppress all its real or imaginary, actual or potential rivals.

Reorienting Policies of Maha Sabha: The RSS

The Rashtriya Swayam Sewak Sangh, the best organised and disciplined non-political national organisation of the Hindus in the country came in for the heaviest blows. It was put under ban and all its known leaders and workers, running into tens of thousands, were arrested and detained without trial. Some of the Maha Sabha leaders were also arrested and the very existence of Maha Sabha as a political organisation came to be threatened. This made the Maha Sabha leaders nervous and those outside the jail decided on the 15th of February, 1948, to accept the advice given by Dr. Mookerjee many months back to re-orientate the policy of Maha Sabha. It decided to suspend its political activities and to concentrate only on social and cultural work. This saved it from the wrath of the party in power. In continued to exist.

Rashtriya Swayam Sevak Sangh

The situation was changed in 1949 by the determined effort of the Rashtriya Swayam Sevak Sangh to assert its right to exist. It sent in about a lakh youngmen to fill the prisons of free India to indicate its right to carry on its perfectly legal nation building activities. The Government had to yield. The ban on the RSS was lifted. The Maha Sabha executive, which had taken the earlier decision under stress of circumstances and not out of conviction, thought the time opportune to return to politics. It resolved to rescind its earlier decision and resumed political activities early in August, 1949.

Resignation from Executive of Maha Sabha

Dr. Syama Prasad Mookerjee could not re-concile himself to this decision of Maha Sabha executive. He was not opposed to its resuming political activities but in that case he wanted it to open its doors to all citizens of India, irrespective of caste and creed, who may be willing to subscribe to its creed and policy. He therefore decided to disassociate himself from the policy making of Maha Sabha. He resigned from its executive, but as a Hindu he continued to be an ordinary member of Hindu Maha Sabha which had been founded primarily for the cultural and social uplift and consolidation of Hindu society.

Dr. Mookerji's attitude towards Maha Sabha during this period has been subjected to uncharitable criticism from some quarters. He has been charged with weakness and bad faith towards Maha Sabha. But the facts prove the contrary. His critics do not seem to realise the significance of the change that partition and freedom had wrought in the politics of the country after 15th of August, 1947. But a dynamic mind like that of Dr. Mookerjee could not fail to grasp it. He wanted Maha Sabha to grow with the times. It was only when he found that it had lost the will and strength to grow that he left it. He outgrew it.

RSS: A Non-Political Organisation

The one organisation outside the precincts of Congress and its satellites, which had demonstrated its will and right to exist and keep the torch of true nationalism, rooted in the age old culture of the country, aflame in face of all odds was the Rashtriya Swayam Sewak Sangh. It had come out of the ordeal of ban and the country wide Satyagraha that it launched against it, with flying colours, keeping its ranks as united and disciplined as ever. Its past record of service coupled with the demonstration of its strength made it look the organisation of the future. It had begun to capture the imagination of the Indian masses. It had its network of branches and a cadre of tried and selfless workers.

Dr. Syama Prasad Mookerjee had come into contact with the great founder and leader of this movement. Dr. Keshav Bali Ram Hedgewar, in the mid-thirtees at Calcutta. He had seen the work of this organisation in the pre-partition days. Addressing a rally of RSS at Lahore in 1940 he had described it as the "only silver lining in the cloudy sky of India." The grand work done by its Swayamsevaks in Punjab, Kashmir, NWFP and Sind during 1947, their self-immolation for the cause of their country and countrymen and the guts and strength they had shown against brutally violent Pakistanis had won his unqualified praise and respect. The restraint of the strong that this organisation had shown after the murder of Gandhiji, in face of the most cowardly attacks on its leaders and workers by the members of the party in power with the connivance of the police and custodians of law and order, and the proof of its strength given by it during its Satyagraha in 1948-49 had raised its prestige and credit even with its opponents and critics.

But RSS was and wanted to continue as a non-political organisation, devoted to the work of character building, cultural uplift, social cohesion and awakening of true national consciousness in the people in general, in the hope that change in the outlook of the people coupled with the respect for the national ideals and 'Sanskriti' that it was inculcating in them, will automatically be reflected in the political life of the nation. It, therefore, gave perfect freedom to its members to join any political party they liked.

RSS Need for Political Affiliation

But the developments and happenings during the post-partition years had forced the RSS leaders and workers to do some hard thinking. They had found that the party in power, blinded by self-interest, had not hesitated to give what it wanted to be a death bow to the organisation which had done the noblest work during the partition days and which was doing the most essential national work of building up character and unity in the country. They had also begun to realise that it was not very easy for ordinary members to influence the policies of well organised and well entrenched parties like the Congress from within, simply because the men who controlled them would not allow fresh blood and fresh ideas to disturb them in their position of power and influence.

They had, therefore, begun to feel the need of a political organisation which should reflect the ideas and ideals of the RSS in the political sphere and which should, therefore, be able to command the willing allegiance of the RSS workers and supporters. This need, it was felt, would become more pressing after the introduction of adult franchise. Every adult who had a vote must have some political understanding and affiliation to be able to exercise his right of vote usefully. The growing influence and scope of politics also pointed to the need of shaping it according to the ideals which RSS cherished in politics cuts deep allround" had begun to face them as a bitter reality.

Dr. Mookerjee was aware of this trend of thought in the RSS circles. He knew that the attitude of the RSS which drew its main strength and sustenance from the lower middle and working classes, towards social and economic problems of the country could be anything, but reactionary. The RSS approach to the problems of culture, nationalism, and partition had his fullest approval. He, therefore, instinctively felt that any political organisation sponsored by or enjoying the confidence of the RSS could surely and speedily become such a force in the political life of the country as may command his fullest allegiance and succeed in mobilising and consolidating the non-Congress and non-Communist nationalist public opinion into an effective opposition.

But the initiative to create such an organisation lay with the RSS leaders. It was, however, pretty certain that they would not bring RSS as such in the political arena and would concentrate on their nation building activities unshakled by any political inhibitions or prejudices. Moreover the RSS was at that time concentrating upon the work of rehabilitating itself after the ban and Satyagraha. It, therefore, did not want to create any diversion for its workers.

The Birth of Jan Sangh

A beginning, however, was made on the 16th of January, 1951 when about a dozen prominent citizens of Punjab and Delhi including L. Hansraj Gupta, Shri Dharam Vir, Pt. Mauli Chander

Sharma, Bhai Mahavir, Mahashe Krishan, Ch. Siri Chand of Rohtak, L.Balraj Bhalla of Jullundhar and Balraj Madhok met in New Delhi to draw up tentative plans for starting a new political party for Punjab, PEPSU, Himachal Pradesh and Delhi, where the need for it was most badly felt because of the utter failure of the party in power to tackle the pressing problems and needs of the people, particularly of the large number of refugees from West Pakistan, and its policy of surrender to the separatists demands of Akalis, who held the balance between the warring factions of Congress legislators. Dr. Syama Prasad Mookerjee was specially invited to this meeting to give it the benefit of his counsel and sober guidance.

While appreciating the pressing necessity of doing something immediate for Punjab, PEPSU, Himachal Pradesh and Delhi, Dr. Mookerjee stressed the need of the formation of an all India Party, without which the Provincial parties could not get the proper status and impetus, at an early date. It was therefore decided, on Dr. Mookerji's suggestion, to start the preparation for the formation of the all India party, whose basic principles and main items of programme were discussed in the meeting in a general way, and a sub-committee was set up to draw up the draft manifesto and constitution for the proposed party in the light of those discussions. It was in this meeting that the proposed party was tentatively christened "Bhartiya Jan Sangh."

In the discussions of the day the approach of the proposed party to the word Hindu Rashtra and its political, social and cultural implications figured prominently.

Concept of Hindu Rashtra

Some of the persons present argued that though they were in full agreement with the concept of Hindu Rashtra yet they would not like it being incorporated or used in the objective of the proposed party because that might create misunderstandings in the minds of some people. That provoked Dr. Mookerjee who have a convincing exposition of the concept of Hindu Rashtra as he understood it. He explained that the British had deliberately given a narrow sectarian connotation to the word Hindu for their imperialist ends and the Congress leaders had played their game in denouncing everything Hindu as Communal. It should be the duty of the new organisation, he pleaded, to dispel these misconceptions and make the world familiar with the broad national import of the word Hindu, the geographical and historical name of the people of Hindustan. Hindu Rashtra, he argues, was a noble concept. It brought out the basic oneness and the common tradition of all the different sects and creeds of India. It did not denote any particular religion but a common wealth of all the religions and sects of the country because, whatever may be the way of worship of any particular individual, he could not, if he was to be a national of India, cut himself asunder from the common cultural and historical traditions of India. As such it is not and never was a communal or narrow concept. Those, he argued, who were scared away by the very word Hindu could not be depended upon for safeguarding the cultural and territorial heritage of the country.

But he was opposed to the word being imposed on those who were not, for the time being, prepared to accept it. He, therefore, suggested that the word Bharatiya and Indian, which are synonyms of the word Hindu but are more acceptable to the westernised as also to those who lack the courage of conviction, should also be used along with the word Hindu till such people shed their inferiority complex and learn to take pride in their own name and traditions.

Pending the formation of the All India organisation it was decided to go ahead with the formation of Jan Sangh for Punjab, PEPSU, Himachal Pradesh and Delhi. It was also decided to form Jan Sangh in as many other States as possible so that the new party should take the shape of growth from below.

Accordingly a convention of some three hundred representative citizens of Punjab, PEPSU, Himachal Pradesh and Delhi was called at Jullundhur on 23rd of May, 1951 to form Jan Sangh for these four contiguous States which for all practical purposes were one unit. The response was most encouraging. Almost all the invitees responded to the invitation.

The attitude of the party in power towards the new organisation became evident even before it was formally born. The reception committee had made arrangements for the convention in the compound of the Anglo-Sanskrit High School, within the municipal limits of Jullundur. But just on the eve of the convention, literally 24 hours before it was scheduled to meet, the District Magistrate, presumably under instructions from above, banned all meetings within municipal limits of Jullundur. All efforts to secure permission for the convention which, as was clear from the very nature of the task for which it had been convened, was to be a sort of private deliberative meeting of the invitees alone, proved of no avail. Therefore, the venue of the convention had to be shifted over night to the compound of a cold storage plant just outside the municipal limits.

The convention resolved to form itself into Bhartiya Jan Sangh for Punjab, PEPSU, Himachal Pradesh and Delhi which were treated as one unit for the purpose of Jan Sangh organisation. L. Balraj Bhalla, an ex-revolutionary (he was sentenced to transportation for life in connection with Hardinge Bomb Case) and a top educationist of Punjab, was elected the first President.

About the sàme time Dr. Syama Prasad Mookerjee called a similar convention of representative Bengalis at Calcutta which resolved to form a Jan Sangh, also called Peoples Party, for West Bengal with Dr. Mookerjee as its first President.

Similar conventions were held during the next two months at Lucknow and Indore for forming Jan Sangh in Uttar Pradesh and Madhya Bharat. The Lucknow convention elected Shri Din Dayal Upadhayay, the reputed social worker, writer and orator of that province, as the first General Secretary of Uttar Pradesh Jan Sangh with Rao Krishan Pal Singh as President.

All India Convention of Jan Sangh

On the 9th of September, 1951, the Presidents, Secretaries and some other prominent workers of the above mentioned Provincial Jan Sanghs of Punjab, PEPSU, Himachal Pradesh and Delhi. Bengal, Uttar Pradesh and Madhya Bharat met in Delhi and decided that time had come to give an all India form to Jan Sangh to which Provincial Jan Sanghs may get affiliated. The task of convening an all India convention for the purpose was entrusted to the Jan Sangh of Punjab, PEPSU and Delhi. The Jan Sangh of Punjab, PEPSU, Himachal Pradesh and Delhi thereupon decided to call the convention at New Delhi on the 21st of October, 1951, and appointed its General Secretary, Prof. Balraj Madhok, to be its convenor.

Before the all India convention met, Provincial conventions were held at Jaipur, Nagpur and Patna to form provincial Jan Sanghs for Rajasthan, Madhya Pradesh and Bihar. Thus, Jan Sangh had come into existence in all the States of North India except Assam and Vindhya Pradesh before it took an all India form.

13

Leading the Jan Sangh as President

Before, the Jan Sangh was formally launched the like minded people searched for the appropriate person to preside over the new outfit, who was to be formally elected as its first head at the Convention. It did not, however, take long for the sponsors of the new organisation to decide that the honour must go to Dr. Syama Prasad Mookerjee. There was no other person in the country with the stature and strength required to carry the burden of an organisation which was destined, from its very inception, to become a force to reckon with.

It was eleventh of October 1951, when at about 8 a.m. Lala Hansraj Gupta, Pandit Mauli Chander Sharma and Prof Balraj Madhok reached 10, Pusa Road, New Delhi, where Dr. Mookerjee was then staying, to request him to give his consent to the proposal. Dr. Mookerjee received us with a broad smile in the verandah of the house and led us into a small study where he had been working, as was usual with him, since 6.30 a.m. after returning from his morning walk. He was sparsely dressed. A coarse cotton 'dhoti', a 'kurta', a 'chaddar' of coarse silk and country made slippers constituted his whole dress. The room had not enough chairs to seat us all. So Dr. Mookerjee himself went to the drawing room of his host to fetch chairs. He took his seat only after all of us had been comfortably seated.

After formal courtesies, L. Hansraj Gupta broached the subject in his own inimitable way, half serious, half humorous, enlivened by some homely touches and references. There was a lull after L. Hansraj had finished. Dr. Mookerji's demeanour became serious. He threw his large body comfortably into his arm chair and plunged right away into deep thought. After a few minutes, he broke the silence with the following measured words.

"It is a great responsibility that you want me to shoulder. I will try to do it in the spirit of humble duty to my motherland. But before I accept it, I want to be clear in my mind about the character and the future working of the organisation you want me to lead".

Again after a pause lasting about a minute and with a question mark on his face, he dilated in some detail upon what he thought the character and working of Jana Singh should be, particularly emphasising its relationship with other nationalist forces and organisations in the country, cultural, social as well as political.

Spearhead of the Nationalist Forces

He visualised Jana Singh as the spearhead of the nationalist forces in the country and, therefore, wanted it to be so broad based as to able to comprehend and consolidate all of them into an effective political organisation. It should be open to all citizens who owed unalloyed allegiance to India and her great culture and heritage which is essentially Hindu in character.

From that very day Dr. Mookerjee put his heart and soul into the making of the new organisation. Day after day he sat for long hours with Pt. Mauli Chander Sharma and Prof. Balraj Madhok to give final touches to the draft manifesto of the Jana Sangh to be placed before the All India Convention. It was during the course of discussions about different aspects of the economic programme of the new party that he showed deep insight into the economic ills of the motherland and his realistic and constructive approach towards them. There was an impression in some that Dr. Mookerjee was more on the side of capitalistic economy than on what is popularly known as Socialistic economy, which was wrong. His approach to the economic problems was not coloured by any text-book maxims or pet theories. His was essentially a practical approach guided solely by the stark realities of the Indian economic situation and the urgent need for speedy economic recovery and welfare of India and her teeming millions. That is why in certain respects his approach appeared to be rather drastic and radical while in others it could be called conservative. In fact, it was neither of the two. It was essentially Indian, Hindu, or Bhartiya, geared to meet the special needs of India.

An interesting anecdote made this fact amply clear. A leading economist and industrialist, who was lending his helping hand in the formulation of the economic programme, on coming across the proposal for profit sharing between capital and labour, in the chapter on industrial relations, felt somewhat shocked. He remarked humourously, "Our young professor seems to be a Communist." But he was soon disillusioned. Dr. Mookerjee defended profit sharing as the only practical means of making the labour interested in increasing production which, he held, was the first essential for solving the economic problems of the country. That perhaps explains why a number of people, who joined the Jan Sangh in the beginning under the impression of it being an extreme right wing party, left it when they found it following an independent national policy, untrammelled by ideological inhibitions of the right or the left in a more progressive and radical manner than what they could swallow.

Another incident just on the eve of the convention demonstrated the selfless devotion of Dr. Mookerjee to the cause he held dear and his disregard for personal name or fame. Shri Dwarka Prasad Mishra, the ex-Home Minister in the Congress Ministry of Madhya Pradesh, had resigned from the Congress and the cabinet in September and had started a crusade against what he called "communal" and "anti-national" policies of Mr. Jawaharlal Nehru. Shortly afterwards he undertook a short tour of North India. Bhartiya Jan Sangh offered him its stage in Delhi and half a lakh people head his tirade against his old organisation and its lord in pin drop silence. The Uttar Pradesh Jan Sangh also, out of courtesy, arranged public meetings for him in some of the cities that he visited in that State. It was then openly discussed that he would join Jan Sangh. But on his return to Madhya Pradesh he floated on organisation of his own under the name of 'Lok Congress'. This came as a surprise to the sponsors of Jan Sangh convention who had invited him to attend it. He came, Dr. Mookerjee and others had long walks with him. But he was found to be hesitant to join Jan Sangh. Some one suggested that perhaps he would not work under any body else. Without a moments hesitation Dr. Mookerjee said, "But let him become the President. I will work under him." His face glowed with an honest and natural earnestness as he said this. It showed his selflessness, his spirit of keeping the cause he loved and principles he cherished above his person. No wonder he became the idol of all those who came in contact with him. Much against the general belief that distant lends charm, his greatness and charm appeared to grow as one came near him.

Unanimous Election as President Jan Sangh

The convention was held in the Ragho-Mal Arya Girls Higher Secondary School, New Delhi. A spacious pandal was constructed in it which accommodated about a thousand special invitees from among the citizens of Delhi besides five hundred delegates that had come from all parts of India.

All India Bharatiya Jan Sangh was formally launched by the unanimous vote of the convention which also adopted its draft constitution and manifesto. The most thrilling part of the proceedings, however, was the election of Dr. Syama Prasad Mookerjee to lead the new organisation as its first President. His name was proposed by L. Balraj Bhalla of Punjab and was seconded by a number of prominent delegates from different provinces. All of them paid glowing tributes to Dr. Mookerjee for his noble record of selfless service to the motherland and his great qualities of head and heart.

For Dr. Mookerjee it marked the beginning of a new, and as later events were to prove, the most momentous phase of his dedicated life. He knew that his task would not be easy. But he had confidence in himself and the teams of young workers that were there to assist him in all the provinces in which Jan Sangh had been formed. For the all India work he selected Pt. Mauli Chander Sharma and Prof. Mahavir, the young and versatile son of late Bhai Parmanand, to assist him as General Secretaries.

Presidential Address by Dr. Mookerjee (1951)

His Presidential address to that historic gathering summed up his political philosophy, his approach to the national and international problems and the lines on which the organisation that he was to lead was to be run.

Just as he rose to speak a number of delegates, who were eager to hear him speak in English, requested him to deliver his

Presidential address in English. Dr. Mookerjee was one very well up in Hindi till then. But he insisted upon speaking in Hindi, the national language, at that national gathering.

He made it clear at the very outset of his address that Bharatiya Jan Sangh was not coming into existence merely to fight the forthcoming general elections and that whatever the result of the elections, "our party must continue to function thereafter carrying a message of hope and goodwill to all classes of people and trying to draw out from them their best efforts in re-building a happier and more prosperous free India."

Explaining the need for the new party he said:

> "one of the chief reasons for the manifestation of dictatorship in Congress rule is the absence of well organised opposition parties which alone can act as a healthy check on the majority party and can hold out before the country the prospective of an alternative government".
>
> "Bharatiya Jan Sangh" he declared, "emerges today as an All India Political Party which will function as the principal party in opposition." Opposition, he added, "Does not mean senseless or destructive approach to all problems that confront responsible Government. While, therefore, we may have to attack or criticise official measures or acts, our aim will be to approach all problems in a constructive spirit so that we may keep the public vigilant and make our humble contribution in developing a real democratic structure for the sound administration of our country".

Dilating upon the composition and character of Bharatiya Jan Sangh he declared

> "We have thrown our party open to all citizens of India irrespective of caste-creed or community. While we recognise that in matters of customs, habits, religion and language Bharat presidents a unique diversity, the people must be united by a bond of fellowship and understanding inspired by deep devotion and loyalty to the spirit of a common motherland.
>
> While it will be dangerous to encourage the growth of political minorities on the basis of caste and religion, it is obviously for the vast majority of Bharat's population to

assure all classes of people, who are truly loyal to their motherland, that they will be entitled to full protection under the law and to complete equality of treatment in all matters, social, economic and political. Our party gives this assurance unreservedly".

He laid great stress on the need for adopting proper approach to the age old culture of the country. "Our party", he declared, "believes that future of Bharat lies in the proper appreciation and application of Bharatiya "Sanskriti" and "Maryada". Let all true sons and daughters of India pride themselves in the thought that the heritage that has come to us from ancient days is something noble and enduring, that it must not be allowed to stagnate and degenerate and that free India's future must be closely linked up with Bharatiya ideals, which must, if necessary, undergo charges from time to time so as to make them respond to the needs of modern and scientific age. This must be suitably reflected in our system of education. While we, therefore, aim at a 'Dharma Rajya' or a Rule of Law, we only abide by the highest traditions of Bharatiya Sanskriti that bind all people together in ties of real amity and fraternity".

Regarding the "most acute problem of deteriorating economic condition of the people" he explained that his party stood for a "well planned decentralised national economic plan" on the lines of Sarvodaya scheme. "Our party" he said, "is against concentration of economic power in the hands of small groups and cartels. Sanctity of private property will be observed and private enterprise will be given a fair and adequate play subject to national welfare. State ownership and State control will be exercised when found necessary in public interest. The party will stand for progressive decontrol. Social and economic exploitation must be checked, distribution must be fair and equitable and an atmosphere created so that all may jointly work for increased production."

His view about India's foreign policy was that "it should be more realistic, primary consideration being the advancement of the cause of our own country and the maintenance of peace and goodwill in international sphere." "We believe", he declared, "in democracy and in the maintenance of civil liberties. We are against totalitarianism of any kind whatsoever. We recognise that every nation must have the right to shape its national policy and attitude towards life according to the genius and traditions of the people themselves. Bharat's message to the world has been the doctrine of "live and let live". So long as India's right to determine her own pattern is not interfered with, there is no reason why we should not maintain friendly relations with all other countries.

He stood for reconsideration by India of the decision to stay within the Commonwealth because of "strange policy of partiality towards Pakistan observed by Great Britain".

Regarding Pakistan he had very definite views. "We hold the opinion", he declared, "that partition of Bharat was a tragic folly. It has served not purpose and has not helped to solve any problem economic, political or communal. We believe in the goal of reunited Bharat. We will like it to be achieved through peaceful means and through the realisation by the people of both states that such reunion will be of benefit to the masses and will make the country a real bulwork of peace and freedom. So long as Pakistan continues we will urge a policy of strict reciprocity. Our party lays great stress on the need for a satisfactory solution of post-partition problems of minorities in Pakistan and evacuee property which Congress Government systematically try to shirk. Our approach to these problems is not at all communal. They are mainly political and economic, and they have to be settled between the two states in a fair and straightforward manner."

Referring to Kashmir which had already begun to loom large on the political horizon, he declared: "Our party feels that the case should be withdrawn from UNO and there should be no further question of plebiscite. Kashmir is an integral part of India and should be treated as any other state".

Refuting the charge of communalism that had already begun to be levelled against him and the Jan Sangh by

Mr. Nehru, he pointed out that "having repeatedly sacrificed Indian Nationalism at the altar of Muslim Communalism, and even after partition having surrendered to the whims and howls of Pakistan Government, it does not lie in the mouth of Mr. Nehru to accuse others of communalism. There is no communalism in India today except the new policy of Muslim appeasement which has been started by Mr. Nehru and his friends for the purpose of winning their votes at the forthcoming election. We have provincialism and other types of class or caste differences in the country today. Let us jointly try to remove these evils so as to lay the foundation for a truly democratic India. The cry of communalism raised by Mr. Nehru is to side-track the real issues now before the country. The problems before the country today are clearly related to hunger, to poverty, to exploitation, to mal-administration, to corruption, to abject surrender to Pakistan, all being evils for which the main responsibility rests on the Congress and the Government under it."

He concluded his remarkable address with a note of confidence in the new organisation to tackle the problems before the country and a fervent prayer for its success. "We enter upon our task", he said, "with full faith, hope and courage. Let our workers constantly remember that only through service and sacrifice will they be able to win the confidence of masses of the people. The great task of revitalising and re-constructing free Bharat awaits us. The mother calls her children irrespective of class, caste or religion to come to her and serve her. However dark the present clouds may be, Bharat has a great destiny to fulfil in the years to come. May our party whose symbol in the forthcoming elections is a humble earthen "Pradip", try to carry this 'light' of hope and unity, faith and courage, to dispel the darkness that surrounds the country. The journey has just begun. May providence endow us with strength and fortitude to remain ever on the right path, not cowed by fears or tempted by favours, and to help to make Bharat great and strong, spiritually and materially, so that she may become a fit and noble instrument in the preservation of world peace and prosperity".

Addressing a huge public meeting in the evening of the same day in the Gandhi Ground he recalled that Netaji Subhas Bose had launched the Indian National Army on that very day — 21st of October. He hoped that Bharatiya Jan Sangh will carry on the fighting tradition of the INA in the service of the motherland. He also referred to Mr. Nehru's threat that he would crush Jan Sangh and declared amidst loud applause, "I say, I will crush this crushing mentality."

Re-election as President (1952)

Dr. Mookerji's political career saw its last and most momentous phase with his re-election as President of Bharatiya Jana Sangh followed by the first plenary Session of the Sangh at Kanpur in the last week of December, 1952. The tumultuous welcome he received from the people of Kanpur when he arrived there to preside over the Session and the momentous decisions that Jana Sangh took there under his leadership marked the pinnacle of his political career.

Reports had been constantly reaching Dr. Mookerjee about the heroic and patriotic struggle of the people of Jammu for the integration of their State with the rest of India and the terrible repression the Sheikh Abdullah's Government had let loose on them with the connivance and support of the Pandit Nehru's Government at New Delhi. He had already expressed his fully sympathy for and solidarity with the Praja Parishad by giving a call for the observance of December 14 as Jammu and Kashmir Day all over the country. It was therefore clear to him as also to one thousand delegates that had assembled at Kanpur from all over India that a decision would have to be taken to extend the active support of the Jana Sangh to the struggle being waged by the Praja Parishad for the cause of Indian unity. For Dr. Mookerjee it was a challenge and opportunity to galvanise Bharatiya Jana Sangh and make it an effective instrument for the protection of the rights and liberties of the Indian people. It also provided him the occasion to make his considered views on national and international problems known to the rank and file of his young organisation and establish a close personal touch with its workers.

Presidential Address (1952)

The Presidential Address and other utterances of Dr. Mookerjee during the three-day session laid down the guidelines for the Jana Sangh and gave a clear and bold lead to the whole country. His personal conduct which was watched by the workers from close quarters endeared him to all of them and established that rapport between him and the organisation which proved to be the biggest asset of the Jana Sangh in the difficult days ahead.

Aims and Objects

Referring to the character of Bharatiya Jana Sangh in his Presidential address which he delivered in his forceful Bengali Hindi, he said that "It will be a fatal mistake to confine the membership of any political party in free India to sections of the people based on caste, community or religion. But while extending its hand of equality to all citizens, Jana Sangh", he declared, "does not feel ashamed to urge for the consolidation of Hindu society nor does it suffer from an inferiority complex to acknowledge proudly that the great edifice of Indian culture and civilisation which has stood the test of thousands of years has been built most of all by the labour, wisdom and sacrifice of Hindu sages, savants and patriots throughout the chequered history of our Motherland".

"If India's freedom is to be purposeful" he continued, "a correct appreciation of the fundamental features of Indian culture is highly essential. A nation that fails to take pride in its past achievements or take inspiration therefrom can never build up the present or plan for the future. A weak nation can never attain greatness".

Referring to the First Five-Year Plan that had just been made public he pointed out: "India today needs a big psychological shake up and the plan unfortunately does not fulfil this essential requirement." But he recognised the "laborious and intelligent" activity that had gone into the making of the plan and declared, "there is no question of opposing the plan even if it does not fulfil our expectations".

He dealt at length with the problems of Kashmir, East Bengal and rehabilitation of refugees. Regarding Kashmir, where the Praja Parishad satyagraha was daily gaining momentum, he pleaded for sympathetic understanding of the fears and doubts of the people of Jammu. "Even at this late stage," he said, "I would appeal to Mr. Nehru and Sheikh Abdullah to cry a halt and not to stand on false prestige. They must open negotiations with the Parishad leaders and arrive at a settlement which will be fair and just to all. Meanwhile", he declared, "our active sympathy must be extended to all those in Jammu who are facing bravely the wrath of the authorities and silently suffering for a noble cause".

Referring to the plight of Hindus in East Pakistan who "if they live there as at present will live as serfs or converts", he deplored the spirit of helplessness shown by India. "It is tragic," he said, "that our stock should be so low in the eyes of Pakistan that it dares humiliate us in season and out of season and our Government should stand by as helpless spectator incapable of taking any effective action". He also warned that activities of fifth columnists within India were steadily on the increase. "If this state of affairs," he declared, "continued, our freedom may become short lived and we will be leading towards a grave catastrophe". Regarding rehabilitation he demanded that an independent commission be appointed to consider the nature and extent of rehabilitation already effected and to suggest lines of action for the future.

Deprecating the tendency to over-emphasise internationalism to the neglect of the basic problem of national solidarity, he said, "Internationalism can thrive only if there is a sound base of national solidarity. We should, therefore, strive hard to keep our home front safe and sound. It is not armies or navies or air forces or arms or ammunitions that ultimately constitute the strength of a nation. Real strength of a nation emanates from the people themselves. If they are contented, if they are united, if they are determined to retain their freedom at any cost or to face any sacrifice or suffering for building up their national life, there is no power on earth that can destroy such a nation. We have attained our freedom after nearly a thousand years. Whatever differences there may be among political parties, whatever may be the hopes and fears of sessions of our people, we must learn the lesson of history and not allow disunity in our ranks to be a cause of our ruination in future".

India with her past traditions and with immense possibilities of her future development," he declared "could play a very large part in creating an atmosphere for peace. But a distorted conception of secularism along with grave economic disabilities is arresting the natural growth of country's manpower and material resources". He concluded this historic speech with the prayer that the organisation he was leading may succeed in fulfilling the mission of rebuilding India on right and progressive lines. "There is no hope for India," he said, "unless the worthily develops herself taking firm root in her culture and civilisation, advancing with the changing needs of the times and marching ahead with the torch of equality, progress and righteousness in hand. In this mighty task of national reconstruction may Jana Sangh play its part with the goodwill and support of the people throughout the country".

But more important than his able enunciation and presentation of the policies to be pursued by Jana Sangh, was the contribution, he made towards revitalising Jana Sangh through his personal contacts with the workers at various levels, proper and correct appraisal of men and situations, and the momentous decisions the party took under his guidance.

Selflessness Simplicity and Devotion to Duty: Instances

The pandal for the session as also "Deep Nagar", the village of tents for the delegates to stay, were constructed in the spacious grounds of Phool Bagh. But, the Reception Committee had arranged for Dr. Mookerjee to stay at the house of Shri Narendrajit Singh, Barrister-at-Law, where he could have all the comforts of home. But Dr. Mookerjee insisted that he must stay amongst the delegates in a tent and share their daily life. This little incident shows the great quality of leadership that he possessed. He never liked "leaders" and "workers" to be treated as two separate classes. All leaders, he held, must be workers first. He who cannot be a worker cannot be a leader.

He also preferred to take his daily meals together with the delegates in the common mess. One day a Harijan worker found himself seated next to him. He was deeply impressed and said in an apologetic tone, "I am an untouchable".

"We are all untouchables here," replied Dr. Mookerjee, "I

am political untouchable number one in this country". This sent all those present into peels of laughter.

The busy schedule of Dr. Mookerjee included an address to a rally of the RSS volunteers early in the morning on the 31st of December. He had gone to bed very late the previous night and his sleep had been disturbed by heavy rain that continued the whole night. Yet he was ready in the morning for going to the rally at 6 a.m. As he was addressing the Swayamsewaks, rain started once again. A worker rushed to him with an umbrella. But he would have none of it. "Why cannot I stand this rain when so many hundreds of Swayamsevaks are sitting in rain. Do you not consider me a Swayamsevak?"

It was little thinks like this that endeared him to the workers who began to look upon him as one of them. Again it was this mutual trust and understanding which enabled Dr. Mookerjee to get the best out of them.

One another occasion some unscrupulous persons, taking advantage of their personal relations with him and his simplicity of heart, tried to rush him into taking decision that might have proved very harmful to the growth of the young organisation. But they had misunderstood Dr. Mookerjee who always held his duty and interests of the cause for which he stood above all personal considerations. He gave them a rebuff and took the correct decision and thereby saved an awkward situation.

The most momentous decision taken by Jana Sangh at Kanpur was to actively support the Satyagraha movement of the Praja Parishad in Jammu for the integration of Jammu and Kashmir State with the rest of India. The younger delegates in their over-enthusiasm wanted Jana Sangh to give an ultimatum to the Government of India either to take concrete steps to meet the patriotic demands of the Parishad within a fixed period or face the Jana Sangh Satyagraha in its support in the rest of India as well. But Dr. Mookerjee counselled patience. He was not the man to take a hasty decision in a fit of emotion. He wanted to explore all avenues of a peaceful settlement and an honourable compromise, before taking the extreme step of Satyagraha. It was, therefore, resolved that he should write to Pandit Nehru and Sheikh Abdullah in a final bid to find a solution.

It was in pursuance of this resolution of his Working Committee that Dr. Mookerjee started correspondence (discussed in the next chapter) with Pandit Nehru and Sheikh Abdullah which, like his correspondence with Sir John Herbert before his resignation from Bengal Cabinet, has become a historic record of his fearless and well reasoned advocacy of what he considered was a righteous cause.

14

Promoting Culture: Interest in Buddhism

Promoting Culture and Sanskriti

Dr. Mookerjee developed keen interest and devotion from his early youth towards literature and Indian culture — the Bharatiya Sanskriti. The great culture and ideals of India, the moral and spiritual values for which they stood, had always had a special appeal and fascination for him. He imbibed them in his own life and tried to live up to them.

He took a very comprehensive view of the term culture or 'sanskriti'. He considered it to be the sum total of the highest achievements of a people in the realm of thought and action which imperceptibly moulds the mind and influences the conduct of that people, individually as well as collectively.

History, literature, lives of great men and social and religious festivals, he held, play a great part in this process of influencing the race conduct. In India all these are essentially Hindu. Therefore, he considered Indian culture to be a essence Hindu culture which has come down in continuous flow right from the Vedic times, absorbing and assimilating the contribution of a number of new elements which, in the course of History, got absorbed into the Hindu or Bharatiya society. Some basic features of this Bharatiya culture according to him, are:

- Philosophy of rebirth
- Philosophy of 'Karma'
- Equal rights to all
- Equal opportunities to all
- Respect and reverence for the learned and the pious as distinct from the rich.
- Balance between the rights of individual and society.

- Right to live for all
- Freedom of thought — Tolerance
- Emphasis on character.

Views on Indian Cultural Missions Abroad

It is the historic mission of Bharat, he held, to give her cultural message to the world to restore balance between the moral and material aspects of man's life.

He, therefore, held that Indian missions abroad instead of trying to emulate their western counterparts in pomp and show and external luxury, should try to interpret India's culture and ideals through their own lives and conduct.

He believed that men like Swami Vivekananda and L. Hardayal had done more to raise India in the eyes of the West than all the political missions that India has sent out since her freedom because, they lack that faith in the destiny and understanding of the ideals and culture of India which distinguished those unofficial cultural ambassadors of India in bondage.

Interest in Following up of Missions Abroad

It was his keen desire that their work of interpreting real India and her thought and culture to the people of the West as also of the East should be continued and he himself had a strong urge from within to go on a lecturing tour of U.S.A. and Britain for the purpose. He had actually got an invitation from the U.S.A. for such a tour and it was his plan to fulfil this mission after settling the Kashmir issue.

As President of Mahabodhi Society of India

But though the cruel hands of death did not permit him to play the role of India's cultural ambassador to the West — a role for which he was eminently fitted — he did play that role in the countries of South East Asia which he visited in 1952, as President of the Mahabodhi Society of India.

Dr. Mookerji's interest in this society and Buddhism was born out of his conviction that Buddhist thought and culture, which is essentially Indian or Hindu in its inspiration and essence, could act as a great unifying force to bind the Buddhist world, particularly the South Asian countries, with India. Consciousness of such a community of thought and culture, he felt, could create an abiding unity between these countries and India transcending any differences in the economic or political sphere and enable Bharat to play her ancient role of a world teacher — "Jagat Guru".

He looked upon Mahatma Buddha as a world teacher who gave the best in Indian thought and culture to the world through his life and teachings. It was wrong, according to him, to say that Buddhism had disappeared from India. Buddhism as taught by Mahatma Buddha, he would say, has been assimilated by the age old current of Hindu culture of which it was an aspect. The fact that Mahatma Buddha has been accepted as one of the ten 'Avtars' or incarnations of God by the Indian people, he believed, was the most convincing refutation of the belief that India had rejected Buddhism. What she rejected was not the essence of Buddhism which Mahatma Buddha gave, but the over-coating given to it many centuries later which transformed it from a reform movement, that it essentially was, into a religion with separate rituals and dogmas. India rejected that over coating and assimilated the spirit within it.

Dr. Mookerjee was attracted by that spirit. He did not mind what rituals and dogmas were adopted or developed by different sects of Buddhism so long as they did not lose sight of the spirit which was common between them and all the sects constituting the common wealth of Hindu Dharma. He tried to emphasise and popularise that common spirit among the Buddhists and thereby rendered a very great service to the cause of cultural unity of India and the countries of South East Asia whose geographical position, economic interests and needs of security also point to a closer unity between them all in the political sphere as well.

Visits to South Asian Countries

The occasion to demonstrate this unity of thought and culture between India and the Buddhist countries of South Asia was provided by his visits to Burma and Indo-China along with the sacred relics of Sari-Putta and Maha-Mogallana, the two chief disciples of Mahatma Buddha, prior to their re-enshrinement in the new Vihara at Sanchi on November 30, 1952.

These relics had been taken out of the ancient Stupa of Sanchi by General Cunningham in 1851. They were then sent to England and were kept in the British museum. They were returned to India after the attainment of freedom and were handed over to Dr. Syama Prasad Mookerjee, as President of the Maha Bodhi Society of India, by the Prime Minister, Pt. Nehru, on the 14th of January 1949 at Calcutta with great ceremonial.

It was followed by requests from different Buddhist countries like Ceylon, Burma, Cambodia and Tibet for an opportunity to worship the relics in their own lands before they were re-enshrined. On their invitation Dr. Mookerjee visited, Burma in March and Cambodia and Indo-China in October 1952, along with the sacred relics.

He visited Burma at a time when Communist rebels were making the life there miserable both for the Government as also for the common people. Even Rangoon, the capital city, was not safe from their depredations. The whole of Burma was in turmoil.

The visit of Dr. Mookerjee with the relics and the mass enthusiasm and devotion they created in the people's minds changed that situation. The people of Burma who had been torn between different political factions and loyalties rediscovered their unity in the common reverence for the gospel of the Buddha. It created a reaction in their minds against Communist irreligiosity and cult of violence. Since that day the situation in Burma has been improving and the Communists have been put on the run.

"You do not know how great a service you have rendered to any country", said Thakin Nu, the Premier of Burma, to Dr. Mookerjee at Sanchi in November, 1952 when he visited that place to take part in the ceremonies connected with the reenshrinement of the relics. "Your visit with the relics brought about a wonderful change in my people. They have found their soul."

The Indian community in Burma also gave him a royal reception. The volunteers of Bharatiya Swayam Sewak Sangh, a cultural and social organisation working among Indians oversea, gave him a guard of honour at the airport, the Burmese Indian Congress gave him a reception in the Congress hall and he addressed a mass meeting of the Burmans and Indians in Bandula Square.

He created a tremendous effect on the minds of the Burmans who heard from his mouth the message of the Buddha, whose memory binds them to India as no economic and political pacts can. They began to think of him as one of them, a sage who had come to re-awaken in them the faith that had been shaken by the stress and strain, the confusion and turmoil, that came in the wake of the violent end of British rule in Burma at the hands of the Japanese. As he was talking to the Premier of Burma just before emplaning for Calcutta, a Burman lady standing near-by remarked in her own tongue "He looks to be a Burman". It drew loud laughter from everyone standing there. On being told the reason for it, he felt elated because he could appreciate the deep feeling of oneness which must have drawn that remark from her.

In Phnon Penh and Saigon

On the 6th October, of the same year he visited Phnon Penh, the capital of Cambodia, with the sacred relics on the invitation of the Cambodian Government. The scenes of pious devotion that he saw there had a very deep effect on his mind. Over a million monks and laymen lined the route from the aerodrome to the Silver Pagoda where the relics were to be kept for worship. He addressed half a million of them in the main square of the city about the message of Mahatma Buddha and the cultural ties between India and the Buddhist countries. As his speech was translated into the language of Cambodia by an interpreter, thousands actually shed tears of joy and devotion. They prostrated before him as if he was a Messiah who had come to re-awaken them on behalf of their spiritual mother-India.

He also visited the ruins of the world famous Hindu Temples at Angkor Vat which still contain 1737 images and on the walls of which the stories of *Ramayana* and *Mahabharata* are presented in exquisite carvings in stone that remind the visitor of the glory that was India in the past.

From Phnom Penh he visited Saigon, the capital of Indo-China. There too he saw similar scenes of devotion and respect for India.

On his way back his plane stopped at Bangkok for a few hours to enable thousands of Siamese who had collected there to worship the relics. Indian diplomats at the Thai capital also met him there. He also came to know there to his great disappointment that the reports of such pro-India feelings of those people, which pointed to the advisability of developing closer cultural relations with them, were usually not sent to Indian foreign office at New Delhi as they were not liked there.

He had been invited by the Government of Ceylon as well. He wanted to visit that country where economic and political causes have given rise to an unfortunate antipathy between the Indian settlers and the Ceylonese. Had he visited Ceylon, he might have brought about a transformation in the hearts of the people there, which no political pacts can, and without which the problem of status of Indians in that country cannot be satisfactorily solved.

International Cultural Conference (Sanchi), 1952

The last great performance of Dr. Mookerjee as the cultural leader of South East Asia came towards the end of November, 1952, when the New Vihara at Sanchi was opened and the sacred relics were re-enshrined in it. An international cultural conference was also held on the occasion which was attended by statesmen, ministers and religious leaders from all Buddhist countries of the world except Communist China.

In his welcome address to the cultural conference, which was presided over by India's Vice-President Sir S. Radhakrishnan, Dr. Mookerjee pointed out the great utility of the genuine cultural contacts such as that conference had produced.

> "Many of these countries in S. E. Asia" Dr. Mookerjee said, "after attaining independence are striving hard to receive the highest elements of Buddhist cultural and religious thought. In this respect India occupies the role of their spiritual mother"
>
> "With a true sense of humility and responsibility," he added, "India can re-establish bonds of- friendship and understanding with them so that this fraternity will not only be welcomed by the peoples of the countries concerned but

will also create mighty source of strength and solidarity which can worthily contribute to the maintenance of world peace and freedom."

The following day the new 'Vihar' was opened with full religious rights. Speaking on that occasion Dr. Mookerjee dilated upon his idea about the role of cultural centres like Sanchi. "Such centres," he said "must not remain confined to the educated few; but from them must flow currents of thought and service so that the poorer people suffering from ignorance, disease, poverty and superstition might receive their due inspiration and be helped to raise themselves socially and economically so as to become worthy citizens of free India".

It was his plan to open schools and dispensaries in the villages surrounding Sanchi to be maintained and manned by the monks of the Sanchi Vihar so that the common people of the region could feel the presence of the great men whose memory was preserved by the stupas of Sanchi.

Paying his tribute to the memory of Mahatma Buddha he said, "Gautam Buddha was not born on the soil of India by accident. The genius of India from time immemorial has been reflected through the words and deeds of mighty men, sages and savants, who gave to their country and to the world the benefits of their wisdom and guidance consistent with the changing needs and aspirations of society. When stagnation came, when the external manifestations of religious rites destroyed the life blood of true religion, these savants appeared on the scene and served to maintain her soul from destruction. Gautam Buddha represented, 2500 years, ago, a unique challenge of the scientific spirit of man when he declared his unwillingness to accept anything as true without full and searching analysis and self-satisfaction."

Referring to the need of peace in the world and the path shown by Mahatma Buddha to achieve it, he said: "Buddha showed the path of peace, peace not of the grave but of the living, peace born out of deep understanding and proper appreciation of the realities of life. Peace can only be permanent if it conquers evil and brings about a true harmony between spiritual and material impulses of man so that both by his preaching and practice he may prove himself the image of his Maker."

Celebrations at Sanchi, incidentally, provided the last occasion when Dr. Mookerjee and Pt. Jawaharlal Nehru met face to face outside the Parliament and talked about culture and peace in the whole world.

15

The First General Elections

Incidentally, All India Bharatiya Jan Sangh, was born just on the eve of the first General Elections on the basis of the new constitution of free India, though the ramblings of its birth had begun to be heard many months earlier. It had not come into existence, as Dr. Mookerjee pointed out in his Presidential Address, merely to fight the general elections. It would have rather liked to establish itself well organisationally before entering into the election arena. But it was impossible for it to ignore the imminent general elections on whose results depended the political shape of things to come during the next five years. The importance of elections for carrying the ideology of the new party to the masses also could not be under-rated. It, therefore, decided to contest the elections to the State and Central legislatures wherever circumstances might permit it.

Need for Electoral Understanding

Dr. Mookerjee was fully conscious of the strength and resources of the Congress and determination of its leaders to come back to power by fair means or foul. He was also fully aware of the probability of the opposition vote getting divided among different parties to the advantage of the Congress. The elections to Delhi Municipal Committee in October of the same year had painfully demonstrated that fact. He was, therefore, keen for some electoral understanding at least between those parties which had a similar or common approach to the major problems of the country. The time at his disposal was too short for contacting and negotiating with all India leaders of other opposition parties which had almost started their election campaigns by that time. Therefore, on his suggestion, the Provincial units of Jan Sangh were asked to form electoral pacts with other parties wherever possible on the basis of mutual give and take. Dr. Mookerjee himself met Swami Karpatriji of the Ram Rajya Parishad at Banaras as also the leaders of Hindu Maha Sabha to persuade them to give a similar directive to their Provincial branches. The criteria for choosing the candidates, he suggested, should be the integrity and popularity of the candidate. It must be left to the candidates to choose the party label and the symbol. Such candidates should be given the fullest support by all the three parties.

Limitation of Experience and Central Control

In some States such arrangements worked well while in others local rivalries and personal prejudices of party bosses marred them. A high power central board of the three parties with overriding powers might have provided the remedy. But apart from the shortage of time to work out any such thing, the weakness of the central control of Maha Sabha and Ram Rajya Parishad over their Provincial units made the efficacy of such a remedy extremely doubtful.

Bharatiya Jan Sangh had a band of trained and zealous workers everywhere. But they lacked political experience and the party as yet had no standing. Its very name was yet unknown to an over-whelming majority of the people. Most of the people were to hear its name during the next two months not from its workers and advocates but from its ruthless critics and opponents like Pt. Jawahar Lal Nehru who saw in the new organisation and its redoubtable leader the potentiality to displace Congress. Dr. Mookerjee was painted by this campaign of vilification started against the new party by the Prime Minister from its very inception without caring to understand what it was and what it aimed at. But he was also thankful to him for acting as "honorary publicity Secretary" of the new-born organisation which was too poor to arrange for proper and speedy publicity for itself.

Opposition Campaign by Nehru

But this determined opposition by Pt. Nehru, who made Jan Sangh the sole target of his wrath and criticism throughout his electioneering tours, and the campaign of deliberate misrepresentation of the character, aims and objects of the new party started by the Congress, the Socialist Party and the Communists Party, made it imperative for Dr. Mookerjee to undertake a tour of the country to explain the programme and policies of Jan Sangh immediately after the Delhi Convention.

Fighting the Odds

It was not an easy job. Jan Sangh had neither the resources nor as yet the organisation to ensure for him even the minimum comforts and quickest means of transportation. The Press too, particularly the English Press, which took the cue from the Prime Minister, was generally hostile to the infant organisation.

But undaunted by all these handicaps, Dr. Mookerjee embarked upon the arduous task of awakening the countries population of the situation and making them familiar with Jan Sangh's call for duty to the motherland. He began with the Punjab. On some days he had to cover as much as two to three hundred miles by train and motor car and address a dozen meetings. The usual programme was to travel by night, cover two or three important places within easy motorable distance from one another during the day, and catch the night train again for the next centre.

Dr. Mookerjee was accustomed to sustained hard work from his very childhood. He used to get up whether in train or home at about 5 a.m. and was ready for work after his morning duties and prayers at about 6.30 a.m. He generally worked non-stop from that hour right upto 10 p.m.

But the work that he was now called upon to do was of a different nature. It put on him more physical strain than he had ever stood before besides straining his vocal chords too much. He attracted huge audiences wherever he went. Hundreds and thousands waited for him even on the small way side stations. His fame seemed to have spread fast. He had begun to be looked upon by the intelligent people all over the country as the real leader of the opposition.

In Stark Contrast with Nehru: A Comparison

The only other man in the country who was subjected to that kind of ordeal in those days was the Congress President-cum Prime Minister, Pt. Jawaharlal Nehru. But he had all the resources of the Government at his command. He moved in Government planes or military dakotas. He also had the benefit of a fine health and balanced body coupled with unique agility.

They presented a contrast in their behaviour, both mental and physical, towards the people whom they wanted to serve and lead. Pt. Nehru in his power consciousness indulged in physical theatricals and fits of temper as a matter of right. At Ludhiana, he gave such a wild push to the local Congress President that only luck saved him from falling down from a dozen feet high rostrum. On the mental plane the burden of his speeches which lacked coherence, logic and argument used to be "after me the deluge". A close analytical study of all the election speeches of Pt. Nehru will reveal that he devoted more than half of his total speaking time in denouncing and abusing the opposition parties, particularly the Jan Sangh, and he had little to say about the positive achievements of his party for the four years it had been in power.

Dr. Mookerjee on the other hand never lost his temper. He sweated and perspired, he looked pulled down and tired, but he never quarrelled with the people for that. He took them to be quite natural and inevitable concomitants of crowded public life in a country like India. At times when the strain appeared unbearable he would still go on with the scheduled programme without betraying any kind of uneasiness. It was only a string will and keen sense of duty which enabled him to go on like this for days and weeks together.

His election speeches, which were mainly delivered in Hindi in which he was not very proficient at that time, mirrored his agonised but confident mind, his deep distress over the things as they were moving in the country and his robust confidence in the destiny of Bharat. He touched on all subjects and problems facing the country. He laid special stress on the problem of providing food, clothing and shelter to the common man failure to solve which, he held, "would shake the very foundations of our social and economic structure and bring about a revolution". "Bharatiya Jan Sangh", he repeatedly declared "was not wedded to any ism but it will not hesitate to take any action, however drastic, to provide for these."

But he cautioned his countrymen at the same time not to

think that economics was the be all and end all of life. He wanted the economic uplift of the people to go side by side with their spiritual and cultural uplift. It is the spiritual and cultural values for which Bharat has stood from the dawn of her history which are and will continue to be her distinctive features and bring her the respect of the world. To ignore them in the wild goose chase of mere economic prosperity would not solve the real problem of restoring and revitalising the moral back-bone of the people which, he felt, was fast decaying.

Condemning Nehru's Foreign Policies

Pt. Nehru's foreign and domestic policies, particularly his policy towards Pakistan and Muslims came in for most eloquent and trenchant criticism from him. He had studied the working of Pt. Nehru's mind from close quarters. He had seen that whatever had been achieved by free India during the first years of her independence had been achieved not because of Pt. Nehru but inspite of him. He would recall with visible anguish how Pt. Nehru had been riding roughshod over the vital interests of India and her millions just to win cheap praise from foreigners. His betrayal of the Hindus in Pakistan, whom he had given solemn pledges on the eve of partition of the country, was considered by him as most unworthy of him and of the great country which had the misfortune to be ruled by him.

Dr. Mookerjee was amused when he heard people saying that Pt. Nehru with all his faults and failures had proved a successful foreign minister who had raised India's name in the international field. He held that the sole test for the success or failure of a country's foreign policy was the good it might have done to the country itself. Pt. Nehru's foreign policy, he would argue, had rendered our sixteen hundred miles long northern frontier which had been absolutely safe all through the ages, unsafe and vulnerable by allowing Communist China to swallow Tibet, it had isolated India from the democratic world without obtaining any advantage from the Communist World, which would not trust India till she went completely red, it had made the lot of the people of Indian origin wherever they might be outside India miserable, it had failed to liquidate foreign pockets within the country while he always made loud noise against colonialism elsewhere and, above all, it had enabled Pakistan to forcibly grab one-third of Jammu and Kashmir State including the strategic region of Gilgit, which she has since been dangling before the eyes of Anglo-Americans as a bargaining counter to secure diplomatic support and military aid from them to be used against India.

Dr. Mookerjee knew a lot about Pt. Nehru's pusillanimity and un-Indian cowardice in dealing with India's enemies particularly when they happened to be Muslims. He could not reveal many of the things that transpired in the cabinet when he was in it. But he would often tell his intelligent listeners in the big meetings that he addressed in English : "when I scan the whole course of Indian history, I do not find a single man who has done more harm to this country than Pt. Nehru."

He was not happy to pass this judgement on Pt. Nehru. But he could not help it. The deliberate persistence of Pt. Nehru in wrong, anti-national and unrealistic policies in spite of repeated appeals and warning from his colleagues and compatriots could lead him to no other conclusion. He held Pt. Nehru to be mainly responsible for the partition of India and terrible carnage and suffering that followed it. The up-rooting of millions of Hindus, from the areas where they had stood the onslaught of foreign Muslims invaders and rulers for centuries, was to his mind the greatest blow to India as a nation. He held him responsible for the slow extermination of the Hindus of E. Bengal as well.

Nullifying Allegations of Partition and Communalism

Dr. Mookerjee also cleared some of the points that were made against him by Pt. Nehru in the course of his election speeches. One such point was that he and Master Tara Singh were also parties to Indias partition because they had demanded partition of Bengal and Punjab. Speaking at Jamshedpur in early January, 1952, Dr. Mookerjee declared:

> It is painful and shameful for a leader like Nehru to indulge in untruths and half truths and say that myself and Master Tara Singh were also parties to partition".
>
> "When it became apparent to me", he explained, "that the Congress, the League and the British had made up their

> mind to partition the country, and that we were powerless to prevent it, I demanded the partition of Punjab and Bengal. I demanded that at least a part of these provinces be salvaged from the wreck. What I agreed to and worked for was partition of the proposed Pakistan comprising all Bengal and all Punjab and not the partition of India. That betrayal had been decided betwixt themselves by the two political parties without the consent and against the express wishes of the vast mass of the people."
>
> "If this was a sin", he concluded "I stand before the bar of opinion of my countrymen for a verdict".

Another main charge of Pt. Nehru against him and his organisation, which he hurled at them time in and time out, was that of communalism. He called Dr. Mookerjee and Jan Sangh communal.

Dr. Mookerjee was both amused and pained by this charge which amounted to the kettle calling the pot black. He held that the one organisation which had encouraged and sustained communalism in the country was the Congress itself.

> "It surrendered itself during the last 35 years at the feet of the communal leaders. "Did you fight," he would ask them, "against the communal award"? Who gave the communal percentages for the purpose of having some pact with the Muslim League? Who agreed to partition the country? You might have done it with the best of intentions, because you thought that you could thereby get rid of the British Government, but having sold the country at the altar of communalism to come forward and say that we are communalists is a perversion of truth".
>
> "But it is to be communalist", he argued, "to love one's country, to love one's community and not think ill of other communities, if we feel with and attempt to unite 30 crores of Hindus living in India that have been liberated after 1000 years. If we try to recover out lost position in a manner which is 100 per cent consistent with the dynamic principles of Hinduism for which Swami Vivekanand stood, I am proud to be a communalist".

Neither Pt. Nehru nor any other Congressman has ever tried to reply to this argument and stand of Dr. Mookerjee. They have no reply. So they took recourse to abuses and vilifications with the help of their kept press, secure in the thought that Dr. Mookerjee agrumentative replies to their criticism will never reach the electorate whose minds they had been poisoning.

Dr. Mookerjee considered it the greatest misfortune of India that she had fallen in the hands of one who had yet to discover what real India was, in the most formative and crucial stage of her long and chequered history. "Pt. Nehru" he said in a very pathetic tone in a meeting of the elite of the Punjab at Simla , "claims that he has discovered India. But he has yet to discover his own mind which has got a heavy over coating of what is un-Indian and un-Hindu." The course of events in Kashmir during and after his martyrdom have proved the truth in Dr. Mookerji's reading of Pt. Nehru's policy in respect of that state at least.

But Dr. Mookerjee was not dismayed by the situation. He had faith in India's destiny and confidence in himself as one of her humble devotees. "I will set this man (Pt. Nehru) right," he had once said to the General Secretary of his party returning from Simla, "if I can take even ten members with me into the Parliament". The occasion for this significant and prophetic remark was provided by his brooding over the prospects in the election of his new party, for which he was campaigning, in a moment of retrospection when the motor was gliding down the tortuous bends of Simla-Kalka road through delightful mountanious scenery. "Have we done a correct thing in entering the election arena in the name of our new party which is barely two months old" he had asked. And after a moment's silence, without waiting for the reply, he had added, "But now the die is cast, we are in the game".

As is well known, he did set Pt. Nehru right to some extent even though he could get only two members besides himself into the Parliament on Jan Sangh ticket; and he would surely have set him right completely if the cruel hand of conspirators had not removed him from the earthly stage so soon.

Encouraging Young Leaders in the Party

After touring the length and breadth of India during the election months, Dr. Mookerjee arrived at the conclusion that it was not conducive to the healthy growth of the organisation to have retired people, out of tune with the new generation, to lead the organisation he was building up.

He encouraged young leaders and himself took a hand in training them. He always attached much weight and importance to the views of young workers and entrusted most responsible jobs to them. He never made any important decision after becoming the President of Jan Sangh without first ascertaining the views of young workers. He would encourage them to think and write by entrusting the drafting of most important resolutions at the various meetings of his working committee to its youngest members. He would encourage them to speak by insisting that some young workers should speak before him whenever he was to speak. His personal interest and solicitude for the betterment and development of his young workers served as an incentive to them to come up to his expectations. As a result he could build up a second line of leaders drawn from the comparatively younger workers, though he himself too was quite young as compared to the leaders of the Congress in Bharatiya Jan Sangh.

Election Results

Dr. Mookerjee himself stood from his home constituency of South Calcutta. It was not an easy constituency. It had about seventy thousand Muslim voters out of a total vote of about three lakhs. They had been misguided by the Congress propaganda to look upon the Jan Sangh and Dr. Mookerjee as their worst enemies. So they were expected to vote solidly against him. The Congress had put up one of the richest men of Calcutta against him. The Communists also had a strong candidate in the field.

To Parliament from Calcutta

Dr. Mookerjee lacked resources. He was not a rich man nor could he ever think of stooping to the methods and means that the Congress and Communists were adopting. But the voters knew him and his services to Bengal and India. They returned him with a thumping majority even though he could give very little time to his own constituency.

Here again he presented a contrast to Pt. Jawaharlal Nehru. Pt. Nehru had declared that he would not visit his home constituency of Allahabad from which he was seeking election. But he had to eat his words and make tremendous efforts to get elected. His friend, Sh. Abdullah, sent Government jeeps and cars and score of workers all the way from Kashmir, a distance of over 1000 miles, to help him. All his family members and a number of central ministers spent sleepless nights, canvassing votes for him. All the Muslim votes were in his pocket. Still his pennyless adversary, Brahmachari Prabhu Datt, was able to secure about 30 per cent of the polled votes.

A Poor Performance

But on the whole the election results were none too flattering for Jan Sangh. It was rather a debacle. Only three of its candidates, including Dr. Mookerjee, out of the 93 who contested on its ticket for the House of the People could get elected. It fared no better in respect of State Legislatures. It had put up 742 candidates out of which 33 could get in. In some provinces like the East Punjab, where Jan Sangh appeared to be the strongest, it could not secure a single seat.

Many factors contributed to this failure at the polls. The most important of them was the infancy of the organisation whose name even had not reached the ears of most of the rural electorate in the country. Much of the publicity it had got by that time had come from its critics who painted it in very lurid colours and created a prejudice in the minds of many people before they had known anything about it. It was thus condemned without a hearing.

Secondly it had not been able to set up its organisational structure in most of the constituencies where its candidates fought elections. It got support from towns and those villages where RSS had some work. But most of the villages had no one to speak for Jan Sangh.

In-experience of the young workers for whom it was a novel experience and lack of resources also accounted to a good extent for this failure. But generally speaking the inexperience of workers was counterbalanced by their enthusiasm and hard work. But nothing could counterbalance the superiority of Congress and Communists, the two richest parties in the country, in resources.

The undue pressure by the party in power through the official machinery and actual tampering with the ballot boxes was another major factor in the defeat of Jan Sangh. That the ballot boxes were tampered with was admitted by Pt. Jawaharlal Nehru in the Parliament. He cited an example where the symbol of one party was removed from the ballot box and that of another party was pasted instead. But more glaring were the examples of opening the ballot boxes, which, as was demonstrated by a number of people, could be opened without damaging the protective seal to take out ballot papers from the ballot boxes. The proof of such happenings came to light at a number of places.

In Punjab the Akali question also was an important factor. Their separatist demands had scared the general mass of Hindu voters. They wanted to vote solidly for a party which might be able to take an effective stand against them. Jan Sangh was yet too young to inspire confidence that it would come in majority. On the other hand Pt. Nehru made an unequivocal declaration at Patiala that Congress would not concede the separatist demands of Akalis. The electoral arrangement between Jan Sangh and Akalis in the State of Delhi, where the issues agitating the minds of Punjab Hindu did not exist was exploited by the Congress, which had itself entered into electoral arrangements with Muslim League in Madras, to blacken Jan Sangh. This confused the voters who for fear of splitting the nationalist vote to the advantage of Akalis voted for Congress.

But it was admitted by all, friends and critics of Jan Sangh alike, that it had given the most determined fight to the Congress wherever it had entered the election ring. It, generally speaking, fought a clean fight and thus set a new standard of behaviour in elections so necessary for the success of democratic experiment in the country.

Dr. Mookerjee was convinced by the evidence that he received about the tampering of ballot boxes and use of other undemocratic and even immoral methods adopted by the men in power to secure victory in the elections. He, in his own inimitable way, smashed the party in power in Parliament when he declared in thunderous voice that "Congress has swept, not the polls but the ballot boxes." But he paid a handsome tribute to the Government servants and the election machinery for efficient organisation of the elections, the most gigantic democratic experiment wherein 170 million voters went to the polls without any kind of clashes or untowards incidents. The responsibility for the mischief, wherever it was done, he declared, lay with the ministers, Central and Provincial, who in their unholy anxiety to come back to power misused their position and not on those entrusted with the actual conduct of election who had to carry out their instructions.

But to his own workers he would say, "We must admit the failure to be due to our own shortcomings and inexperience and handicaps beyond our control. Let us not console ourselves by shifting the whole blame on the party in power. That would be suicidal for the growth of our party. We knew that the party in power would do all that lay, in its power to defeat us. So why complain about that".

As an optimistic, that he was, he would emphasise the bright side of the election results. "We began with zero", he would argue, "and we have now got something plus everywhere. We have gained something and lost nothing". He counted the gains not strictly in number of the seats won. To him the chief gain was that the Jan Sangh had, through the elections, made its existence felt everywhere. Its name and ideology had reached the remotest villages in the areas in which it had contested any seat. It had secured a foothold in the country and in the hearts of the people.

The most significant gain was the recognition of Jan Sangh as one of the four all India Parties by the Election Commission of India on the basis of the number of votes polled by it. The elections brought Jan Sangh in the front rank of the political parties contesting for the affection of the people, leaving a number of much older parties behind in the race.

But all those who had entered the Jan Sangh on the eve of elections had not that idealism, faith and optimism. Many of them had come to Jan Sangh to serve their own political ends. Others belonged to that extensive class of people who worship the rising sun. They thought Jan Sangh to be a new luminary on the political fermament of thè country and bowed before it. But when they realised that the Congress star was still in the ascendant, they beat the retreat with indecent haste. Even some of the top and trusted leaders of the new party like Pt. Mauli Chander Sharma, got disheartened for some time and began to harbour pessimistic thoughts about the party which they thought might prove a flop.

But Dr. Mookerjee on the top and the young rank and file below remained constant. They had entered the field as a matter of duty with the words of the Lord "You have the right to do your duty but not to the reward," on their lips. They honestly felt that they had done their duty. Dr. Mookerjee by his robust confidence inspired them to remain constant to built a greater and rosy future for the motherland.

It was thus due to the steadfastness and self-confidence of Dr. Mookerjee and enthusiasm and capacity for sustained hard work of the young workers that the infant Jan Sangh could stand the stunning blow of defeat in the general elections and raise its head again after lying low and inactive for a few months. The achievements of Dr. Mookerjee in the Parliament where he came to be recognised as the virtual leader of the Opposition, and the persistence of the young workers in the Provinces in the task of revitalising and strengthening the infant organisation ultimately succeeded in rehabilitating Jan Sangh within a few months of the debacle of general elections.

The Election Break-up

In Lok Sabha, the final picture of the party position as it emerged out of the general elections was anything but encouraging for the opposition parties separately as also collectively. The opposition had collectively secured more than 55 per cent of the total votes polled as against 44.63 per cent polled by the Congress party alone. But the Congress had won 364 seats as against 125 won by the entire opposition. The Congress strength was further augmented by the six members from Jammu and Kashmir State who were nominated by Abdullah's Government and not elected by the people of the State and the five nominees of the President from among the Anglo-Indians and tribal people of Assam.

To make things worse, the opposition strength of 125 was

badly divided. The Communists and their allies who had 26 members in the new Parliament formed the largest organised group in the opposition. But in keeping with the Communist tradition all over the world, they were incapable of making a common front with any other group or party except on their own terms, which invariably amounted to the absorption or extermination of the junior ally. They tried to rope in a few independents. But none liked to walk into their parlour.

The Socialist had 12 members and the Kisan Mazdoor Praja Party of Acharya Kripalani had 10. Their merger to form the Praja Socialist Party raised their combined strength to 22. The Communists tried to form a combination with them and even offered the leadership of the combined group to a PSP nominee as a bait. But the Socialists who had grown wiser after their experience of alliance with Communists during 1935-40 spurned this offer.

The Bharatiya Jan Sangh, the only other all-India party had only three members, Ram Rajya Parishad had three, the Hindu Maha Sabha had four and the Provincial or sectional parties like the Gantantar Parishad, the Akali Dal, the Jharkand party of the tribals of Bihar and the Tamilnad Toilers party had five, four, three and four members each respectively. The independents who numbered 36 were, as their very title indicated, incapable of united action. Some of them conscientiously felt that they should remain completely independent. Others wanted to use their independence to good purpose by taking sides at will or at the command of their self interest.

Dr. Mookerjee: Opposition Leader of First Elected Parliament

Another notable feature of this motley opposition was that it lacked talent though not to the same extent as did the party in power. None of the top leaders of the Communists and the Socialists and the KMPP had been able to get in. The one man in the opposition who stood head and shoulder above all others, just as Pt. Nehru stood among the Congressmen, was Dr. Syama Prasad Mookerjee. His pre-eminence was recognised by all and it was accepted by his friends and opponents alike that he would be the chief spokesman of the Opposition in the first elected Parliament of free India.

But technically only that party or group could be given recognition as the opposition party and its leader treated as the leader of the Opposition which had a minimum strength of 50 members. It was felt by many prominent members of the Opposition as also by some Congressmen that such a combination could be formed only under the leadership of Dr. Mookerjee. So efforts were set on foot by a number of such members from the Opposition soon after the final party position became known to create such a combination with the approval and support of Dr. Mookerjee. With this end in view an invitation was issued to most of the non-Communist members in the opposition under the signatures of Dr. Mookerjee, Shri N.C. Chatterji, President of Hindu Maha Sabha, Shri Rajendra Narain Singh of Patna, leader of the Gantantra Parishad, Sardar Hukam Singh, leader of the Akali Dal, Shri Jaipal Singh, leader of the Jharkhand party and a few independents for an exploratory meeting at New Delhi, before the inauguration of the Parliament.

This meeting was held on the 28th of March, 1952, in the Constitution Club and was attended by about 20 individual members and group leaders who together represented about 45 opposition members. There it was decided to form a combined opposition Parliamentary party on the basis of a minimum common programme.

National Democratic Party

But some of the members who had originally signified their consent to join the proposed party got nervous about associating with Dr. Mookerjee for fear of incurring the displeasure of the Prime Minister. They formed an independent group of their own. Dr. Mookerji's proposed opposition party in the Parliament, therefore when it was actually formed under the name of National Democratic Party could count only 30 members. But it included some of the fine intellects and Parliamentarians like Shri N.C. Chatterji, Sardar Hukam Singh, Shri U.M. Trivedi and Shri B. Ramchander Reddi.

The New Parliament thus opened without any recognised opposition party. The speaker however gave recognition to those parties or combinations in the Opposition which had more than twenty five members as "Parliamentary groups."

The Question of Official Recognition as Opposition Party

But soon after the Praja Socialist Party leaders suggested to Dr. Mookerjee that the PSP members in the Parliament were prepared to accept him as their leader within the Parliament in combination with his own National Democratic Group so that they may together form the official opposition party in the Parliament, provided he was prepared to drop the Hindu Maha Sabha members from the proposed combination.

Dropping the Hindu Maha Sabha Offer

It was a flattering offer. It had all the advantages and no handicaps. By accepting it Dr. Mookerjee would have become the official leader of the Opposition in the country with all the privileges and advantages that go with that position. He would have got some striking power to support his relentless logic and elocution which would have enabled him to set the Prime Minister with his stream roller majority right more effectively.

But the democrat in him revolted against the condition about dropping Maha Sabha from the combination. He argued with the PSP leaders that this suggestion betrayed a narrow mindedness worse than communalism of which they charged the Maha Sabha because it amounted to condemnation of that party outright without a hearing. Communalism, he argued, was no charge. The PSP he reminded them, had been blaggarding him and his Jan Sangh also as Communal and reactionary during the elections. But now they were prepared to treat him and his party as national and progressive. The same, he agreed, could be true of Maha Sabha. He suggested that a minimum programme be drawn up. Those who would agree to abide by that programme should be accepted into the combination. Others would automatically be dropped.

But the PSP leaders feared the reaction in their own ranks against their association with Hindu Maha Sabha in any shape or form. They, therefore, insisted upon exclusion of Maha Sabha. They perhaps had not understood Dr. Mookerjee. He preferred principles to personal aggrandisement. The PSP offer was rejected by him.

His decision created genuine regret in the hearts of many people who thought that the Jan Sangh - PSP combine in the Parliament could have paved the way for the fuller unity of these two parties which, they thought, would have ideally complemented each other. The pure nationalism of the Jan Sangh based on the allegiance to the age old culture of the land, they felt, together with the economic programme of the PSP would have created a truly popular and effective opposition party in the country. But it was not realised by them that the PSP was not a homogeneous party and that its components varied from the extreme leftists of Marxist brand to sober nationalists like Shri Jai Prakash Narain, who had begun to understand the importance of culture and spiritual values in the life of the nation. Therefore, no lasting combination with this party was possible till it had set its own house in order and developed a clear cut ideology distinct from that of the Congress and the Communists.

The Inevitable Opposition Leader

It, however, became established in the very first session of the New Parliament, which opened on the 11th of May 1952, that Dr. Syama Prasad Mookerjee was the leader of the Opposition whether he had the requisite party strength or not. All the groups in the Opposition, including the Communists, began to look to him for guidance. They all considered him to be their chief spokesman and conceded to him, by implication, the right to reply on behalf of the Opposition on all major questions. Even more than the Opposition, the party in power looked upon him as the unofficial leader of the Opposition. His stature and acumen as a statesman, his Parliamentary skill and elocution, his deep understanding and constructive approach to all the problems facing the country and his following outside the Parliament made him look the real democratic adversary of the Government. Many of the Congress members who in their heart of hearts shared his approach to the problems of the country, had deep admiration for his person and his able advocacy of the policies he considered correct and his fearless and trenchant criticism of what he thought to be wrong and not in the best interests of the country. The Treasury Benches respected him for his deep study and application of the problems before the Parliament. They unconsciously treated him as their superior, both as a man and as a statesman. Most of the ministers had known his work and worth as a cabinet minister.

His searching and enlightened probe into their policies and affairs made them nervous and the ease and cogency with which he demolished their arguments made them fear him.

Nehru's Chief Adversary

The one man who looked upon him as his equal was the Prime Minister, Pt. Jawahar Lal Nehru. He had seen him and his work in and outside the Cabinet. He had been deeply impressed by his incorruptibility, irrepressible independence, nobility of mind and behaviour and, above all, by his great intellectual attainments and Parliamentary skill. But he had never liked his views and approach to the national problems which was always as refreshingly realistic and practical as his own was devastatingly utopian and unrealistic. He lived in air while Dr. Mookerjee walked on earth.

Having been brought up from his early youth in an atmosphere of unquestioning submission to his whims and fancies by the high and low he had developed fascist tendency of intolerance for all criticism coupled with an exaggerated sense of self righteousness. This tendency in him had become very marked since the death of Sardar Patel. The consciousness that the Congress success at the polls in the general elections had been mainly due to him had somewhat swollen his head. There was none in his cabinet and his party who could stand up to him or question him. He had literally become the monarch of all that he surveyed.

Dr. Mookerjee was the only man in the Parliament who would not only tell him on his face that he was wrong but who would also demolish his arguments and expose the hollowness and un-national character of his internal and external policies with such relentless vigour and adroitness, supported by irrefutable facts and figures, that Pt. Nehru would feel crest fallen before his camp followers. This made him very bitter. Failing to find facts to meet facts and arguments to counter arguments of Dr. Mookerjee, he would lose temper which resulted in those flashes of repartee in which Dr. Mookerjee used invariably to outshine Pt. Nehru. By his behaviour he tacitly accepted Dr. Mookerji's position as the leader of the Opposition, his chief adversary in Parliament and his substitute before the country.

16

Historic Speeches in Parliament

Historic Speeches

Dr. Mookerjee was painfully aware of the temper of Pt. Nehru and his tendency to regard all criticism as malicious. He knew that such an approach towards the Opposition would reduce democracy to a farce and spell disaster for the country. So in his very first speech in the new Parliament on the address of the President on the 21st of May, 1952, he made a sincere and passionate plea for a correct approach towards the position. He said:

On Resolving Differences

"As was looking to this House for the last two days, I felt, as must have been the feeling of many members of this House, that here we witness the epitome of free India. We here are representative men and women coming from all parts of India elected on adult franchise, representing diverse view-points, varied outlook, but I know it, all imbued with one idea and one alone: how to make our freedom effective and how to advance the interests of the millions of people of India. It is one of the greatest experiments of history that we are making. Every one of us, no matter to which group or party we may belong, whether we are independents or dependents, must be able to look at the problems from the widest stand-point and while appreciating the differences among ourselves we must try to resolve these difficulties and come to conclusions which will be to the good of the country. If we fail to adjust our differences, what is the alternative before the country? If this great experiment fails, if we go on according to the old fashion with the tyranny of the majority or under a megolomaniac dictatorship, if we do not accept that there are diverse view-points honestly expressed and an adjustment of these view-points is an essential ingredient of the successful working of democratic government, the alternative will be chaos. The alternative will be a sense of helplessness, frustration in the minds of the people and things who go beyond the control of every one".

Had any heed been paid to this fervent plea for tolerance of the view-point of others by the party in power, much of the unfortunate developments that followed could have been avoided and Dr. Mookerjee might have been spared to serve the country for many years more.

On Various Problems Being Faced by the Country

He also briefly touched, in this first speech, all the big problems and issues that were then, as now, facing the country which thoughts, should be handled not on party lines but as national problems demanding the cooperative effort of all. The first in importance, he held, was the problem of food. He reminded the Parliament that scarcity conditions still prevailed in Rayalseema and parts of West Bengal. He exhorted the government to give first priority to this question and see that no one died of starvation. He warned that failure to solve this problem would spell disaster because the people, who had become politically conscious, could not be expected to tolerate any government that failed to meet their basic need of food, shelter and clothing.

His sympathy was not merely verbal. He made a practical suggestion, which revealed his truly human heart that would go out for the relief of human suffering wherever he found it and which, if accepted, would have made the five hundred members of the Parliament actual sharers in the hardship of their suffering country-men. "We get now Rs. 40 per day", he said. "I do not know what the allowance of the members of the House of the People will be hereafter. Let us agree to a voluntary cut of Rs. 10 per day and let us set apart this sum for the purpose of opening homes where these women and children (of famine affected areas) may be housed and fed."

He also drew pointed attention to the dangers of growing

casteism, provincialism and communalism to the national unity. He pleaded for putting a check on them by eradicating the causes which were giving rise to them. He pointed out "that the very communalism, casteism and provincialism which have been so rightly condemned in the President's address were taken full advantage of in every suitable place by the Congress party for winning elections." This, he declared, was very deplorable. He appealed to the men in power to set an example in respect by their own behaviour.

On Jammu and Kashmir Problem

He also referred to the problem of Jammu and Kashmir which had begun to threaten the integrity and unity of India and for a just and honourable solution of which he laid down his life a year later.

He appealed to the Prime Minister to consider the forces which were then at work in Kashmir and which had been revealed by Sh. Abdullah's declaration that Indian Parliament had no jurisdiction over the Kashmir State.

The interruption that Pt. Nehru made while Dr. Mookerjee was making this appeal was characteristic of that conceited man. "I know more about Kashmir than Dr. Mookerjee", he interrupted. The reply Dr. Mookerjee gave to this retort was equally characteristic of the man and revealed his clear understanding of the grave implications of the policies being pursued by Sh. Abdullah in Kashmir with the connivance of Pt. Nehru, and his determination to got to be brow-beaten where the interests of the country happened to be at stake.

"The whole difficulty", Dr. Mookerjee said, "is that the Prime Minister knows more about anything throughout the world than anybody else and he will not accept any advice from anybody. Now how can any Parliamentary work be carried on if that is the attitude. If I make any suggestion he says: I know more than you do. Undoubtedly he does, but I will give some suggestions, place some point of view before him which he must consider".

I would like to know", he continued, "are Kashmiris Indian first and Kashmiris next or they are Kashmiris first and Indian next or they are Kashmiris first, second and third and not Indian at all? That is a very important point which we have to settle." He thus put the real problem of Kashmir in a nutshell for the Prime Minister and the Parliament to consider.

On Problems in East Bengal

He also referred to the problem of Hindus of East Bengal which had always been worrying him and which had again been getting serious. According to his information large number of Hindus were being driven out of East Bengal. He, therefore, expressed surprise at the speech of Pt. Nehru of an earlier day in the course of which he had said that though papers had reported that an exodus had started, the figures proved otherwise. Dr. Mookerjee pointed out that it was that failure to realise the gravity and urgency of the situation at critical times, that had been responsible for the loss of lives, honour and safety of many people in that area. He wanted that mistake, should not be repeat again.

Repartees with Nehru

This remark infuriated Pt. Nehru and there followed the following brilliant repartee between the two that continued to be a regular and enlivening feature of the Indian Parliament so long as Dr. Mookerjee lived. It gives an insight into the character, nature and approach of the two men as perhaps nothing else does.

Pt. Nehru : "Was my statement wrong."

Dr. Mookerjee : "It is wrong. Let the Prime Minister instead of depending on the reports of his.."

Pt. Nehru : "If I place the whole facts and exact figures."

Dr. Mookerjee : "The general statement and approach of the Prime Minister were absolutely wrong. It is a matter of verification. I say it is a matter of verification. What I suggest to him is this. He may get some figures from official sources. I cannot blame him for that. But if any Hon'rble Member gets up and says that he has information that the exodus has started, it is the duty of a responsible Prime Minister to get up and say : We will take that into consideration and see how to prevent it......"

Pt. Nehru : "The Hon. Member is challenging my statement."

Dr. Mookerjee : "I am not."

Pt. Nehru : "I challenge him to prove his and I will prove mine."

Dr. Mookerjee : "This challenge and counter challenge will be carried on for the whole of the session".

It literally continued for the whole of the remaining period of the life of Dr. Mookerjee.

On Railway Budget (1952)

His speech on the Railway Budget on the 26th of May, 1952 was equally remarkable. He was opposed to the way the re-grouping of the railways had been done, particularly in regard to certain portions of the E.I. Railway and the location of its head-quarters, which were to be shifted from Calcutta contrary to the original plan. It was a question about which Bengal was very much agitated. Calcutta had observed complete Hartal for a day on the call of Dr. Mookerjee to register its protest against the decision. In his well reasoned and documented speech he exposed how the pulls and counter pulls on the provincial basis from Congress high-ups had resulted in alteration of the original plan drawn up by experts. His plea to the Government was : "Do have the matter re-examined by an expert Commission". He was actuated not by narrow provincial feeling but by considerations of efficient administration and the necessity to avoid dislocation of low paid as far as possible.

On General Budget

He was very unhappy over the sense of self-complacency that he found was creeping over the men in power, who cared more for the chits and praises of obliging or interested foreign dignitaries than what the people of the country felt about their policies. He was particularly worried about the food situation in the country. He made an impassioned plea for looking to the needs of the common man in the course of his speech on the General Budget on the 4th of June, which was acclaimed to be one of his greatest speeches in the Parliament: He said :

"The Prime Minister said the other day that today foreigners are coming and praising Government a lot for what it has done. Undoubtedly there are some achievements to the credit of the Government. But let us not only think of what Mrs. Roosevelt has said about us, or some other gracious lady has said about us. Let us find out what our own people are saying about us. If you are not able to supply food to the people at some reasonable price, if disease and poverty stalk the land, then the foundation for your existence as a Government disappears. This is not being said as a measure of treat. This is a matter which must be taken above party politics. Unless we are able to solve the food problem and to give some measure of economic stability to the common man, whatever big scheme we may talk of, all will disappear into the limbo of oblivion. You will not be able to ensure sufficient public support for the purpose of making your planning schemes a success. I, therefore, say that so far as the present budget is concerned, it is a cheerless budget, it is a colourless budget, a budget that might satisfy the capacity and efficiency, which undoubtedly the Finance Minister possess, to manipulate dry facts and figures in a manner which he thinks would satisfy the conscience of the Chief Accountant; but if you think of a budget which carries a message of hope and of good cheer, indicating sharing of sacrifices in a common measure with all classes of people, leading to removal of basic wants and privations, then the budget fails and fails miserably."

On Reorganisation of States

Dr. Mookerjee was very much opposed to the policy of drift, of letting things take their own course, where vital interests of the country and the people were concerned. He stood for quick and practical decisions and then standing by them. His approach to the problem of reorganisation of States on linguistic basis is a fine example of this quality of his mind. While speaking on the resolution on linguistic States in the Parliament on the 7th of July, 1952, he urged the Prime Minister to take initiative in his own hands instead of allowing the things to drift. He said :

"Before things deteriorate I will beg of this House that this question should be gone into... It is no use adopting an ostrich like policy and thinking that everything is going on all-right. If you say : Let us not redistribute the boundaries of India for any consideration, if that is the policy of the Government, let them announce it and face the consequences. Then the people will know where they stand. If you say there is to be redistribution consistent with the declarations that Congress has made for the last 35 years, then do not leave the matter to be decided by the parties concerned but take the initiative in your own hands. This is my appeal to Pt. Jawahar Lal Nehru. Let him take the initiative in his own hands, appoint a commission, appoint Advisers or call informal conferences of the leading representatives of the areas concerned and try to adjust matters in such a way that they may come to a decision which will be mutually acceptable to all. It is not a question of making some debating point from the Congress side or the non-Congress side. It is a first class national issue which has got to be settled on a national basis not on party basis."

However, his words of practical wisdom fell on deaf ears. The men in power allowed the things to drift till the martyrdom of Potti Sri Romulu and campaign of lawlessness and destruction that came in its wake. The belated decision of the Government to appoint a high power commission to go into the question of reorganisation of States all over the country is a tribute to the realism and statesmanship of Dr. Mookerjee.

On Preventive Detention Act

His greatest speech of the session was the one he made on the Preventive Detention Act on the 2nd of August. It literally brought the whole of Opposition, including the Communists, under his wings and completely floored the Home Minister, Dr. Katju, who was piloting the Bill.

Dr. Mookerji's opposition to Preventive Detention Bill, the principle of detention without trial, sprang from his inborn love of democracy and freedom. Protection of Civil Liberties of the People of his country was one of the three great aims Dr. Mookerjee aspired to achieve from his early youth; the other two were re-organisation of the post-graduate studies in the Calcutta University, a task left unfinished by Sir Ashutosh, and the writing of the biography of his illustrious parent. The last task he took in hand during his detention in Kashmir. But the cruel hand of death did not allow him to complete it.

What amazed and annoyed the Treasury Benches most was his resourcefulness in collecting apt passages from their own speeches and writings as also from those of their forbears like Pt. Moti Lal Nehru to condemn the principle underlying the bill which, he declared, "is repugnant to any democratic constitution in any part of the civilised world except at a time of emergency or crisis."

In Dr. Katju whose own words :

> "Detention on mere undisclosed and often on groundless suspicion without charge or trial is opposed to all notions of natural justice and all canons of civilised administration."

He quoted with telling effect would not listen to his voice of reason. Secure in the steam-roller majority of his party he shook his head at all his arguments and pleadings and drew from Dr. Mookerjee the famous retort : "He (Dr. Katju) will never learn anything, forget everything and make a mess of everything."

On Kashmir Issue

Five days later he delivered another great speech. It was on Kashmir, a subject on which he had made a great speech on the 26th of June as well, and which shall be dealt in a separate chapter. It was a marvellous speech and was listened to with "rapt attention" by a full House and record number of visitors: One of the visitors of the day, Shri C. L. R. Sastri, later wrote about it in the *Modern Review* (Nov. 1952) as "one of the most brilliant orations that has fallen to my lot to hear whether inside or outside Parliament."

Compared to Sardar Patel

By the time the first session of the first elected Parliament of free India came to a close in August, 1952, Dr. Mookerji's position as unofficial leader of the Opposition had been firmly established. The Press, which being mainly controlled by the party in power was by no means friendly to him, admitted this fact and many of the papers editorially commented on it. The most remarkable tribute came from the *Times of India* which commented that "mantle of Sardar Patel had fallen on Dr. Syama Prasad Mookerjee." It was a most befitting tribute because Dr. Mookerjee had been exercising the same sort of sobering and restraining influence on the Nehru government which Sardar Patel had been doing from within so long as he lived. The approach of Dr. Mookerjee to most of the national problems was essentially the same as that of Sardar Patel whom he paid an eloquent tribute— "he was fearless, realistic, bold whenever a case demanded as to how he should act" —in his speech on Kashmir on the 26th of June. Both were practical men of affairs, deeply rooted in the soil of India, who never allowed the considerations of name and international fame to take the better of the considerations of real interest of the country. Sardar Patel continued to work with Pt. Nehru even after Dr. Mookerjee resigned from the Cabinet because he knew that his withdrawal would mean the end of Congress. Love of the organisation to the making of which he had given his life blood kept him tied to Pt. Nehru against his better judgement.

Another remarkable tribute came from the pen of Prof. Indar Vidya-Vachaspati M.P., who then edited *Jan Satta,* a Congress Hindi daily of the capital. In a half humorous tone he wrote that the one man whom all restaurant and cafeteria keepers in the Parliament buildings cursed was Dr. Mookerjee, because whenever he had to speak no one stayed back to patronise them.

The second session of the Parliament which began in early November, the same year, saw him rise even to greater heights. He made three great speeches in this session on The Estate Duty Bill, the Five Year Plan and the running sore of East Bengal.

On the Estate Duty Bill

He gave his general support to the principle underlying the Estate Duty Bill. But he demanded from the Government to tell the Parliament and the country how they were going to utilise the income from it. "Let us know from the Government," he pleaded, "what their proposals are for tackling the grave and widespread economic discontent in the country."

On the Five-Year Plan

His speech on the Five-Year Plan on the 16th of December, 1952, was an excellent example of constructive criticism of a thing of vital national importance. He paid handsome tribute to the authors of the Plan. But at the same time he pointed out with the help of facts and figures the lacuna in it — the uncertain and undependable premises in respect of finance on which the Plan had been built and the scant attention paid by it to the basic questions of education, health and industrial self-sufficiency.

He drew pointed attention of the Government to the question of popular enthusiasm and cooperation for the Plan without which the Plan, he said, would not be able to achieve its objective. The public cooperation, he pointed out, would come only if the party in power would handle the plan on national and not on party lines. "Do not say you want public cooperation and you have got the Bharat Sewak Samaj for that," he thundered, "and at the same time go on developing it as a 'Benami' Congress show. Do not allow that to be built on party lines".

> "Public cooperation" he declared : "will come provided certain essential conditions are fulfilled. If you come forward with a sincere call that you really want to build up an economy not meant mainly for the privileged or the favoured few but for the millions of downtrodden people, not on paper but in reality ; if you take such a message to them there is bound to be public cooperation."

"We are anxious to give, you cooperation" he asserted. "We are not enemies sitting face to face before each other. You feel for the country ; we feel for the country as well. We want that the country should develop. We know that political freedom will be meaningless and fruitless if it is not followed by economic freedom and by social equality. But let us proceed not on party lines. Let there be more tolerance, let there be more appreciation of the other man's point of view. If some of us do not agree with you, do not see eye to eye with you, do not immediately think that we are traitors or enemies of the country. We are here to serve the country and that is the spirit in which I have spoken."

Unfortunately this noble idealism and spirit of surrender for the good of the country was not shared by the idealistic Prime Minister, Pt. Nehru, who thought and acted either as an individual and a partisan or as an internationalist but seldom as a nationalist.

The Final Appeal in Parliament

The final act in the Parliamentary life of this great Parliamentarian was enacted during the budget session of the Parliament in 1953. His mind was by that time fully engrossed with the problem of Jammu and Kashmir. His heart was full and his mind was being agonised by the reports of repression and suffering of the people of Jammu. He was convinced of the justice of the cause of the people of Jammu and its wider implication for the unity of India as a whole. He wanted an honourable and fair settlement of the issue and had been carrying on correspondence with Pt. Nehru with that end in view. He, therefore, took the opportunity to make an eloquent and fervent plea in the course of his speech on the budget on the 14th of February, 1953: to the men in power" to look at the issue dispassionately". "Let us not hurl abuses at each other", he appealed to them. "There may be other occasion when we may do so. But if once we decide to not to cast motives at each other, if once we proceed on the assumption that all sides are proceeding in a bonafide manner and yet not agreeing with each other, it is only then that it will be possible to come to a settlement which will be fair and just".

Referring to the charge of communalism that was being used to malign him and his organisation as also the Praja Parishad, he asked the Prime Minister to tell him concretely what was communal about him and his party and their stand instead of making vague charges.

On Communalism

"I know", he thundered, "the Prime Minister levels the charge of Communalism on all of us. Whenever he cannot meet an argument that is the answer that he has to give. I am quite prepared, I am not making a challenging suggestion, because I am getting sick of this charge which is unfounded, if we want to consider whether Communalism exists in the country or whether it is openly advocated as a plank by any political organisation, let us fix a date for a debate and let us discuss the matter. Let Government bring forward its charges. Let us have a chance of replying. We do not want Communalism in this country. We do not want that on the basis of religion or on the basis of caste one section of Indians should go on hating other sections. We want to see developed a society where people of diverse religions will be able to live as common citizens and enjoy common rights".

> "If there is a feeling that something is being done" he continued, "opposite to this policy which we say not — instead of talking in an abstract way, let us meet privately if he so desires, let us all against whom such charges are levelled sit together and discuss. We are no enemies of this country. We are not people guilty of treason because we do not agree with you. It does not matter to which party people may belong. None of us is here for doing harm or deliberate injury to the State. Therefore, if Government comes forward with such a charge-sheet it is only fair and just that it must be a real charge-sheet and we must be able to understand each other's point of view. We may differ. But let us agree to differ in a gentlemanly way and not go on exchanging fireworks and hurling abuses at each other because it does not carry us anywhere".

On Repression of Dogras

He also pointed out the futility of repression and vilification to cow down the Dogras.

"You will not be able to destroy the Dogras", he declared. "I have seen some of them, fine elements. It brought tears to my eyes. I saw some men and women great people, patriotic people, fearless people. They have not been violent uptil now. I advise them that if any movement, any protest is to be carried on, it must be on the basis of nonviolence because you cannot fight the organised violence of the State and you will lose the sympathy and cooperation of the people. It is a question of civil right. It is a question of their life and death, of their very existence. Believe them. I have seen Prem Nath Dogra whom I respect with all my heart. I am not ashamed of that. I have met many people in my life. There may be men good or bad or greater than Prem Nath

Dogra. He is a loyal citizen and a quiet sufferer. He is a leader who does not lose his head".

On Kashmir Issue

Towards the end of this memorable speech he made another plea for a peaceful settlement of the issue. "Even now my appeal to the Prime Minister" he said, "is this. Let us forget the past. Let him take up the matter. He can rise equal to the occasion. He can deliver the goods with Sh. Abdullah. I do not wish for a moment that you should humiliate the Government because. Then, whom do I humiliate? Our own Government elected by the people of the country. It is not a question of mutual humiliation or gaining one point here or losing another point there. It is the question of settlement of an issue which is of national importance, which may create serious problems and destroy the peace and happiness of large parts of India and I appeal to the Prime Minister to move before it is too late."

But Pt. Nehru, because of his deep prejudices and lack of touch with the actual realities of the situation in Jammu, had become impervious to all such arguments and pleadings. His inability to meet argument with argument and facts with facts made him sullen and full of anger which was touched off by the casual remarks of Dr. Mookerjee about the results of the four recent bye-elections to the Delhi State Assembly, in which Congress had been badly trounced by the Jan Sangh—Hindu Maha Sabha combine, towards the close of his speech. This resulted in the last of those great wordy duals between him and Pt. Nehru which had become a feature of the Indian Parliament so long as Dr. Mookerjee was alive.

Nehru-Mookerjee Repartee on Elections

"Let me assure the Prime Minister" Dr. Mookerjee said, "that however much he may decry and distrust us, we also have a little hold on this country. The elections were fought a few days ago. So far as these elections are concerned they are important for this reason. I saw with my own eyes how powerfully the resources of the Government can be made to operate for the purpose of winning the election. I can tell the Prime Minister sometime later.

He does not know that money and wine played their part in many a sphere. You talk of Gandhiism......"

Pt. Nehru: "It is disgraceful the way this charge is being made."

Dr. Mookerjee : "I am glad the Prime Minister said it is disgraceful. It is indeed disgraceful that such things should happen."

Pt. Nehru : "Is it right that in the course of this debate the Hon'ble Member should bring these charges? To make these wild, irresponsible and fantastic charges is perfectly disgraceful for the Hon. Member. This itself shows the nature of his entire speech."

Dr. Mookerjee: "Good, very good."

Pt. Nehru : "The mentality behind it, the irresponsibility behind it."

Dr. Mookerjee : "His temper shows more than anything else his incapacity to rule over this country. Let us not cloud the issue."

Pt. Nehru : "I ask the Hon. Gentleman. I challenge him to either prove or withdraw his remark about wine and women."

Dr. Mookerjee : "I said money and wine. I do not know whether women were used, but I never used the word 'women'."

Pt. Nehru : "I challenge the Hon. Member to prove his irresponsible statement,"

Dr. Mookerjee : "There is no use losing any temper."

Pt. Nehru : "It is only the Hon. Member's right, I suppose, to lose his temper and say these things."

Dr. Mookerjee : "It is the eternal right of Shri Jawahar Lal Nehru always to lose his temper and our eternal duty to submit to it."

It was clear to all those who heard and read this brilliant repartee that Pt. Nehru was wrong and that he had been badly outwitted.

Offer of Unconditional Support

But Dr. Mookerjee was not happy over it. He had been trying to persuade the House and particularly Pt. Nehru to save the daily worsening situation in Jammu. Uppermost thought in his mind was good of the country. He therefore rounded off this last of his great speeches in the Indian Parliament with an ennobling and patriotic offer of fullest cooperation to the Government in the case of any emergency. "Whatever may be said against us", he declared, "whatever motives may be ascribed to us, I can give this assurance to the Prime Minister that in case an emergency arises in this country, in behalf of the party I represent including the much maligned group, I offer our unconditional allegiance and support to the Government."

A few days after this historic speech Dr. Mookerjee was arrested for alleged violation of Section 144 in Delhi in connection with a procession of the remains of some victims of police repression in Jammu. He got his last opportunity to speak in the Parliament on the 26th of April, 1953, when he once again pleaded for justice to the people of Jammu and a re-orientation of Kashmir policy.

But it all fell on deaf ears. Pt. Nehru seemed to be determined to not to hark to his voice of reason. He, it appeared, had made it a question of personal prestige. This lowered him in the eyes of many of his own party men as well who genuinely felt that he was wrong and Dr. Mookerjee was right. But no one dared to tell this to him on his face. That revealed the moral degradation and the rot that had set in Congress party and highlighted the pressing need for an alternative leadership in the country.

That alternative, now it was universally accepted in and outside the Parliament, could be none else than Dr. Syama Prasad Mookerjee. He had developed that stature and country wide following which was so essential for a man who might be called upon to lead the vast and varied country like India. He had been leading the Opposition in the best traditions of Parliamentary life, not opposing for the sake of opposition but for the sake of improvement and betterment of the country. He never grudged paying tribute to the Government and offering it his fullest cooperation whenever the occasion demanded. His touch stone was good of India and her teeming millions and not any particular ideology or its homeland which must be upheld and praised at all times. This distinguished him, from the Communists. The contrast between his attitude and that of the Communists was best brought out by the following repartee between him and Mr. H. N. Mookerjee, the deputy leader of the Communist group, in the course of his speech on railway budget on Feb. 25, 1953, when he was praising the Chitaranjan Locomotive Factory for its being in a position to manufacture 70 per cent of the component parts of the locomotives.

H. N. Mookerjee : "They are not manufacturing locomotives".

Dr. Mookerjee : "Perhaps my Hon. Friend does not know that... We have yet to see a country which manufactures all the hundred per cent parts required for locomotives."

H. N. Mookerjee : "There are".

Dr. Mookerjee : "It may be Russia about which my Hon. Friend knows better than I do. Actually let us look at matters as an Indian and not as a Russian for the time being".

This constructive and nationalistic attitude coupled with his determined but enlightened resistance to all anti-national and totalitarian policies and trends of the men in power made him one bulwork of freedom and democracy in the country. To the common man he had become the most redoubtable fighter for his rights who could teach even Pt. Nehru a lesson. The staff of the Parliament and the Secretariat who often found him in action in Parliament had begun to call him "The lion of the Parliament". Dr. Mookerjee rules the Parliament though Pt. Nehru may rule the country, they used to say. And to all those interested in the progress of democracy in the country, he appeared to be the coming man, the prospective Prime Minister and hope of the democratic millions of the country.

17

The Kashmir Movement

Dr. Mookerjee in his impressive logical style wrote many a letter to Pt. Nehru and Sheikh Abdullah, during the period of crisis, but to no avail. The failure of the protracted correspondence to bring about a change of heart in Pt. Jawaharlal Nehru and Sh. Abdullah without which no fair and just settlement of the Jammu impasse was possible, created genuine regret in all patriotic hearts. Some distinguished people like Sir S. Radhakrishnan, the Vice-President of India, who had high regard for Dr. Mookerjee, his burning patriotism and leonine heart which could go to any length to effect a compromise with his own people, as he thought Pt. Nehru to be, for the national good, tried to act as intermediaries. But unlike the British Viceroys who, with all their authoritarian and bureaucratic outlook, had training in democracy in their own homeland and therefore could be amenable to reason and sober counsels if they came from people for whom they had respect, Pt. Nehru was living in the atmosphere of the Mughal Court and only psychophants could catch his ears. Moreover, there was no escape from the veto power that he had given to Sh. Abdullah. So his efforts failed. And where Radhakrishnan failed no one else could hope to succeed.

Of Right against Might

But Dr. Mookerjee was not the man to sit on his oars because he had failed to persuade Pt. Nehru to see reason. The reports of the reign of terror that had been let loose in Jammu were daily reaching him. He sincerely believed the cause of the Praja Parishad to be the cause of Indian unity. It was his own cause and the cause of every patriotic Indian. Right was on the side of the Parishad, might on the side of the government. The path of duty was clear before him. As a Karam-Yogi he had tried what Samarth Ram Das called "Dharm Shakti" and "Niti Shakti", but in vain.

The "Rajya Shakti", the argument of power, which Samarth Ram Das advocated as the last measure to achieve a noble end, he did not possess. But he was a democrat. He knew that the power which had intoxicated the Congress rulers of the country and the monster they had raised in Kashmir, came from the common people who were the ultimate masters of the country. So he decided to make a direct appeal to them so that such a strong public opinion in the country might be created as it would be impossible for the government to ignore with impunity.

Non-Cooperation by Government

But the Government would not allow him to do even that. They had already taken steps to deprive Bharatiya Jan Sangh and its allied parties of their democratic right to educate and organise public opinion about an admittedly vital national problem. The Punjab government in its over anxiety to prove its loyalty to Pt. Nehru, had already struck at the Jan Sangh and detained most of its top leaders under Preventive Detention Act. It had promulgated Section 144 in almost all districts which, in practice, was meant for Jan Sangh only. The spokesmen of the Congress and the hired agents of Sh. Abdullah were allowed to carry on their propaganda against the Praja Parishad and Jan Sangh without let or hindrance. The metropolis was not to lag behind. Soon after meetings and processions were banned in Delhi as well and there too the ban was meant mainly for Jan Sangh and its supporter.

This created a new situation. Preservation and protection of civil liberties had been one of the main tasks set before himself by Dr. Mookerjee from the day of his entry into public life. He had fought for civil liberties of his people in Bengal even when he himself was a member of Bengal government. It was his firm conviction that democracy could not function without civil liberties. He, therefore, looked upon ban on peaceful public meetings and processions in Delhi and elsewhere as a challenge to democracy. It amounted to adding insult to the injury being caused by the government's anti-national and repressive policy towards the Praja Parishad.

Call for Jammu and Kashmir Day Against Kashmir Repression (1953)

To protest against the growing repression in Jammu and to demonstrate people's will to protect their democratic right of free association and free expression of their views on national problems, he gave a call to observe March 5, 1953 as Jammu and Kashmir Day all over the country. The programme of the day was to include public meetings and peaceful processions for explaining to the people the stand of Jan Sangh and allied parties on Kashmir.

Electoral Victory

That the public opinion was appreciating the viewpoint represented by Dr. Mookerjee was proved by the results of four bye-elections to Delhi State Assembly which were held just when Pt. Nehru was spurning the appeals of Dr. Mookerjee and saying: "We have no intention of abdicating and running away from the duty that has been entrusted to us by the people and the Parliament."

Jan Sangh-Maha Sabha combine captured three seats while it lost the fourth by only a few votes to a millionaire sitting Congress member. Kashmir policy had been made the main issue of the election by both the parties and the Congress had, besides making full use of official machinery and patronage, brought a number of Kashmir ministers and M. Ps to help it.

Had the Congress rulers been responsive to public opinion they should have realised that the people had begun to disapprove the policy they had been following in regard to Jammu and Kashmir and they should have adopted a more realistic attitude towards the Parishad and its supporters in India. But that was not to be.

All India Tour to Garner Public Support for J&K

In the meantime Dr. Mookerjee undertook a tour of western districts of U.P. to explain Jan Sangh stand on Kashmir. He visited Muzaffarnagar, Saharanpur, Hardwar and Dehra Dun. At Dehra Dun he performed the opening ceremony of a four mile long irrigation canal built by Jan Sangh workers with the help of the local people. Everywhere lakhs of people heard him and assured him of their support.

Proceedings at J&K Day

As fifth of March approached, the authorities in Delhi became nervous. They had been watching the rising tempo of public opinion in favour of Jan Sangh and they realised that the meeting announced for the day was going to be held in spite of the ban. So they thought discretion to be the better part of valour and lifted the ban just before the meeting was scheduled to begin.

The meeting was held in the Queens Garden. It was presided over the Swami Karpatri ji and was addressed by Shri N.C. Chatterji and Pt. Mauli Chandra Sharma besides Dr. Mookerjee. The atmosphere was tense. Few among the half a lakh people who had assembled there knew that the ban on the meetings had been lifted and that the meeting they were attending was a lawful one. They had come with the determination to suffer for their convictions. Many had brought wet piece of cloth with them to protect themselves against the affect of tear gas.

Dr. Mookerjee's Speech

Dr. Mookerjee made one of the most powerful speeches of his life that evening. Every word seemed to come from the depth of his heart. He explained his efforts to place the cause of the Praja Parishad which, in its ultimate analysis, was the cause of the whole of India before the powers that be. He wanted them to call the leaders of Parishad and explain to them their point of view if they could not do anything else just then. He had implored them to not to treat the patriots of Jammu as untouchables. But all his efforts had failed. It was now for the democratic people of India, he told his audience, to assert their right to be heard in the interest of the nation as a whole.

Other speakers compared the role played by Dr. Mookerjee to that of Lord Krishna who had gone to the extreme length to persuade the ruling 'Kurus' to do justice to the `Pandvas'. That was a correct appraisal of the situation, Dr. Mookerji's advocacy of the cause of the Praja Parishad had been no less sincere than that of the Pandavas by Lord Krishna, and the patience and tact he had shown could not be surpassed.

Seeking Public Opinion and Support

The only path open to him then was to give to the people, who looked to him for lead and guidance, a call to share the suffering of the people of Jammu by starting a peaceful and non-violent struggle in the rest of India also in the hope that might change the heart of Pt. Nehru some day or, failing that, awaken the conscience of the nation to the wrong his mistaken policies were doing to the country as a whole. The fighter in him urged him to give this call. But the democrat in him wanted to avoid it, as far as possible, because he thought that it would be an abnormal thing in a democratic set up where normally the authorities should be amenable to the pressure of the public opinion.

But a pre-requisite for that was that the democratic government should allow the public opinion to be expressed and mobilised. Dr. Mookerjee still had some hope that the democrat in Nehru may assert itself against the Fascist that, he thought, he was fast becoming. So he decided to test him once again much against the wishes of the people who were looking for a call of action.

March against Repression

It was announced that the ashes of some of the victims of the Police firing in Jammu shall be taken out in procession on the next day, the 6th of March, from the Railway Station and that the procession would be led by Dr. Mookerjee, Shri N.C. Chatterji and Shri Nand Lal Sastri MP. The idea was to inform the people of the extent and nature of repression that was going on in Jammu.

Mookerjee and others Arrested

Just before the procession was going to be taken out the next day, ban was re-imposed. Dr. Mookerjee and his companions, however, reached Chandni Chowk from where they were to lead the procession at 4 pm, the appointed time. But as soon as they reached there they were taken into custody under Section 188 of the I.P.C., on the charge of contravening the order against public meetings and processions.

Arrest of Dr. Mookerjee

The news of his arrest created a stir in the country. Crowded protest meetings and Hartals were observed all over India. In

Delhi large crowds paraded the streets. They were lathi charged and tear gassed a number of times.

His arrest became a signal for the start of a peaceful and non-violent struggle which was as much in sympathy with the struggle of the Praja Parishad in Jammu as in protest against the suppression of civil liberties in India.

Unfortunately for the government, the Magistrate who arrested Dr. Mookerjee in his over-zeal failed to fulfil the elementary demands of law regarding the presentation of his august prisoners before the court of law within the fixed time. Babu Ram Narain Singh MP., therefore, filed a habeas corpus petition before the Supreme Court which ordered Dr. Mookerjee and his companions to be set at liberty on the 11th of March.

But a charge under Section 188 was framed against them and a regular case was instituted. Dr. Mookerjee did not like to defend himself because he asserted that freedom of association and expression was his fundamental democratic right and that he had committed no offence by attempting to join the Procession. But Shri N.C. Chatterji wanted the defence to be put up. His counsel also raised some technical law points which had to be referred to the High Court and which unnecessarily prolonged the trial.

Release from Jail

At the time of his release by the Supreme Court Dr. Mookerjee agreed to execute a personal bond for Rs 100 in respect of the case under Section 188. He had thought that the trial would be soon completed and he would get the usual sentence for which he was prepared. But the prolongation of trial made him uneasy. He wanted to be with his younger companions who had been taken into custody along with him and who were living in jail as under-trials. The reports of repression from Jammu as also from different parts of India pained him. He wanted to share the suffering of the Satyagrahis by being with them in jail. He, therefore, tried a number of times to surrender his bail and go back to jail. But the government wanted to avoid his return to jail because that would have created a stir in and outside the Parliament. So Dr. Mookerjee had to remain out much against his will.

All India Tour After Jail Release

But he made the best use of this enforced liberty to educate his countrymen about his stand about Kashmir and the circumstances which had forced first the Praja Parishad and then the Jan Sangh and its allied parties to take resort to the path of suffering and self-sacrifice. He visited Gwalior, Indore, Jaipur, Calcutta, Bombay, Bangalore, Patiala and Patna during the months of March and April. Everywhere literally lacs of people turned out to listen to his voice of reason and call for action. The people had begun to appreciate the stand he had taken on Kashmir and had begun to see in him the alternative leadership that the country so badly needed to save it from megalomaniac dictatorship of one man.

Massive Public Support

Everywhere he received assurances of cooperation from the big and small, the rich and the poor.

A popular slogan of those days was, which meant:

"The more Nehru will shout at us, the stronger Jan Sangh will grow."

At Bombay more than a lac of people assembled at Chaupaty sands to listen to him within a few hours of his unexpected arrival there. At Patiala he thrilled the people by his unequivocal declaration that he looked upon Sikhs as a part and parcel of Hindu Society. Therefore, their unity with other Hindus could not be made a matter for bargaining. He asked them to talk as Hindus and have all they wanted.

Atal Behari Bajpai as Emissary

The demand for him from different parts of the country was so pressing and persistent that it was not physically possible for him to meet it. So his message was taken to those provinces which he could not visit by Shri Atal Behari Bajpai, who played the role of his personal representative with distinction.

Satyagraha Movement

The Satyagraha also showed in action his great qualities of leadership, the capacity to inspire love and confidence in the common workers, to judge people and to distinguish the genuine from the spurious. He had the knack of winning the hearts of all those who came in contact with him, particularly the common worker, by a winning smile, a word of cheer and wit and his own earnestness which was contagious.

He was very particular about the work in Delhi, the capital of the country and hub of all political activity. It is why he had selected it to be the main centre of Satyagraha. The movement revealed the fine stuff that the RSS trained workers were. He had so far heard about their devotion to duty and spirit of self-sacrifice. Now he saw these qualities in action. Young men like Durga Das Varma, the underground General Secretary of the Praja Parishad, who visited Delhi thrice in the course of the movement to meet him, Shri Rameshwar Das who risked his everything to do his duty, Shri V.P. Joshi who came up to his expectations in every way after he had left on his last and tragic journey to Jammu, Shri Vijay Kumar, the Joint Secretary of Delhi State Sangh and Shri Jagdish Abrol who between themselves organised the whole movement in Delhi, appeared to him the type of men that can make a fine job of anything entrusted to them.

Intensification All-Over India

The response from UP, which alone sent about 2000 Satyagrahis, confirmed the faith he had developed in the leaders and workers of Jan Sangh in UP. He would often tell Nana Deshmukh humorously, "Half of the central cabinet comes from UP because they say, UP is equal to Bharat. So your contributions to the Satyagraha must be equal to that of the rest of Bharat." UP did fulfil his expectations.

A distinctive feature of this movement was that the rank and file that joined it came from educated and politically conscious section of the society. It was estimated that out of about 10,000 Satyagrahis who courted arrest all over the country about a thousand were professional men, graduates, doctors, lawyers teachers and professors and about three hundred paid income tax. Quite a large number of Satyagrahis came from villages. A number of batches came on foot right from Indore and such other distant places. Batches of Satyagrahis came from Maharashtra, Bombay, Andhra and Karnataka as well. This fact gave a lie direct to the

Congress propaganda that it was a localised affair in which the people of the country in general were not interested.

As the movement gained momentum in Punjab, Delhi, UP and other parts of India, Shri Abdullah's Government intensified the repression in Jammu where a no tax campaign had also begun. The Dogra police was replaced by Kashmiri Police and Militia, which was predominantly Muslim. They let loose a reign of terror in the countryside of Jammu. The villagers were hounded out of their homes, their properties were looted and their women insulted. This sent a wave of indignation throughout Jammu. The patience of the warlike people, many of whom were ex-servicemen, came to a breaking point. They began to press the Parishad dictator, Durga Das Verma, to allow them to meet violence by violence. "We are soldiers", a number of them wrote to him, "and have seen fighting in different parts of the world. We have been so far obeying your instruction to remain non-violent in face of all provocations. But we cannot remain non-violent spectators when our women are insulted before our very eyes."

The statement issued by a number of retired civilians including an ex-Inspector General of Police, who visited the scenes of such occurrences of their own, confirmed these reports.

This made Dr. Mookerjee very uneasy. He did not want violence to break out in any case. He, therefore, decided to send two of his colleagues, Shri U. M. Trivedi Bar-at-Law, M. P. and Shri V. G. Deshpande MP, to Jammu to see things for themselves and console the people. But the Defence Ministry refused to issue permits to them for entry into the State and when they expressed their intention to proceed even without permit, they were arrested under Preventive Detention Act at Jullundur in mid April.

Soon after a delegation of some retired ministers and high dignatories of the State visited Delhi. They again drew the attention of the people and Government of India to the fast deteriorating situation in Jammu. The situation there demanded immediate attention. The government seemed to be utterly impervious to the appeals of even their friends and its false sense of prestige prevented it from taking any initiative in the matter. In view of this situation Dr. Mookerjee began to think of his own going to Jammu to see things for himself and to meet people there including

Sh. Abdullah, if possible, in an attempt to find a solution of the impasse.

But the continuous hearing of the case under Section 188 in the court of the A.D.M., Delhi, stood in his way. He needed recess of at least a week to be able to visit Jammu. Before that he wanted to tour Punjab for a couple of days because of the pressing and persistent requests from the workers of that State.

Appeal to Nehru

In the meanwhile he made his last appeal to Pt. Nehru in the course of his speech in the Parliament on the 26th of April, to rise to the occasion and take the initiative to settle the question. He told him that he would be satisfied if Pt. Nehru invited Pt. Premnath Dogra and explained to him his view-point and difficulties instead of talking about them to him. But it had no effect on him. He appeared to be determined to crush Praja Parishad and the Jan Sangh as they had dared to challenge his might. Just about that time I brought to his notice a prophecy published in "Filmindia" which said that he would replace Pt. Nehru towards the end of 1953. Dr. Mookerjee felt perturbed over it." It will further harden him (Pt. Nehru)" he remarked, "and make a solution more difficult."

Determination to Go to Jammu

Dr. Mookerjee had seen how permit to visit Jammu had been refused to Shri Trivedi and Deshpande and prior to them to the fact finding mission consisting of a number of legislators, including the Deputy Speaker of Rajasthan, which he wanted to send to Jammu in January. He was also aware of the fact that permit system had been introduced to prevent Pakistani agents and spies from entering Kashmir and that it could not be lawfully used to stop responsible men, like members of Parliament, to visit that State. He, therefore, wrote a letter to the Defence Minister asking him the legal position about the Permit System. The Minister gave him no reply.

Dr. Mookerjee's Last Journey

Before starting on what was to prove his last journey, he paid a hurried visit to Calcutta to pay his respects to his aged mother. On his way back he stopped for a day at Patna. There he expressed his intention of going to Jammu to his host, Shri Thakur Prasad Advocate. This came as a surprise to him. His aged father who had served as Dewan in a number of Muslim State tried to dissuade Dr. Mookerjee from going to Jammu. "I will never advise you", he pleaded, "to put yourself on the mercy of Sheikh Abdullah. My experience has taught me never to trust men of his tribe."

But Dr. Mookerjee dismissed his suggestion with a laugh. He was not the man to change his plan for fear. Thereupon the old man entreated: "Go, if you must. But please see that you do not take anything there unless it is first tasted by one whom you trust. One does not know the ways of such rulers. They are capable of anything." Dr. Mookerjee agreed to abide by his advice, as far as possible.

Jailed by Sheikh Abdullah

Just a day before he left Prof. Johnson, Personal Secretary of Mr. Adlai Stevenson, the defeated Democratic candidate for American Presidency, who was then on a short visit to India, met him at his residence to fix an appointment for his chief. It was fixed for 13th of May, by which time Dr. Mookerjee was expected to be back in Delhi after spending two days in Jammu. But he had a premonition that he might not be able to keep the engagement. So he told Prof. Johnson while he was leaving him, "It is possible that I may not be able to keep the engagement. Anything may happen." His premonition proved correct. The 13th of May saw him a prisoner in the jail of Sheikh Abdullah.

18

Vitiating Kashmir Problem

Dr. Mookerji's main pre-occupations, outside Parliament, during the year 1952 were the problem presented by the continuously worsening situation in East Bengal and the resultant exodus of Hindus from there, the work in connection with the visit of sacred relics of Sriputta and Mahamoggallana, the two disciples of Mahatma Buddha, to the Buddhist countries and their re-enshrinement in the new Stupa at Sanchi, which he had to attend as President of Mahabodhi Society of India, and the problem of Jammu and Kashmir State's relationship with the rest of India to which he devoted himself fully during the closing months of his crowded life.

Switch-over to Kashmir Problem

His interest in the problem presented by Jammu and Kashmir State grew casually. As a member of the Central cabinet he had been instrumental in India going to the defence of that State after it had formally acceded to India on the 26th of October, 1947. Since then Pt. Nehru had taken sole charge of Kashmir and others were seldom consulted in regard to the policy about it, particularly that pertaining to its internal developments. Nor did other ministers, including late Sardar Patel, feel like giving their unsolicited advice to the Prime Minister in matters concerning Kashmir because he was known to consider Kashmir to be the one feather in his cap for which he must have the whole credit alone. Furthermore many of them did not know much about Kashmir except what came to them from Pt. Nehru and Sh. Abdullah.

But disconcerting reports about the policies that Sheikh Abdullah had been pursuing within the State had begun to pour into the Indian capital as early as November and December 1947.

Justice Kanwar Dalip Singh who was sent as Agent General of the Government of India to the Jammu and Kashmir State early in November, 1947, soon found to his utter disillusionment that Sheikh Abdullah was determined to go his own way unmindful of the plans and policies laid down by the Government of India. He reported the matter to New Delhi. But he was over-ruled and he, therefore, resigned.

Arrest of Pt. Prem Nath Dogra

Soon after Justice Mehar Chand Mahajan, the Prime Minister of the State, whose presence as a check was irksome to Sheikh Abdullah, was driven out of the State in a most humiliating way. It was a pointer to the shape of things to come in Kashmir which was taken note of by shrewd men like late Sardar Patel. Then came the arrest and detention without trial and without even any charges being framed, of Pt. Prem Nath Dogra, the undisputed leader of the people of Jammu, along with a number of his co-workers in the Praja Parishad. This sent a wave of indignation throughout Jammu. After some months of futile efforts to draw the attention of the Government of India to the discriminatory policies of Sheikh Abdullah against the people of Jammu in general and Dogras in particular and complete suppression of civil liberties, the Praja Parishad launched a peaceful and non-violent Satyagraha. Its main demands were that the policy of discrimination against Jammu be stopped and Pt. Prem Nath Dogra be released.

Hundred of men and women from all parts of Jammu, including some Muslim Dogras, courted arrest during this Satyagraha. Sheikh Abdullah's government adopted a policy of heartless repression to suppress the movement. Even women were not spared. A number of them were insulted and lathi charged indiscriminately. Thereupon a deputation of some respectable ladies of Jammu city came to Delhi and met a number of members of Parliament and ministers to apprise them of the true facts of the situation in Jammu. They met Dr. Syama Prasad Mookerjee as well in October, 1948. He was deeply moved by the facts they placed before him. But he expressed his inability to do anything in the matter. He advised them to see the Prime Minister who, he told them, was directly handling the Kashmir issue.

Pt. Prem Nath Dogra was released by Kashmir Government towards the end of 1948, on the intercession of the Government of India and the Praja Parishad was given the assurances that no hindrance will be put in the way of its normal constitutional activities.

Constituent Assembly Elections in J&K

A few months later the decision to have an elected constituent assembly for the State which will "ratify the accession of the State of India" was announced. The Praja Parishad decided to contest the elections to this Assembly and began to make preparation for that.

Partisanship of Government to National Conference

The rejection of 42 of the 59 nomination papers of its candidates by the returning officers on most flimsy and even whimsical grounds set the Praja Parishad leaders a thinking. They began to consider whether it would be worthwhile for them to contest the elections in face of this unabashed partisanship of the Government for the National Conference. Pt. Prem Nath Dogra then visited New Delhi to draw the attention of the Government of India to the new situation and consult the leaders of public opinion in the country about the course of action his organisation should adopt. The attitude of the Government of India appeared to him to be quite discouraging. Many of the leaders outside the Government, including some ex-top dignitaries of the Congress, advised him to boycott the elections. He wanted to consult him to boycott the elections. He wanted to consult Dr. Syama Prasad Mookerjee, who had by that time come out of the Government, as well. But Dr. Mookerjee was not in Delhi. He therefore entrusted the task of consulting Dr. Mookerjee to Balraj Madhok the General Secretary of Jan Sangh.

In New Delhi, Balraj Madhok met Dr. Mookerjee in the Western Court where he used to stay after his exit from the cabinet. After he had explained the whole situation to him he opined that elections should be fought in spite of all odds. His view was that legislatures were the only effective forums for giving vent to diverse view-points on Governmental policies. Therefore, it would be worthwhile fighting the elections if thereby the Praja Parishad could send into the Assembly even one single spokesman.

Praja Parishad's Decision to Boycott Elections

But before this weighty opinion could reach the Praja Parishad leaders they had decided to boycott the elections. As a result Sheikh Abdullah could fill the State Constituent Assembly with his hand picked nominees, many of whom happened to be known Communists or Pakistanis, who were all returned unopposed.

Special Treatment to Kashmir

This Communist cum communalist dominated one party Constituent Assembly, contrary to all expectations, set about breaking or weakening the ties that already bound Jammu and Kashmir State with the rest of India instead of strengthening them. Under the Communist inspiration Sheikh Abdullah began to take a strictly legalistic view of the Article 370, the temporary Provision about the special position of Jammu and Kashmir, which was incorporated in the Indian Constitution on the request of Sheikh Abdullah and against the definite opinion of Dr. Ambedkar, the chairman of the Drafting Committee of the Constituent Assembly, who smelt the motives behind his insistence upon it. When late Shri Gopala Swamy Aiyangar placed that Article before the Constituent Assembly, many of the members objected to it. Thereupon Shri Gopala Swamy tried to remove their fears and doubts by saying that the discrimination in favour of Kashmir made in the said Article was due to special condition of Kashmir which made that State then unripe for fuller integration. But he added that "it is the hope of everybody here that in due course, even Jammu and Kashmir will become ripe for the same sort of integration as has taken place in the case of other States".

Sheikh Abdullah thereafter began to proceed on the basis of Kashmir being an independent State which had acceded to India for limited purpose of defence, foreign affairs and communications. Even respect of these three subjects he had mental reservations. Even though defence was a central subject he insisted upon raising a many thousand strong Militia force to be equipped by India but controlled by him. He evaded the transfer of State telegraphs and telephone departments as also the strategic highways within the State, to the Central Ministry of Communications. Even in respect of foreign affairs he dodged the Government of India by using his trade agents at Delhi and Bombay as his diplomatic missions for developing contacts with foreign missions in India. He could do all this because of the doting support of Pt. Nehru for everything he said or did.

Resentment amongst People to Kashmir Special Status

This policy was resented by the people of Jammu who wanted fuller integration of their State with India like other acceding states. They resented the exclusion of the Indian national tricolour flag from all public buildings and functions in the State and the use of National Conference party flag instead. They also resented the insulting attitude adopted by Sheikh Abdullah towards the Dogra Maharaja who had, on the behest of Pt. Nehru, invested him with power against his own better judgement. The systematic elimination of Hindi from educational curricula as also from offices, the talk of the Kashmiri nation as distinct from the Indian nation, the transfer of all State valuables, rare manuscripts and some of the institutions from Jammu to Srinagar, vivisection of Jammu to carve out its parts adjoining the Kashmir valley into new Muslim majority districts and open propaganda for Pakistan by some high and trusted officers of Sheikh Abdullah's Government created genuine doubts and fears in the minds of all nationalists in Jammu and Kashmir about the future of the state with which their own future was so intimately connected.

The matters were brought to a head early in February, 1952, when students of the Government Gandhi Memorial College, Jammu, protested against the compulsion to salute the National Conference party flag at an official function. They were dealt with very harshly. As a reaction the students of the college went on strike. They also gained the sympathy of the general people who considered their stand to be correct. This gave to the students agitation the colour of a mass movement. The Kashmir Government exploited the situation to arrest Pt. Prem Nath Dogra and many of his other workers, all of whom were detained without trial, after clamping an eighty-two hours curfew on Jammu city.

These developments drew the attention of the whole country for the first time the internal situation in the State and it began to be realised that there was something wrong with Abdullah's internal policies. It created the curiosity and desire to know the true facts about the internal situation in the State all over the country.

Pompous Declaration by Sheikh Abdullah and his Lieutenants

This was followed by a number of ominous statements by Sheikh Abdullah and his lieutenants in and outside the Kashmir Constituent Assembly. On 24th of March, 1952, Mirza Afzal Beg, the Revenue Minister in Sheikh Abdullah's cabinet, declared in the State Constituent Assembly:

> "The Jammu and Kashmir State will be a republic within the Indian Union.... So far as the constitution of the State is concerned we aim at making its frame-work such that the state will be a republic like other republics. According to our plans the State will have its own President, a separate National Assembly and a judicial set-up".

This was followed by the pompous declaration on the 29th of March in the State Constituent Assembly by Sheikh Abdullah himself, who had returned a few days earlier from Paris where he had been sent by the Government of India as its delegate to the UNO, that

> "we are a hundred per cent sovereign body. No country can put spokes in the wheels of our progress—neither the Indian Parliament nor any other Parliament outside the State has any jurisdiction over us."

He followed this up by a more damaging speech at Ranbir-singhpura on the 10th of April, in the course of which he said:

> "Kashmir's accession to India will have to be of a restricted nature so long as communalism has a foot-hold on the soil of India". He called the arguments in favour of full accession to be "childish, unrealistic and savouring of lunacy." And then he threw a fling on India by saying: "Many Kashmiris fear what will happen to them and their position if, for instance, something happens to Pandit Nehru. We do

not know. As realists we Kashmiris have to make provision for all eventualities."

These outburst of Sheikh Abdullah coupled with the reports of happenings in Jammu pricked the bubble of complacency about Kashmir in India. The Press and public opinion reacted sharply to this attempt of the Kashmir tiger to bite the hand that had been feeding him. Only Pandit Nehru tried to minimise the gravity of the situation by making the Praja Parishad the scape goat for the indiscretions and ebullitions of his creature.

Dr. Mookerjee's Concern on Kashmir

Dr. Mookerjee was deeply perturbed over these developments. He was not happy with the turn things had been taking at the UNO in regard to Kashmir. He was pained by the continued occupation of 1/3rd part of the Jammu and Kashmir State by Pakistan and he considered it to be a dangerous blow at the integrity of truncated India. These new developments indicated that the part of the State that was, technically at least, still part of India was also slipping away. He strongly condemned in a public statement this volte face of Sheikh Abdullah, whom he compared with late Mr. Jinnah, and described his speech to be an "offer of accession with his left hand with secession up his sleeves."

But he was not the man to sit content merely with issuing a statement where the integrity and honour of India as a whole was at stake. He became keen to know full facts of the situation so that he might educate and guide the public and Parliament in time about the real situation about which they had been so far kept in dark by the Government and the Press of the country. This created in him a desire to meet Pt. Prem Nath Dogra who had just then been released from jail under the pressure of the Government of India.

Prem Nath Dogra's Revelations of Sheikh Abdullah's Designs on Kashmir

He had not to wait long for that. Pt. Prem Nath Dogra visited New Delhi by the end of April, 1952, to place his case before the leaders of public opinion in India. He met Dr. Mookerjee in his suite in the Western Court early in May.

The meeting, judged by the later results, was a momentous event in the life of both of these great men. Pt. Prem Nath Dogra, who was then in the 70th year of his dedicated life, was a picture of humility and self surrender. But his spirits were high. He narrated to Dr. Mookerjee the events that had preceded and succeeded Sheikh Abdullah's elevation to power, how he would not enter Jammu without getting an assurance of support from him, how he had publicly accepted that the responsibility of what happened in Jammu in October, 1947, lay mainly on the shoulders of Pakistan and her agents who forced the people of Jammu to fight in self defence, how he pressed him to join National Conference as a pre-requisite to his being taken into his cabinet and how his refusal to sell his conscience for loaves and fishes of office made him his enemy. He also explained how the hand of cooperation offered by the Praja Parishad for the defence and betterment of the State and her people was spurned by Sheikh Abdullah and how he had started the process of Muslimisation of the State in the name of secularism, and of establishing a totalitarian one party regime in the name of democracy. The Praja Parishad, he explained, had been putting up with all this under the impression that Government of India was giving a long rope to him for securing his support towards the final settlement of the Kashmir problem. They had hoped that all this would end after the integration of the State with the rest of India like other acceding States and consequent application of the constitution of India to the State of Jammu and Kashmir as well.

"But this hope", he said in a voice choked with emotion, "has been dashed to the ground by the recent developments in the State. Sheikh Abdullah and his Communist and Communalist supporters are now bent upon cutting Jammu and Kashmir State from India for different reasons. The Communists want to make Kashmir their stronghold which they might be able to use as a jumping ground for a red revolution in the rest of India at the opportune moment. They, therefore, want the Indian control over its affairs to be reduced to the minimum. With this idea they are trying to equip the State with full paraphernalia of an independent State. Communalist and pro-Pakistan supporters of Sheikh Abdullah are also encouraging him in this policy because they feel that it would be easy for Pakistan to grab Kashmir once its ties with India have been loosened.

All the nationalist elements in the population of the State including the Buddhist of Laddakh, the Dogras of Jammu and a good section of the Kashmiris as well," he added, "are opposed to this policy. They feel that Sheikh Abdullah is making Jammu and Kashmir into another Pakistan. The people of Jammu are particularly scared by it. For them it is a question of life and death. They are determined to resist this policy of cutting Jammu and Kashmir asunder from the rest of India. Their one aspiration is to be governed according to the constitution of India under the Indian tri-colour and they want to owe allegiance to none but the President of India". The people of Jammu, he emphatically told Dr. Mookerjee, were united to a man in this matter and they were prepared to make any sacrifice for asserting their right to be one with India, their common motherland.

The whole thing came as a revelation to Dr. Mookerjee who listened to him with rapt attention. He began to see the real purpose and motive behind Sheikh Abdullah's utterances referred to above. He saw the justice of the stand of the Praja Parishad and its wider implications for the unity and integrity of India as a whole. He was impressed by the transparent sincerity of the aged man who had the spirit of the youth in him, and he was visibly moved by his appeal for his support to the cause for which Praja Parishad was struggling.

But Dr. Mookerjee was not the man to rush to conclusions without mature thought. He wanted facts to substantiate what Pt. Dogra had narrated to him and also wanted to be sure of the popular support to the Parishad because, as a democrat, he was the last man to go against the wishes of the people.

Pt. Prem Nath Dogra was ready for it. He placed before him facts and figures, supported by documents and official records and publications, in support of his contentions. As regards the popular support for the stand of the Parishad, he invited him to visit Jammu to see things for himself.

Dr. Mookerjee was convinced by the facts and evidence placed before him about the righteousness and genuineness of the cause of the Praja Parishad. It did not, therefore, take him long after that to determine his course of action. He told Pt. Prem Nath Dogra that he would do whatever lay in his hand to persuade the Government of India to change their policy and stop Kashmir from becoming a sovereign republic within the Indian republic with a separate to Pt. Dogra to place all the facts and figures he had got before the Prime Minister also.

Nehru's Refusal to Meet Prem Nath Dogra

Pt. Dogra tried to meet the Prime Minister. But Pt. Nehru refused to see him in spite of his repeated requests because he seemed to have developed some deep prejudice against him on the basis of false and misleading report from Sheikh Abdullah.

Dr. Mookerjee was pained when he came to know about the democratic Prime Minister's refusal even to see a recognised leader of public opinion in a very important part of the country in which the whole country was deeply interested. It became clear to him that Pt. Nehru was not prepared to listen to the pleas and requests of the people of the State to reconsider his policy about Kashmir unless popular pressure was put on him by the rest of India as well.

Jan Sangh Resolution (1953)

Dr. Mookerjee gave the lead to the country in the matter by getting a resolution passed by the Working Committee of Bharatiya Jan Sangh on the 14th of June, 1953, which emphasised that Jammu and Kashmir State was an integral part of India and declared that:

> "The decision of the State Constituent Assembly concerning an elected President and a separate flag coupled with the recommendations of its Basic Principles Committee that Kashmir will be an autonomous republic are in clear violation of India's sovereignty and the spirit of India's constitution". It further added that :
>
> "The committee takes a serious view of this development and wants to remind the people and the Government of India that the Cabinet Mission Scheme of 1945 envisaging a week centre with only three subjects was opposed by the Congress and a large section of Indian opinion as being inimical to India's unity and interests. The fissiparous

tendencies of the Muslim League, however, succeeded in dividing India leading to disastrous consequences. To allow the Jammu and Kashmir State to proceed along the same path now looks like permitting history to repeat itself. It might mean a fresh call to disruptive elements in India to break its unity and integrity which has been achieved at such tremendous cost."

Call for All India Kashmir Day

The resolution also called upon the people of India to observe June 29th as Kashmir Day and hold public meetings and demonstrations in support of the stand taken by Bharatiya Jan Sangh.

On the 26th of June, three days before the appointed all India Kashmir Day, Dr. Mookerjee made first of his great speeches on Kashmir in the Parliament. Earlier on the same day the people of Delhi staged a huge demonstration before the Parliament to condemn Sheikh Abdullah's policy of separatism.

Speech in Parliament on Sheikh Abdullah's Separatism

In the course of this speech Dr. Mookerjee dealt with the question of separate flag, elected head in the place of hereditary Maharaja as the constitutional head of the State, and the Article 370, on the basis of which Sheikh Abdullah wanted a separate constitution for the State, point by point and demolished completely the case of Sheikh Abdullah and his Indian supporters.

Referring to the question of flag he pointed out :

> "You cannot have divided loyalty. Sheikh Abdullah has said : We will treat both flags equally, you cannot do it. It is not a question of fifty, fifty. It is not a question of parity. It is a question of using one flag for the whole of India, India that includes Kashmir. There is no question of having a separate Republic of Kashmir having a separate flag."

Regarding the move to replace the Maharaja by an elected head of the State he declared:

> "The Maharaja is gone. There is no question of the continuance of his autocratic administration. He functions as

> the constitutional head of Kashmir with his bands completely bound, a dignified rubber stamp. But if you want that no Maharaja should remain in any part of India even as a constitutional head over a particular unit let it be done soberly, properly and constitutionally. If the Parliament of India considers that the constitution of India should be amended and there should be no Maharaja's rule, no Rajpramukh in any part of India, let us discuss it."

He also pointed out the inconsistency between the attitude of the Congress party towards Article 370 when it was placed in the constitution by late Gopala Swamy Aiyanger and its present attitude of defending Sheikh Abdullah on the basis of the same Article. He also referred in detail, with facts, figures and documents, to the suppression of civil rights, elimination of Hindi, vivisection of Jammu on communal lines, expropriation of Dharamarth property and funds, communalism in services, discrimination against Jammu, the double game of Sheikh Abdullah in giving different version of his speeches to the press and people of India from the one meant for the home consumption in the State and the iron curtain he had drawn around the State to prevent true facts from being known outside. He made a passionate plea

> "For being clear in our own minds as to what we want and," he added prophetically, "if you just want to play with the winds and say " We are helpless and let Sheikh Abdullah do what he likes" then Kashmir will be lost. I say this with great deliberation that Kashmir will be lost."

On 29th of June, Kashmir Day was observed all over the country with great enthusiasm. Dr. Mookerjee himself addressed a mammoth public meeting in Delhi.

The sharp reactions of the Press and the people of all shades of opinion to Sheikh Abdullah's utterances and the tremendous popular response to the Jan Sangh's call for observance of Kashmir Day made even Pandit Nehru a bit restive. He summoned Sheikh Abdullah to New Delhi to be able to persuade him to stop his fire eating. But Sheikh Abdullah evaded compliance with his request on one pretext or the other. On the other hand he sent a team of his constitutional advisers to negotiate with the Government of India an agreement which may give recognition to his decisions about separate flag and constitution for the State. He himself came down on the 16th of July, to extract more concessions and give final touches to the deal that his agents had negotiated. It was placed before the Indian Parliament by Pt. Nehru on the 24th of July, and has since come to be known as July Agreement.

The July Agreement

This Agreement was a victory for Sheikh Abdullah's separatism. It conceded to him the right to have separate citizenship, separate flag, elected head of the State in the place of hereditary Maharaja and separate constitution. The concessions he made to the Indian view-point were all hedged in by so many 'ifs' and 'buts' that they could be nullified without much ingenuity by any dishonest man.

Dr. Mookerjee disapproved of this Agreement. The very idea of an agreement which aimed at abridging the constitution and overriding the sovereignty of India in respect of one of its constituent parts, was repelling to him because he felt that it would be the first step towards constitutional disintegration of India, which would be exploited by the disruptive forces elsewhere as well.

He got the opportunity to give vent to his feelings and ideas on this agreement in the Parliament on the 7th of August, 1952. He put two straight questions to Pt. Nehru — one about the areas of the State occupied by Pakistan and the other about the areas ruled by Sheikh Abdullah. Regarding the first he asked: "Is there any possibility of our getting back this territory?" "We shall not get it," he added, "through the efforts of UNO; we shall not get it through peaceful methods, by negotiations with Pakistan. That means we lose it unless we use force and the Prime Minister is unwilling to do it. Let us face facts — are we prepared to lose it?"

Regarding the second his question was : "May I ask — was not Sheikh Abdullah a party to this constitution of India. He was a member of the Constituent Assembly; but today he is asking for special treatment. Did he not agree to accept this Constitution in relation to the rest of India including 497 States. If it is good enough for all of them, why should it not be good enough for him in Kashmir?"

Pt. Nehru had no reply to these questions. He evaded them and talked about the special position of Jammu and Kashmir State. It convinced none—not even his party men. But his condemnation of the Praja Parishad as an organisation which had no following among the people seemed to carry conviction with many who knew little or nothing about Jammu and Kashmir except what was doled out to the Indian Press by Kashmir Government or by Pt. Nehru.

The Praja Parishad had by this time announced its decision to hold a convention of its workers at Jammu on the 9th and 10th of August, to give its authoritative views on July Agreement and decide upon its future course of action. It had invited a number of members of Parliaments and leaders of public opinion in India to attend that convention and judge for themselves the following of the Praja Parishad and the feelings of the people. Dr. Mookerjee had accepted the invitation. He announced his decision to go to Jammu to see things for himself in the Parliament on the same day.

Decision to Visit Kashmir

This made some of the Congress leaders and MP's, who knew the real situation, nervous. They tried to persuade him to drop the idea of going to Jammu. Some of them told him : "Why are you lowering your position Doctor Sahib? You will not find even five hundred people to receive you. Praja Parishad has no following at all."

An unknown astrologer also visited his house and pressed him not to go to Jammu. He warned him that there was danger of his losing his life as a result of an accident. But Dr. Mookerjee was not to be dissuaded. He had planned to leave on the eighth night by Kashmir Mail. Shri U.M. Trivedi and Babu Ram Narain Singh—both members of the Parliament, a good number of Press representatives, and the present writer were to accompany him. But to his utter disappointment he learnt at about 6 p.m. that the Defence Ministry had not issued the permits for entry into the State to him and his party till then. He immediately telephoned to the Home Minister and the Defence Minister and was able to get the permits just before he was to leave for the Railway Station.

On reaching the Railway Station the pressmen who had to accompany Dr. Mookerjee were greatly surprised to find that he was to travel in the third class along with the rest of them. One of them could not hide his amazement and asked: "You must be travelling in the third class for the first time in your life?" "No, I travel third quite often" was the prompt reply. "You know ours is a poor organisation", he added, "the saving made in this way helps us to meet other necessary charges."

Dr. Mookerji's travelling kit consisted of only one suitecase which contained one small pillow, two sheets and a few clothes. He spread one sheet on the wooden seat of the third class coach and used the other for covering his body. That was the kit that he usually had with him except that in winter one cotton sheet was replaced by a blanket. When asked why he had not brought his bedding he smiled and said, "I believe in travelling light." The Indian ideal of simple living and high thinking had become a living reality in his life.

The journey from Delhi to Jammu was a memorable event in his life. Upto Dasuya on the Jullundur-Pathankot line, where the train reached at about 6 a.m., he was not disturbed at any wayside stations because instructions to that effect had been sent by the Jan Sangh headquarters. But from Dasuya onwards every station saw thousands of people waiting to greet their hero. They invariably insisted upon his speaking a few words to them. Dr. Mookerjee was not the man to disappoint them. So the first speech of the day was delivered by him at 6 a.m. At Pathankot where the train reached at about 9 a.m., a huge crowd had assembled on the platform to welcome him. It included Pt. Prem Nath Dogra who had come all the way from Jammu to receive him and welcome him into the State. Dr. Mookerjee was deeply impressed by the devotion and earnestness of Pt. Dogra who at the ripe age of 70 appeared as active as a youngman.

Dr. Mookerjee had to address a huge public meeting just outside the Pathankot railway station before he could proceed to the house of his host Mr. Gopal Krishan Mahajan, the son of Justice Mehar Chand Mahajan, whose interest in the welfare of

Jammu and Kashmir and its people has continued unabated. He had to go through a crowded programme which included a talk to pressmen and meeting a deputation besides taking his lunch during the three hours he stayed at Pathankot. At about 1 p.m. he and his party left for Jammu on a jeep. The press reporters followed him in wagon.

He crossed Madhopur bridge on the Ravi at about 3 p.m. As soon as he set his foot on the territory of Jammu and Kashmir State he was greeted by the resounding slogans which kept ringing in his ears till the last days of his life :

Bharat Mata Ki Jai;
Kashmir Bharat Ka Ang Hai;
Ek Desh Men Do Vidhan,
Ek Desh Men Do Nishan,
Ek Desh Men Do Pradhan,
Nahin Chalenge Nahin Chalenge

The first town of the State, its gateway, to which he was first taken was Kathua, the headquarters of the district of the same name. It is just about four miles from the Ravi Bridge and at that time, had a population of about three thousands only. But more than ten thousand people, men and women, had assembled there on that historic day to receive Dr. Mookerjee who was taken through the tastefully decorated streets of the town to the meeting place.

The enthusiasm, the earnestness and the grim determination that Dr. Mookerjee saw on the faces of the hardy Dogras there removed the doubts that had been assailing him till then in view of what he had been told by his Congress friends, who claimed to know Jammu and Kashmir better than him. What impressed him most was the universal respect for Pt. Prem Nath Dogra and the hold of Praja Parishad over the masses. He gave vent to his feelings in the short speech he delivered there. He said:

> "Before I left Delhi many Congress friends had told me that I should not visit Jammu because Praja Parishad has no following among the people. I would ask them to come here and see whether Praja Parishad has any following or not".

Referring to the slogans that he had been hearing and which were prominently displayed at the meeting place he declared:

"You want Indian constitution, you want Indian flag, you want Indian President to be your President. These are just and patriotic demands. They will have to be met. So far as I am concerned I can only assure you that I will do all I can". And then he uttered the prophetic words:

Ham Vidhan Lenge Ya Balidan Denge

"I will secure for you the constitution of India or lay down my life for it."

Hero's Welcome

Seventy miles journey from Kathua to Jammu was a continuous procession. All along the route people, sturdy men and women from remote villages, were standing to greet the one Indian leader who had responded to their appeal and had come to understand their feelings and sentiments, their woes and problems. They had put up gates on the road here and there with photos of Pt. Prem Nath Dogra, the "State Kesri" prominently displayed on them. After every mile or two Dr. Mookerjee had to stop and say a few words. At Hiranagar and Samba, two tehsil places on the way side, he had to address mammoth meetings.

He was scheduled to reach Jammu by 6 p.m. But he could not leave Samba, a distance of 25 miles from Jammu, before 7.15 p.m. The unexpected enthusiasm of the people who had travelled long distances to have a glimpse of Dr. Mookerjee had caused the delay.

The people of the villages lying between Samba and Jammu had been waiting for him for long hours. As night fell many of them returned to their homes disappointed but many others continued to wait for him with torches and 'Mashals' in their hands. It was a sight to be seen. Beautiful arches and gates surrounded by young and old people with flower garlands in their hand waiting for their hero for hours together in pitch dark. Shri Jagdish Abrol, a co-worker who had been driving the jeep tried to race against time to reach Jammu early and in the attempt just missed a serious accident. The jeep was about to fall in a depression at one sharp bend when he, with great presence of mind, pulled it up with a sharp jerk at the steering.

As the flower bedecked jeep carrying Dr. Mookerjee reached Tawi bridge, the outpost of the city of Jammu, a surging sea of humanity greeted him with full throated Jais. They had been waiting for him since 5 p.m. The two and a half miles route the Tawi bridge to Pt. Prem Nath Dogra's house was tastefully decorated and the whole city had turned out to have a glimpse of their saviour.

As he reached his destination at about 11 p.m. broken and tired after a long days strenuous journey, in the course of which he had delivered no less than twenty speeches, he had become fully convinced of the popularity and strength of Pt. Prem Nath Dogra and the organisation he headed. He had also become fully aware of the strong feelings and sentiments of the people about Abdullah's move to have a separate flag and constitution for the State.

Visit to Srinagar

Within a few minutes of his arrival, the Deputy Commissioner of Jammu came to him to invite him on behalf of Sheikh Abdullah to visit Srinagar the next day and have talks with him. Sheikh Abdullah, it appeared, had been informed by his officers about the charged atmosphere in Jammu and he wanted to place his point of view before Dr. Mookerjee before he gave his advice and guidance to the Praja Parishad convention.

Dr. Mookerjee was not prepared for this invitation. The people of Jammu including his hosts did not wait to be deprived of his presence amidst them even for an hour. But Dr. Mookerjee, the democrat as he was, thought it his duty to hear the other side before he arrived at any conclusion. He accepted the invitation on the condition that he would be sent back to Jammu the same day to be able to keep his engagements there.

He left by plane for Srinagar at 11 a.m. on the 10th of August, and reached there by noon. He was directly taken from the aerodrome to Sheikh Abdullah's residence where he had talks for about six hours with him and his deputy, Bakshi Ghulam Mohammed. The plane had to return to Delhi in the evening. It waited for him for some time. But the talks continued longer than expected and Sheikh Abdullah decided to send him back by car at night. Before he left Srinagar he had a long talk with Yuvraj Karan

Singh, who was then being pressed to become the Sadr-i-Riyast much against his will, as well.

What exactly transpired in the talks between him and Sheikh Abdullah, none can say. But this much is known that at one stage Sheikh Abdullah began to talk loudly and imperiously about his right and powers as was his wont, but Bakhshi Ghulam Mohammed interrupted him by saying that, that was not the way of making one's standpoint understood to the other. Dr. Mookerjee, as was clear from the speech he delivered at Jammu after his return from Srinagar, appreciated the difficulties of Sheikh Abdullah in carrying the Muslims of Kashmir with him. But he was not convinced of the advisability of the ways and methods he had adopted to placate the communalist Muslims. He told him on his face that his policies and utterances made him look more like Mr. Jinnah, who would not accept a strong or even a weak centre on the plea that it would be controlled by Hindus, who happened to be in majority in the country taken as a whole, than like Mahatma Gandhi whose path he claimed to have been following in Kashmir. He particularly advised him not to take any hasty step about the flag about which the people of Jammu had very strong sentiments.

Dr. Mookerjee left Srinagar at about 8 p.m. by car, slept for a few hours at Batote where he reached about 2 p.m. and again continued his journey in the morning so as to reach Jammu by 9 a.m. He was scheduled to leave Jammu the same afternoon.

Immediately after his arrival he was closeted with Pt. Prem Nath Dogra and some other top leaders of the Parishad whom he gave a gist of his talks with Sheikh Abdullah. He advised them patience for some time more. Pt. Dogra asked him to remember the temper of the people he had seen and told him how all the delegates at the convention had been demanding some sort of direct-action. Dr. Mookerji's reply was characteristic of that man of peace. Satyagraha, he said, was an extreme step and it must be resorted to only after all other means have been exhausted. He was, he added, going to meet Prime Minister Nehru, and place the real situation before him. Within the State, he advised them, they should continue to organise and educate the people. He hoped that better counsels might prevail upon Sheikh Abdullah. But if he remained adamant, he assured them, then he would support any action they might take.

He spoke in the same strain to the half a lac people who had assembled in the scorching sun in the Parade ground to listen to him. Some of them were disappointed at his pacifism while the sober section appreciated his tone.

The Special Correspondents of the *Statesman* and the *Hindustan Standard* who had gone there to study the situation wrote about his visit that he had pacified the people whose patience had reached the point of exhaustion, and had thereby done great service to the cause of mutual understanding and peaceful settlement of the vexed question.

Meeting with Nehru on Return

Dr. Mookerjee had a long interview with Pt. Nehru immediately after his return to Delhi. He told him that it was no use minimising the gravity of the situation. Praja Parishad, he informed him, was not the organisation of a few disgruntled and expropriated landlords as he would like him to believe. It was a democratic political organisation with capable leadership and mass following. It was a force, he told him, to reckon with in Jammu and Kashmir and it would be impolitic and dangerous to force decisions, which, besides going against the unity and integrity of the country, were totally unacceptable to him. He advised him to take Pt. Prem Nath Dogra whose integrity and patriotism was beyond doubt, in his confidence so that the Dogras, who happened to be one dependable factor in the Kashmir situation, be harnessed for fortifying the unity of that State with the rest of India.

His advice went unheeded both by Sheikh Abdullah and Pt. Nehru. Secure in their respective seats of power, they failed to understand the strength of feeling in Jammu against their policies and the growing awakening of the Indian public opinion about it.

Approval of July Agreement and Aftermath

Sheikh Abdullah got the concessions made to him by the July Agreement about elected head in the place of the Maharaja and the flag implemented by his Packed Constituent Assembly with indecent haste and postponed any decision about extension of citizenship, fundamental rights and the jurisdiction of the Indian Supreme Court to the State. On the other hand the Constitution Drafting Committee appointed by him prepared a draft Constitution which virtually made Jammu and Kashmir an independent State with its own National Assembly, Supreme Court and flag. The Praja Parishad leaders were able to secure a copy of this draft constitution which made them all the more restive about the future of the State. The efforts made by Pt. Dogra to draw the attention of the Indian authorities through a memorandum to the President, deputation to the minister of States and through other means open to him had failed miserably. So the feeling in Jammu began to grow that they will have to go through the sacrament of sacrifice to awaken to conscience of the leaders and people of India to their pitiable condition and the patriotic nature of their stand which had its importance for India as a whole. They decided to consult Dr. Mookerjee once again before they took any final decision.

Accordingly Pt. Prem Nath Dogra met Dr. Mookerjee at Jullundur on the 8th of November, where the latter had gone in connection with the Punjab Provincial Jan Sangh conference. Pt. Dogra placed before him the full picture of the deteriorating situation and the growing feeling in the people that things could not be set right without a struggle.

Dr. Mookerjee had seen how all his own efforts to make the authorities in Delhi see light of reason had failed. Conviction had begun to grow in him that Pt. Nehru was not susceptible to democratic pressure, that arguments, logic and public opinion had no meaning for him. As a man who had been agitator all his life Pt. Nehru, he felt, had developed a complex for agitational methods. He would bow before force and agitation but not before right or reason if it was not backed by might. He thought it to be a most unfortunate thing as it undermined the people's faith in democratic methods. But he had to see things as they were. He, therefore, told Pt. Dogra that he had tried to secure justice for them and had failed. So he had no right to bind their hands any longer. But the decision, he said, must be taken by Praja Parishad after full consideration of its own resources and strength. Jan Sangh, he assured him, will stand by them and do everything possible to mobilise public opinion in India, because it was convinced that the cause of the Praja Parishad was the cause of the whole of India.

Pt. Prem Nath Dogra took leave from Dr. Mookerjee at Jullundur with a heavy heart. He knew that he would have to lead the people of Jammu in the struggle and he was prepared for the worst. Dr. Mookerjee was deeply impressed by the nobility of character, courage of conviction and winning manners and behaviour of that old man. He had developed sincere respect for him.

Hoisting of the National Conference Party Flag

Soon after Pt. Dogra's return to Jammu, Kashmir Government announced its decision to hoist the National Conference Party flag, which had since been adopted with a minor change as state flag, on the State Secretariat at Jammu with full ceremonial on the 17th of November. It was a direct challenge to the people of Jammu. They took up the challenge. Pt. Prem Nath Dogra declared that none but the Indian National Flag shall fly over Jammu and gave a call to the people to get prepared for making sacrifices for the vindication of their right to be one with their mother-India.

The National Conference flag was not hoisted on the State Secretariat on the appointed day. The government had realised the weakness of their position. They decided to strengthen it by the use of force. The obliging Pt. Nehru lent them battallions of Central Armed Reserve Police and his nominee in Punjab followed suit with the supply of tear gas squads. Having thus equipped themselves, Sheikh Abdullah's government started the policy of repression for which the people of Jammu were well prepared. Pt. Prem Nath Dogra and Shri Shyam Lal Sharma, the organising Secretary of the Praja Parishad, were arrested on the 26th of November when they addressed a public meeting and hoisted the Indian tri-colour in the main square of Jammu city. That became signal for the start of the Praja Parishad Satyagraha.

Dr. Mookerjee took it to be a signal for him also to do whatever he could to secure justice to the people of Jammu and save India from another partition.

19

Journey to Kashmir: Subsequent Arrest and Death

Amid full throated slogans, raised by thousands of people the passenger train carrying Dr. Mookerjee to Punjab enroute to Jammu steamed out of the Delhi Railway Station at 6.30 a.m., on the 8th of May, 1953. The compartment in which he sat had been decorated with flowers and Jan Sangh flags. Vaidya Guru Datt, Shri Atal Behari Bajpai, Dr. Varman, Shri Tek Chand and Balraj Madhok accompanied him in the same compartment. A few pressmen also joined them.

Just before his departure, he issued a statement explaining his purpose in going to Jammu. "The Satyagraha movement has been continuing in Jammu," he stated, "for nearly six months leading to the arrest of about 2500 persons and to the killing of more than 30 Satyagrahis by police firing. In Delhi and Punjab the movement has been going on for more than two months and has led to the arrest of more than 1700 Satyagrahis in these two and other adjoining States. In spite of all provocations and various types of repression and terrorisation, reminiscent of the British regime, the movement has remained non-violent and free from any communal bias.

> "Although the movement has remained confined to Delhi and some parts of the Punjab," the statement continued, "yet a large number of Satyagrahis are pouring into the capital of India from various parts of the country giving the movement an all India character. They are bringing with them the support and blessings of large sections of people living in the area's concerned. In Jammu, in spite of the iron curtain, people have not succumbed to fear and are ready to face the wrath and fury of the authorities whose repressive measures continue unabated."

Referring to the success that the movement had achieved it said:

"During the last few weeks I have visited many parts of India and I have tried to place our viewpoint before our country. I have found that slowly and steadily even those who did not fully support our movement are realising the grave implications of the mistaken policy of Mr. Nehru towards Jammu and Kashmir. From that point of view our movement has been successful. It has aroused widespread public support in favour of the basic objective of the movement.

Explaining why he had not applied for permit the statement said:

"Mr. Nehru has repeatedly declared that the accession of the State of Jammu and Kashmir to India has been hundred per cent complete. Yet it is strange to find that one cannot enter the State without a previous permit from the Government of India. This permit is even granted to Communists who are playing their usual role in Jammu and Kashmir, but entry is barred to those who think or act in terms of Indian unity and nationhood. I do not think Government of India is entitled to prevent entry into any part of the Indian Union which according to Mr. Nehru himself includes Jammu and Kashmir. Of course if any one violates the law, he will have to face the consequences."

Regarding his object in going to Jammu the statement said:

"My object in going to Jammu is solely to acquaint myself with what exactly had happened there and the present State of affairs. I would also come into contact with available local leaders representing various interests, outside the Praja Parishad. It will be my endeavour to ascertain what the intention of the people of Jammu is and to find out if at all there is any possibility of the movement being brought to a peaceful and honourable end, which will be fair and just not only to the people of the State but also to the whole of India. I confidently hope I shall receive the full cooperation and sympathy of all concerned when I proceed to discharge this difficult responsibility. If I am allowed to enter the State, I for my sake do not rule out the possibility of even meeting Sheikh Abdullah and have a personal discussion with him."

It was thus clear that he was proceeding to Jammu on a mission of peace.

The journey from Delhi to Ambala Cantt, his first halt in the Punjab, was a continuous ovation from literally thousands of people, rich and poor townsmen and villagers, who assembled even on small wayside stations in hundreds to express their solidarity with and support to his mission. At bigger stations like Ghaziabad, Modinagar, Meerut, Muzaffarnagar, Saharanpur and Jagadhri gatherings ran to four and five figures.

Just on the eve of his departure some Indian merchants from West Indies had met him. They had requested him to keep an eye on the lot of Indians who had gone overseas. He himself had developed interest in them after his visit to Burma, Cambodia and Indo-China where a large number of them had met him. He thought that an organisation like the British Overseas League should be set up in Delhi to collect and disseminate information about the overseas Indians and watch their interests generally. He wanted that a beginning should be made in that direction. That wish of his still remains to be fulfilled.

Message to Sheikh Abdullah

As he was approaching Ambala Cantt, it struck him that he should inform Sheikh Abdullah of his projected visit to his State. So as soon as he reached there he sent the following telegram to Sheikh Abdullah.

"I am proceeding to Jammu. My object in going there is to study situation myself and to explore the possibilities of creating conditions leading to peaceful settlement. I will like to see you also if possible".

A copy of this telegram was sent to Pt. Nehru in New Delhi.

Because of Section 144, Dr. Mookerjee could only address a private meeting of workers in Ambala Cantt. Later while talking to some pressmen, he stated: "Permit System is meant to prevent foreigners and particularly Pakistani agents from entering Kashmir and obtaining military secrets and not to prevent respectable citizens from moving in the country. As a member of the Indian Parliament I have a right to go to every place within India to study the situation there. It is why I did not apply for a permit."

"Do you think Sheikh Abdullah will meet you?" A pressman asked.

"Why not", replied Dr. Mookerjee, "It is my wish that I should meet him. I see no reason why he should refuse".

From Ambala Cantt, Dr. Mookerjee motored to Karnal where he had to address a public meeting and stay for the night. He was stopped in the way by enthusiastic crowds of thousands at Shahabad and Nilokheri. He made brief speeches at both the places.

He reached Karnal at about 8 p.m. and went straight to the place of meeting where over ten thousand people were awaiting him. As he returned to the house of his popular host, L. Sita Ram, he was dead tried. He wanted to go to sleep immediately after taking his dinner. But workers of the district had assembled there to meet him. They wanted him to speak to them for some time. He turned round to Madhok and said in an appealing voice, "Why don't you help me. You talk to them and let me sleep. I am tired".

Madhok knew his condition and had not mind to be cruel to him. But the workers wanted him to say something. He had to submit. "They have come to talk to you doctor Sahib and not to me", Balraj Madhok told him apologetically.

Without a second word he sat up in the chair and talked to the workers and answered their queries for more than half an hour. He could not disappoint them.

From Karnal he went to the historic city of Panipat early next morning and addressed another huge meeting there. From there he entrained Bombay Express and arrived at Phagwara, his next halt, at about 4 p.m. In the way thousands greeted him on all stations as on the previous day.

Dr. Mookerjee received Sheikh Abdullah's reply to his telegram of the previous day at Phagwara. The telegram read, "Thanks your telegram. I am afraid your proposed visit to the State at the present juncture inopportune and will not serve any useful purpose."

On being asked what he proposed to do in view of Abdullah's reply, he said: "I want to visit Jammu to study the situation there. Therefore, I know its usefulness. If Sheikh Abdullah does not think that it will serve any useful purpose, he may not meet me and may utilise his time for any other useful work".

Pt. Nehru did not care to reply.

From Phagwara he motored to Jullundur where he addressed a Press Conference. Replying to a question regarding the position of UNO *vis a vis* Kashmir he said: "India had taken the issue of Jammu and Kashmir to UNO for stopping Pakistani aggression and for getting her armies out of the State and not to settle how and when plebiscite was to be held there. Pt. Nehru should have protested against this deflection from the main issue and should have withdrawn from UNO if it had failed to accept this."

Replying to another question he explained his stand about the vexed question of Punjabi speaking State.

"It is difficult to say anything about it", he said "so long as one does not know about the geographical limits of such a State. Large number of people from West Punjab have now settled in Ambala division. Therefore, Punjabi speaking areas today are not the same as they were in 1947. The whole matter should be left to the Commission for reorganisation of States which the Government of India must appoint without delay."

Disclosure of Forthcoming Arrest

As he entrained at Jullundur for Amritsar an elderly person who was sitting in the same compartment introduced himself to him as Deputy Commissioner of Gurdaspur. He disclosed to him that the Punjab Government had decided not to allow him to reach Pathankot. "I am expecting instructions from my Government as to where you should be put under arrest," he added.

It now became clear that he would be arrested. Vaidya Gurudatta had been sent to keep company with him if he was arrested. He wanted a younger companion also who besides looking to his personal comforts should "be available for consultations also." He wanted Shri Atal Behari Bajpai for the purpose.

A huge crowd of over twenty thousands received him at the

Amritsar railway station where he stayed for the night. He met the workers and told them about his plan. He declared that Sheikh Abdullah's reply to him was analogous to the reply sent by Maharaja's Government to Pt. Nehru in 1946, when he wanted to visit Srinagar to study the situation created by the arrest of Sheikh Abdullah and that he had decided to go to Jammu whether Sheikh Abdullah liked it or not.

Journey from Amritsar to Pathankot on the 11th of May was again a triumphant march. Thousands greeted him at every station. But to his surprise he was not arrested.

Soon after he arrived at Pathankot, the Deputy Commissioner of Gurdaspur, who seemed to have preceded him there, sought an interview with him. He informed Dr. Mookerjee that he had been instructed by his Government to allow him and his companions to proceed without Permit and added, "Though no limit has been put on the number of companions you can take with you, I will advise you to take only a few."

This information intrigued Dr. Mookerjee because it contradicted the information that had been given to him by the same officer at Jullundur. He could not understand why the Government had changed their plan. He did not then know that a conspiracy had been hatched to push him into the State where he would be out of reach of the protecting hand of the Supreme Court.

Pathankot gave him a right royal send off. Thousands of people with folded hands stood on both sides of the bazar through which his jeep passed. Just before his departure a ninety year old lady blessed him with the following touching words: *We Putra! Jit ke avin, aiwan na avin* — My son ! return victorious, not otherwise.

Dr. Mookerjee and his companions reached the Madhopur Check Post of the Ravi bridge at 4 p.m. The Deputy Commissioner and other officers present there saw him off and wished him good journey. But as soon as his jeep reached the centre of the bridge, he found the road blocked by a posse of Kashmir police. The jeep stopped and a police officer handed him over an order of the Chief Secretary of the State dated 10-5-53, banning his entry into the State.

Dr. Mookerjee read the order and said: "I have been permitted by the Government of India to proceed. What is it now". "I am Superintendent of Police, Kathua", the police officer replied, "I have been instructed to hand over this order to you".

"But I intend to go to Jammu," Dr. Mookerjee declared.

Order of Arrest

Thereupon the police officer took out an order of arrest under Public Security Act of the State issued by the Inspector General of Police, Jammu and Kashmir State on 11-5-53. It stated that Dr. Mookerjee "has acted, is acting and is about to act in a manner prejudicial to public safety and peace."

"All Right", Dr. Mookerjee said after reading the order and got down from the jeep. Vaidya Gurudatt and Shri Tek Chand, who insisted that they would accompany him also got down and were put under arrest. The rest of the company were sent back. Dr. Mookerjee then told his returning companions that he felt that it was a conspiracy between the Governments of India and Jammu and Kashmir. He also sent the following last message for his countrymen through them: "I have entered Jammu and Kashmir State, though as a prisoner".

After a halt of about an hour at Lakhanpur, Dr. Mookerjee and his companions were put in a jeep which dashed towards Srinagar. The people of Jammu who had not got the news of his arrest had assembled in their thousands at Tawi bridge to receive their hero. They waited for him till night. But they could not notice him as the closed jeep carrying him passed the bridge at dusk.

He reached Udhampur at about 10 p.m. He was dead tired by the strenuous and uncomfortable journey in the jeep and wanted to spend the night there. But the officer escorting him told him that night was to be passed at Batot. He reached there at about 2 a.m., slept for the remaining hours of the night there, and was again rushed next morning towards Srinagar Central Jail where he reached at about 3 p.m. From there he and his two companions were escorted by the Superintendent of the jail, Pt. Siri Kanth Sapru, to a small cottage near Nishat garden where he was to spend the last forty days of his life as a prisoner.

The news of his arrest created a stir all over the country. Protest demonstrations and hartals took place at Delhi and other places. It gave a new direction to the Satyagraha. Satyagrahis began to proceed to Jammu without permit instead of courting arrest at Delhi or Pathankot. "Jammu Chalo" became their new slogan".

On the 13th of May, Shri N.C. Chatterji raised the question of Dr. Mookerji's arrest by Kashmir Government after he had been allowed to proceed to Jammu without permit by the Government of India as per information given by the Deputy Commissioner of Gurdaspur to him. But to the amazement of all Pt. Nehru flatly denied the fact of the Deputy Commissioner having met Dr. Mookerjee at all. "Does Pt. Nehru think," commented a Hindi daily of the capital on this denial, "that Dr. Mookerjee is not to return to take him to task for this flagrant lie".

The Prison

The small cottage which was converted into a sub-jail for him was on the slope of the mountain range which flanked the Dal Lake. It had one main room about 10 ft. by 12 ft., in which Dr. Mookerjee was lodged and two small side rooms which accommodated his co-detenus. There was no room in this "bungalow" for a fourth cot. When Pt. Prem Nath Dogra was brought there on the 19th of June, a tent had to be pitched outside for him.

The whole compound was covered with fruit trees and vegetable beds leaving only a small lawn, smaller than a tennis court, for the detenus to move about. It was at a distance of about eight miles from the city. There was no arrangement for medical aid there. Doctor had to be called from the city on being requisitioned. About hundred yards away from the hut there was a canal and a substation of the water-works department, which had a telephone. That telephone served this improvised jail in the wilderness as well.

Only one newspaper—*Hindustan Times*—was supplied to him though later he was permitted to receive *Hindustan Standard* also. But they seldom reached him in time. Usually two or three days elapsed before he got the next consignment of newspapers which, along with his *dak*, were brought to him by the Superintendent of the jail personally. The authorities were most callous in respect of his *dak*. Generally it took about a week for a letter, particularly one written in Bengali, after it had reached

Srinagar, to be delivered to him. Some letters that were sent from Calcutta on the 10th of June and which bore Srinagar Post mark of the 12th and 13th of June, were returned undelivered to his family after his death. On his protest at this inordinate delay in delivering his *dak* to him, he was told that the person who censored his dak written in Bengali was not readily available. Thereupon Dr. Mookerjee suggested that he could supply them English rendering of the letters written in Bengali, which came only from his family members and contained no politics, for the purpose of censor to avoid delay. But no heed was paid to this suggestion. What was worst many letters to and from him were completely suppressed. This was clear on scrutiny of catalogue of letters to and from Dr. Mookerjee, given in the statement issued by the Kashmir Minister for prisons after his death.

He was not even supplied with the books and other necessities of life that he required as is clear from his various letters to his friends like 'Homa' of *Hindustan Standard* and to his daughter in Delhi, for sending him books and articles like a tin of biscuits, Nescafe, a muffler, merocalized wax, a tin of ovaltine a bottle of hair oil, lemon drop lozenges, a *khatta* and a writing pad.

Dr. Mookerjee was in the habit of taking long walks in the morning and evening. That was, in fact, the only exercise he took to keep his body fit and going. He needed it all the more in jail where there was no other activity that could give any exercise to his limbs. But the narrow and short garden path could not serve his need. So he began to loose appetite soon after he reached there. The bracing climate of the valley had no use for him because he suffered from high blood pressure and high altitude was harmful for him. It was medically wrong to keep him in Kashmir. He should have been kept in some jail in Jammu province.

The natural scenery that the cottage commanded was of course good. But it could not give his limbs the exercise they needed on his soul the buoyancy which natural beauty can give to a free man alone. The feelings of Dr. Mookerjee about the place of his confinement are best expressed by him in the following letters to his family members:

> "I am staying in a small bungalow. The bungalow is situated in a small but lovely garden. I walk on the narrow

garden path. When you read this, you will feel how happy I must be. Alas, that is not possible. What physical comforts, what charms of nature, can bring you joy if your freedom is not yours.... Send me a long reply full of news and stories — but not politics of course! For, I am a prisoner here".

Letter dated 18.05-1953.

"Permission is limited only to a walk along the garden path. It takes 2 or 3 minutes to cover the distance. It is there only and in the open space that lies ahead of it that I take my stroll. This house is very small".

Letter in Bengali dated 25.05.1953.

"Permission could not be had for stroll outside the garden in the morning and in the afternoon. I take a walk in the narrow path inside the garden. The garden is not large. There are ten or twelve police men who keep guard—lest there be loss of prestige".

Letter in Bengali dated 25.05.1953.

That he was refused permission to take a stroll, under guard of course, outside the compound throws a lurid light on the working of the mind of Sheikh Abdullah. Colonel R.N. Chopra, the Inspector General of Prisons, visited Dr. Mookerjee in jail a few days after his arrival at Srinagar. On being asked if he could do anything for him, Dr. Mookerjee told him that he was missing his morning walk very much.

"That is a small thing", replied Colonel Chopra, "You can take stroll on the canal bank. Police guard will accompany you".

Colonel Chopra instructed the Superintendent accordingly and he instructed the inspector of police on duty. But when Dr. Mookerjee got ready for walk the next morning, the inspector of police informed him:

"I have not received written order so far. I am waiting for it". He did not get written permission till 20th of June, when Dr. Mookerjee had become physically unfit to move even.

It was later discovered that Sheikh Abdullah had ordered that Dr. Mookerjee not be given any facilities without his express orders.

No Freedom at All

None of his friends or relatives were allowed to interview him while he was in jail. His eldest son applied for permit to visit Srinagar to see him. But he was informed by the permit issuing authority in New Delhi that he could not be allowed to visit Kashmir to see his father. Some of his relatives were in Srinagar at that time. They too sought an interview with him but were refused. The only person from outside who was taken to him for the purpose of interview, except S. Hukam Singh MP. whose visit was purely political and Barrister U.M. Trivedi MP., who met him as his counsel, was a half mad sadhu who was inflicted upon him to hear his nonsense. It was probably done to tell the world after his death that interviews were allowed to him.

Reading the Only Pleasure

Dr. Mookerjee spent his time in jail in reading, writing, meditation and occasional chats with his co-detenus over the cup of afternoon tea which covered a wide range of subjects, from culture and spiritualism to politics and his assessment of men and events. It was his long cherished desire to write a biography of his father. He began writing it there. He also used to write his diary regularly. He took it with him to the hospital as well when he was removed there on the 22nd of June. It would have been the most authentic source of information about his life and work, thoughts and ideals and above all his own feelings and reading about the events that culminated in his tragic death. But is was kept back by Sheikh Abdullah's Government after his death and was not returned in spite of repeated requests. This betrayed a guilty conscience.

One of the books that he read there was *Raj Tarangani*, Kalhan's Chronicle of Kings of Kashmir. This great book gives a pathetic account of the intrigues and treachery that have characterised the rulers of Kashmir, with a few honourable exceptions all through the history.

Letter to Sister-in-Law

Some idea of the sublimity of his thoughts and ideas about himself and the world around can be formed from the following last portion of the letter that he wrote on June 6th, to his sister-in-law, wife of his elder brother, Justice Rama Prasad Mookerjee.

"I do meditate, not simply over the days and years that are past, but also the events which happened then. And when they are mingled with sorrow and happiness, how could I afford to forget them. WWith them I bored over the present men and events. They flash in my mind like pictures — the place one is staying at, the work one is busy with or the how and why of events which are taking place — they crowd into my mind in different ways. Then again, when I ponder over the uncertain and distant future, a different set of ideas prop up in a different fashion. Then, I have a vision of light in the midst of darkness - victory in the midst of defeat. I experience what is good in every body. I have felt very much during these few days, how small and trifling, yet how proud and power drunk we are, and yet how little conscious we are about it. We do not realise that this universe is moving like a machine, nor do we think of Him whose kindness has caused the birth of this creation, and is even causing its growth and destruction. I am at the 'fag end' of my life, yet am not sure what I have done in my life. I just think how I have spent my time in trifling and absurd words and deeds, how many errors and wrongs I have committed.

You know I like books. At present I am going through works on various subjects - new and old - but learning things a new all the same. There is the ardent desire to write but somehow that does not seem to be possible. Even in the past thirty years, a biography of father could not written. This is a thing which I sorely regret. Even if an endeavour was now made many stories and writings of his time could be discovered.

For the past few days I feel moved with a desire to wield the pen for it. My mind also intends to write down the none to small experience that I have gathered during my life time. I do bother myself about you, the children, the grand children and the thousands of boys who have been kept confined behind the prison bars. I am not sure how long will I remain in this State. Nor am I sure about my future programme. But I know it for certain that there is neither sorrow nor worry in my mind. Ràther, I have been able to keep up, during these few days, that unceasing confidence which I used to place in myself and I could maintain my faith in that Unknown Supreme power without whose guidance we cannot move or survive. This really cheers up and gives strength to the mind. This much for the day. Please reply.

Your Mejothakurpo.

A Letter Immersed with Humour

His lively and elegant humour continued to enliven the drab atmosphere of the jail till the end. He was in the habit of seeing the bright side of everything, animate and inanimate. His self-confidence was superb and his optimism was catching. But he never failed to note the inconsistencies and hypocrisies that often go with life and he used both his humour and satire to expose them. The letter written by him on the 7th of June to the columnist "Homa", paying his tribute to Norkay Tensing, is a brilliant example of his humour and satire:

"We are having mixed weather here", he wrote, "like our mixed economy, or if you like, my mixed health or my mixed feelings in detention. The conquest of Everest gave us unmixed pleasure — but Tensing although he reached first and was the real guide, got a mixed world reception. The Calcutta reception will of course be one of unmixed pride and admiration. The real discoverer of this proud and lofty mountain was a Bengali surveyor. Sikdar, I believe, was his name. But the Burra Sahib Everest, got an unmixed dedication. Such is life".

Poor State of Health

Dr. Mookerjee as said above, began to lose appetite soon after his detention at Srinagar. He also developed acute pain in his right leg accompanied by temperature on the 18th of May. He never regained his full health after that.

On the 24th of May, Pt. Nehru and Dr. Katju visited Srinagar for "rest". They had not the courtesy and decency to visit their august prisoner and see how he was being treated there.

The pain in his leg reappeared on the 3rd of June, with greater intensity. In a letter dated 06.06.1953 he wrote: "I was on the whole keeping well, but the pain in the right leg has again increased during the last two days. Moreover for some days I have been running temperature in the evening. There is burning sensation in the eyes and face. I am taking medicine".

On the receipt of this letter at Calcutta on or about 12.06.1953, Dr. Mookerji's brother saw Dr. B C Roy, who apprised him to his health and requested him to contact Govt. of Jammu and Kashmir.

This pain in the leg with fever was a new malady which Dr. Mookerjee had never had before. Because of loss of appetite he was getting weak everyday. Barrister U.M. Trivedi, who had gone to Srinagar to argue his Habeas Corpus before Kashmir High Court and who had refused to take instructions from him on the 12th of June in the presence of the District Magistrate, interviewed him for three hours on the 18th of June, after the Kashmir High Court had directed the Kashmir Government to allow him to take instructions in private. He found Dr. Mookerjee weak and cheerless.

Pt. Prem Nath Dogra who was taken from Jammu to Srinagar on the 19th of June, to meet him was also struck by his poor state of health and low appetite. He asked him the reason and was informed that it might be due to lack of exercise.

The same night he developed pain in chest and high temperature. On the 20th morning the authorities was informed about it. Thereupon Doctors Ali Mohammed and Amar Nath Raina reached the sub jail at 11.30 a.m. Dr. Ali Mohammed diagnosed the trouble as Dry Pleursy and prescribed Streptomycin injections. Dr. Mookerjee protested that his family physician had advised him not to take Streptomycin as that did not suit his system. But no heed was paid to it. Dr. Mookerjee, according to Vaidya Gurudatt, requested the Superintendent on that day that news of his illness should be sent to his relatives. But no such intimation was sent nor any bulletin issued by Government till after his death.

Next day, the 21st of June, except the Jail doctor, a sub-assistant surgeon, no other doctor, not even Dr. Ali Mohammed, visited him. His temperature rose and pain increased during the day.

Because of this sudden collapse he could not have much talk with Pt. Dogra who had been brought to Srinagar for consultations with him regarding withdrawal of the movement in view of the internal developments in the State, which had divided the State cabinet into two camps - Sheikh Abdullah and Mirza Afzal Beg on one side and Bakshi Ghulam Mohammed, Pt. Shyam Lal Sarraf and Mr. Girdhari Lal Dogra on the other. The latter wanted an understanding with the Praja Parishad to checkmate the designs of the former. Pt. Dogra had been brought to Srinagar to meet Dr. Mookerjee in spite of the opposition of Sheikh Abdullah. Dr. Mookerjee, a democrat as he was, was then thinking of drawing up proposals in consultation with Pt. Dogra for the consideration of Jan Sangh and Praja Parishad colleagues outside who, he held, must be consulted before any decision was taken.

At about 4 a.m. on the 22nd of June, he had a severe heart attack. His temperature went down to 97° and he began to perspire profusely. Vaidya Guru Datt administered him some hot cardamom and clove water which gave him some relief.

At 5.15 a.m. the Superintendent was informed about Dr. Mookerji's health and was requested to come with the doctor immediately. Dr. Ali Mohammed reached there at 7.30 a.m. He suggested to the Superintendent that Dr. Mookerjee should be immediately removed to the State Nursing Home. The Superintendent asked him to get orders from the District Magistrate. Thereupon both the Codetenus requested him to get permission for them also to move with him to the nursing home. But Dr. Ali Mohammed refused to do so and remarked: "I understand your anxiety, but you don't worry. He will be in better hands there".

How one wishes that they, particularly Shri Tek Chand, who had insisted to go with him much against his wished, had then insisted to be with him in the nursing home.

At about 11.30 a.m. the jail superintendent reached there with a Taxi car in which Dr. Mookerjee was removed to the nursing home in the State hospital at a distance of about 10 miles from there. He was kept in a room in the first floor.

This removal to the distant hospital, and the exertion it involved, of a patient suffering from acute heart attack was itself wrong from the medical point of view.

Last Two Days

Dr. Mookerjee was shifted to the State Nursing Home on 22nd June, 1953. What took place in the nursing home is still shrouded in mystery. Barrister Trivedi met him at 5.30 p.m. after completing his arguments in the Court. He was confident that he would be set at liberty the next day when the judgement was to be delivered.

He left Dr. Mookerjee at about 7.30 p.m., weak but cheerful, Dr. Mookerjee himself felt better. Doctors on attendance told Shri Trivedi that the worst had passed and that he would be X-rayed next morning and would be all right in two or three days.

But on the 23rd of June at about 3.45 a.m. Shri Trivedi was picked up from his hotel to go to the hospital. Pandit Prem Nath Dogra and the two co-detenus of Dr. Mookerjee in the sub-jail were also asked about the same time to get ready to go to the hospital. They reached there at about 4.30 a.m. and were informed that Dr. Mookerjee had breathed his last at 3.40 a.m.

Suspected Foul Play

The communique issued after his death by the Kashmir Government on June 23rd, gave the report of Doctors Ali Mohammed and Ram Nath Parihar, MD., who were declared as having been attending upon him. The report said that his general condition was fairly good at 4 p.m. Oxygen was given to him at 11 p.m. to allay restlessness which started at that time, that he got pain in the heart area at 1 a.m. and became restless, and that his pulse stopped at 3.40 a.m.

Apart from the criminal negligence in the treatment meted out to Dr. Mookerjee, who had been detained without trial and was, therefore, a national trust in the hands of the Governments of Kashmir and India, there is much circumstantial evidence which goes to suggest something worse.

In the first place the time of his death as given in the official communique is not correct. According to all accounts coming from other patients in the nursing home at that time as also from a hospital official, he died at about 2.30 a.m. and not at 3.40 a.m. as given out by the Government.

Secondly, according to a very reliable information, oxygen

was not given to him at all. In fact only a vain effort was made to get it from the military hospital at the spur of the moment. The name of Dr. Parihar was probably associated with Dr. Ali Mohammed as the physician attending upon him only to lend weight to the official version. He had never examined Dr. Mookerjee since his arrival in Srinagar.

These discrepancies in the official version and the known and uncontradicted facts go to prove that there was something to hide.

Enquiries made on the spot by some very responsible persons later revealed even more damaging facts which called for further investigation. It was, for example, found that it was not a fact that Dr. Mookerji's condition took a turn for the worse at 11 p.m., as given out in the official communique. He was rather feeling better at that time. His condition suddenly worsened only after a particular doctor gave him an injection at 1 a.m. "as a precautionary measure". The same doctor is known to have refused to come and attend upon him after that, even though he was repeatedly summoned on the telephone by nurses on duty to do so in view of the fast deteriorating condition of Dr. Mookerjee.

The suspicions roused by these stray pieces of information are further strengthened by the popular belief in Srinagar, and the ominous warnings that some respectable men gave to Shri Trivedi when he went there. When, on being refused permission to take instructions from Dr. Mookerjee in private, Shri Trivedi was planning to return to New Delhi an important citizen of Srinagar dropped into his hotel room and pleaded with him not to do till he had got Dr. Mookerjee released. He warned him that "Dr. Mookerjee will be killed," if he was not got released early. The same man met him on the 24th morning outside the hospital and reminded him of his earlier warning.

A police superintendent who came to Shri Trivedi before he left his hotel for Delhi was so agitated that he took out his pistol and cried aloud: "They have killed him, killed him. I will shoot them."

What is more important, every one in Srinagar instinctively felt that there has been foul play. The facts about the internal rift in the Kashmir Government, the fact that the Kashmir High Court gave permission to Shri Trivedi to interview Dr. Mookerjee much against the wishes of Sheikh Abdullah and the general belief, and Shri Trivedi's own conviction, that Dr. Mookerji's petition would have been granted and he set at liberty on the 24th of June, point to the same conclusion. "*Vox populi*" they say is "*Vox Dei.*"

It was quite natural in view of these facts and circumstantial evidence that people in India should suspect a foul play. That explains the universal demand for an open and impartial enquiry into the circumstances leading to his death. All political parties and even some leading Congressmen joined in making this demand on the Government of India. But the Government of India turned down this demand for reasons best known to it.

In fact the story of the last forty days of Dr. Mookerji's life in detention at Srinagar culminating in his martyrdom on the 23rd of June, 1953, will go down in history as one of the most tragic and poignant episodes in the political life of free India. It is a sad commentary on democracy as it functioned in India under Pandit Nehru and on the character and behaviour of men who masqueraded as democratic rulers of the country in the most formative period of her life as a free nation.

Public Reaction on Death

Everybody was stunned and surprised at the news of Dr. Syama Prasad Mookerji's death which came as a bolt from the blue to his countrymen who, including his family members, had to information about his illness till then. It shocked, the whole of India.

There was spontaneous and unprecedented mourning throughout the length and breadth of the country. Hartal was observed and condolence meetings held in every town and city of the country. Poignancy was added to the tragedy by the mysterious circumstances in which he had passed away. It intrigued people's minds and created the suspicion of foul play. It added indignation against the Government of Kashmir as also of India, to the grief.

In Jammu people went mad with rage and grief. Every one of them felt that he had become a martyr to their cause — the cause of Kashmir's integration with India, the cause of Indian unity.

In Delhi people demanded revenge — blood for blood — for they felt convinced that their beloved leader had been made to die. But for the patriotic restraint displayed by the Jan Sangh leaders the people's rage might have taken a violent form.

The people of Bengal naturally felt the tragedy most. They were moved to their depths. The whole of Calcutta, where his body was flown from Srinagar, kept a night long vigil to pay homage and have the last glimpse of its departed leader. Over a million people lines the 14 mile long route from the aerodrome, from where the cortege started at 10 p.m. to his house in South Calcutta where it reached at five in the morning. A million followed it when it started on its last earthly journey to Keortala burning Ghat at noon. All along the route lakhs of people showered flowers and shed tears from balconies and house tops. It was something unprecedented even in the history of that city of big things.

Tributes to His Memory

The Parliament, the State Legislatures and other corporate bodies, the Press and the leaders of Public opinion irrespective of party affiliations, as also the leaders and rulers of the Buddhist countries of S.E. Asia mourned his death as a great national loss and paid glowing tributes and homage to his dedicated life of services to his motherland. His achievements as an educationist and a patriot were recalled by all. But the dominating note in the nation wide tributes was his service to the cause of unity of the motherland and to the democratic freedom of the common people.

Shri Guruji, the Leader of RSS had the following words to say on his death:

> "As a true fighter for his motherland Dr. Mookerjee died in the fore front of the battle for integration of Kashmir, which is and which ought to be immediately declared an undivided and indivisible part of Bharat".

"India has suffered an irreparable loss in Syama Prasad's martyrdom for United India" bewailed Tarak Nath Das, the veteran revolutionary leader.

His colleagues in the Parliament and lovers of democracy emphasised the loss to democratic forces in the country.

"Dr. Mookerjee was the only person before whom the Prime Minister bowed and with him Shri Nehru lost many a battle in the Parliament", said Dr. Lankasundram.

"His ability and fearlessness were powerful brakes on the growing arrogance of Treasury benches", said Shri Frank Anthony.

"He was the best Parliamentarian and made his dominating personality felt all the time", said Smt. Sucheta Kriplani.

His colleagues in the field of education, in cabinet and in political life recalled his great qualities of head and heart.

"Public life in India in recent years has not known a more courageous and gifted leader", said Dr. John Mathai, his colleague in the first Union Cabinet.

"Country is definitely the poorer for him. Great things were expected of him", said Shri Purshottam Das Tandon.

"He was a great patriot, a great fighter for the causes he considered right and held dear", said Acharya Kripalani.

"In Dr. Mookerji's Bharat has lost one of the foremost patriots and a born Parliamentarian", said Shri V.D. Sawarkar.

To his colleagues and co-workers of the National Democratic Party in the Parliament, Hindu Maha Sabha, Ram Rajya Parishad and Praja Parishad, and above all, to the Bharatiya Jan Sangh which he led so boldly and successfully that it became the most formidable challenge to Congress misrule within two years of its inception, his death come as a cruel blow and an irreparable loss.

The only tribute that the Jan Sangh could pay to his memory was to re-dedicate itself to complete his unfinished work. That it did.

The most touching and telling tribute came from Dr. M.R. Jaykar the famous Jurist and Privy Councillor who said:

> "To die in a prison house, locked there by his country's Swadeshi Government by persons with whom he shared power as a colleague, is a fitting termination of a warring life. Let us hope that this incident will make the Government of India realise, in their self complacent enjoyment of the chits of American Visitors, the enormity of their behaviour, which ignored all the canons of fairness and justice accepted by civilised Governments."

His was a warring life no doubt. All his life he fought valiantly for his country's freedom both social as well as political, for civil liberties of the people, for the unity of the motherland and, after the dawn of independence, for upholding democracy against growing fascism of the men in power. He ultimately laid down his life for these. He truly became a martyr to civil liberties, to democracy and to the unity of India. Like a true *Karma Yogin*, he lived as a soldier, and died a martyr. He was great in life, greater in death.

Index